Paradise Lost

PARADISE LOST

Rural Idyll and Social Change in England since 1800

JEREMY BURCHARDT

I.B. Tauris *Publishers*
LONDON • NEW YORK

Published in 2002 by I.B.Tauris & Co Ltd,
6 Salem Road, London W2 4BU
175 Fifth Avenue, New York NY 10010
www.ibtauris.com

In the United States of America and in Canada distributed by
St Martin's Press, 175 Fifth Avenue, New York NY 10010

ISBN 1 86064 514 3

A full CIP record for this book is available from the British Library
A full CIP record for this book is available from the Library of Congress

Library of Congress catalog card: available

Set in Monotype Garamond by Ewan Smith, London
Printed and bound in Great Britain by MPG Books Ltd, Bodmin

Contents

Acknowledgements

I am particularly grateful to Professor E. J. T. Collins who encouraged me to write a book about urban perceptions of the countryside in England and who read some of the chapters that resulted. I have also benefited greatly from the comments of Phillada Ballard, Roy Brigden, Malcolm Chase, Philip Conford, Peter Dewey, Yohji Iwamoto, Donna Landry, Derek Roper, Sadie Ward and Roy Wolfe, all of whom read drafts of chapters of this book. Caroline Benson provided invaluable help with the illustrations and I am also grateful to the other members of staff of the Rural History Centre, who have all helped in different ways. Finally, I would like to thank Lester Crook, a generous and unfailingly interested editor. The book is better than it would have been had I not incurred these debts of gratitude; but responsibility for remaining errors is of course my own.

Jeremy Burchardt
The Rural History Centre

Introduction

§ EVEN the most cursory glance at the shelves of a second-hand bookshop will confirm that the English countryside has received more than its fair share of literary attention. It is true that many of the titles on the shelves labelled 'nature', 'topography' or simply 'England' are likely to prove of limited intellectual ambition. Nevertheless, even if these more lightweight books are disregarded, there remains a not unimpressive corpus of academic work relating to rural England – and above all to rural England in the period covered by the current volume (the years since the industrial revolution). Is there then any rationale for another book on this subject? Yes – because most previous works on nineteenth- and twentieth-century rural England have privileged one particular aspect of the countryside (agriculture), and, as the following paragraphs argue, there is scope for an alternative approach.

Most academic histories of the countryside since the industrial revolution place agriculture at the centre of their accounts; indeed, the countryside is frequently more or less equated with agriculture. Farming is seen as the most important dimension of the countryside, and the terms 'rural' and 'agricultural' are often used almost synonymously. More nuanced accounts acknowledge that non-agricultural aspects such as industrial activity and leisure are significant components of the countryside, but most continue to structure their narratives around agricultural change. This approach indisputably has much to commend it. First, it provides a strong linking theme around which a coherent narrative based on the shifting fortunes of agriculture can be constructed. Typical chapter headings include: 'The golden age, 1850–75', 'The agricultural depression, 1875–1896', and 'The era of the Common Agricultural Policy, 1973–2000'. Second, basing a narrative around agriculture helps to sharpen the definition of a potentially amorphous subject. For if the countryside cannot be equated with agriculture, what *does* it consist of? Any alternative definition seems inherently less clear-cut and easily handled. Third, to prioritize agriculture ensures that the narrative remains firmly grounded in socio-economic factors, rather than being ensnared in the intangible, complex and shifting web of attitudes to the countryside existing only in people's minds.

Many fine histories of rural England have been written by making use of the strategy outlined in the previous paragraph. A good example is Howard Newby's *Green and Pleasant Land?*, one of the most eloquent and coherent social histories of the English countryside written in the last fifty years. For Newby, the changing significance of the countryside could be charted only against the economic evolution of agriculture, and it was therefore the technological and institutional changes in farming that formed the basis of his analysis. Many other historians have followed a similar path, including the editors of the authoritative *Agrarian History of England and Wales*. To privilege agriculture as these accounts do, though, is to define the countryside in a certain way: essentially, it is to assert that what matters most about the countryside is that it is a means of production.[1]

Yet there is another countryside besides that dedicated to farming and to the maximally efficient output of wheat, beef, milk and other food products. This other countryside is the countryside of nature, of leisure, of artistic contemplation – the countryside that is enjoyed 'for itself', rather than used as a means to a separate end. This second version of rural England is undoubtedly the one most people at the time of writing are most conscious of when they think of the countryside. It is the countryside as an object of consumption rather than as a means of production – and to this countryside, agriculture is peripheral rather than central. This 'other' countryside has become ever more important over the period covered in this book. At the same time, and perhaps in inverse relationship, the importance of the 'primary' (agricultural) countryside has diminished. As food production has become ever more efficient, fewer and fewer people and a smaller and smaller proportion of the nation's capital have been required to produce an adequate supply of food.[2] This process has continued to the point where it could well be argued that, taking the twentieth century as a whole, it is the countryside as an object of consumption rather than as a means of production that has more significantly affected English society.

The 'other' countryside is not held together by a single easily defined focus of interest in the same way that agriculture unifies the concept of the countryside as a means of production. While the countryside-as-agriculture can be seen as based on the processes of food production, which are amenable to economic analysis and simplification, the 'other' countryside consists of everything that people have thought or felt about rural England. It is therefore intrinsically amorphous and indeterminate, and to construct a history of it is a correspondingly arbitrary and more than usually subjective task. Nevertheless, it seems worth trying to write a history of the countryside from this point of view, displacing agriculture from the centre of the picture, and, in its stead, putting what people have thought and felt about rural England. While such an approach may be handicapped by the lack of a clear focus, it may achieve a new perspective on the countryside which has been incompletely developed in previous accounts predicated on the notion of the countryside-as-agriculture. The present book, which attempts to do this, is therefore to some degree an experiment.

Within the overall aim of achieving this shift in perspective, the book has two subsidiary purposes. First, it aims to show how attitudes to the countryside developed between 1800 (taken as a very approximate date for the onset of the industrial revolution) and the year 2000 (the time of writing). Second, it aims to demonstrate that the 'other' countryside was not merely epiphenomenal. On the contrary, as subsequent chapters explain, changing attitudes to the countryside were deeply implicated in social change, not only in the country-side itself but also in the towns. A good example of this, examined in more detail in Chapter 4, is the urban parks movement. This was inspired in part by the conviction that the countryside was morally and physically healthier than the towns, and that the quality of urban life would therefore be improved if aspects of the countryside were re-created within urban settings. A second example, on a larger scale, is the emergence of the planning system. This was, at least in large part, a response to the powerful development of preservationist sentiment towards the English countryside in the late nineteenth and early twentieth centuries. Yet planning legislation, once enacted, came to have an immense influence on the social evolution of the English countryside, as we will see in Chapter 13. Planning curtailed both house building and industrial development in the postwar countryside, with major consequences for rural social structure which operated differentially between classes. Attitudes to the countryside therefore often powerfully reshaped the rural fabric to which they pertained.

Because of its concern with the imbrication of attitudes in social change, this book is not a pure, rarefied analysis of ideas and sentiments, but rather a socio-cultural history of attitudes *and their consequences*. This, of course, raises the question of what the relationship between the two actually was. Did 'social reality' determine attitudes, or were attitudes more than a mere manifestation of 'underlying' socio-economic trends? This question, although perhaps in-escapable, is of course no more than an aspect of one of the central (and hitherto unresolved) debates in the history of thought: whether what people believe determines their actions, or vice versa. It would be superfluous and invidious to attempt to make a contribution to so complex and long-standing a debate in the context of a work like the present, and fortunately it is not necessary to do so. The position taken in this book is a pragmatic one. It is contended that attitudes can be demonstrated to have influenced socio-economic developments, and also vice versa; but this involves no commitment on the question of whether one is or is not in some *ultimate* sense derived from the other.

Attitudes to the countryside acquired a powerful resonance within English culture and society in the nineteenth and twentieth centuries, largely as a result of industrialization and urbanization, and it is with the years since 1800 that this book is primarily concerned. The word 'countryside' came into common usage only during the nineteenth century, and it could plausibly be argued that any attempt to write the history of the English countryside in the pre-industrial period would be anachronistic. Attitudes to the countryside took shape within the broader context of the relationship between humanity and the natural world, and a brief account of changing attitudes to nature in European (and specifically English) culture in the centuries prior to the industrial revolution provides an essential context for the subsequent chapters of this book. We can begin by looking briefly at attitudes to nature prevalent in the middle ages.

Medieval thought about nature was dominated by theology. Most theologians argued that nature (understood as the entire non-human world) had been created by God for man's express benefit. This interpretation drew heavily on the account of the creation of the world, and the exile from the Garden of Eden, provided in Genesis. A purpose was imputed to everything in nature, and this purpose was presupposed to consist of what would be conducive to God's grand design for the world – the benefit of humankind. In the case of obviously benign aspects of nature it was unproblematic to argue that they had been created to serve man's needs. All those plants which provided food or fuel were easily understood in this way, as were domesticated animals. Inedible or poisonous plants, and dangerous wild animals, were more difficult to account for within this framework. Nevertheless, medieval thinkers were not short of often extremely fanciful inferences about the true purposes of such aspects of nature. Dangerous animals such as wolves could be explained as providing men with an incentive towards activity and courage, or as serving to remind humankind of its weakness and dependence on God's mercy. Destructive weather was equally amenable to a positive interpretation: it could be seen as a punishment for sins which those afflicted had committed. This, then, was an almost completely anthropocentric view of the world, in which nature was understood to exist only for the sake of fulfilling man's temporal and spiritual needs.[3]

Nature seen in these terms was quite separate from humanity, and, at least in the last analysis, benign. While this was the predominant view among theologians, in practical terms nature was characteristically experienced very differently by most people. Far from being quite separate from man, nature was intimately interwoven with human life. The overwhelming majority of the population lived in rural areas, often sharing a single building with domestic animals (cows, horses, dogs, pigs and poultry). Most day-to-day work took place in the fields, in direct contact with plants and exposed to the vagaries of the weather. Furthermore, practical experience of nature also contrasted with the theological perspective in that the former did not necessarily suggest that nature was benign. On the contrary, nature's destructiveness or even apparent enmity towards humanity was all too apparent. Wolves, foxes or birds of prey might carry off young livestock or poultry, while crop and animal diseases could devastate the economic basis of a peasant household. Worst of all were the unpredictable but occasionally catastrophic effects of the weather: floods could destroy houses, ruin crops and drown animals, while frost or rain at the wrong times of year could decimate a harvest.

It was this practical experience of untamed nature as dangerous that largely shaped aesthetic perceptions of and responses to the countryside. Landscapes that were obviously untamed, and therefore potentially dangerous, were rarely admired. Mountains and moorland were more usually associated with desolation, barrenness and extremity than with beauty. In so far as landscape was appreciated for aesthetic qualities at all, this tended to be only the most comprehensively tamed and therefore safest of landscapes – archetypally the walled garden.[4]

Thus in the middle ages, nature was seen as appurtenant to man, and as dangerous when not subdued by him. These assumptions, however, were undermined by the intellectual and socio-economic developments of the seventeenth and eighteenth centuries. A particularly important role was played by the scientific revolution. This had two major consequences for attitudes towards nature. First, nature began to be seen more objectively, rather than in terms of human needs. Nature was more and more regarded as being of interest in its own right, and not just with respect to its uses for and dangers to humanity. This shift in sensibilities was exemplified by the rise of dispassionate observations of nature and, correspondingly, of the forerunners of modern classification systems in natural history (notably through the work of Ray and Linnaeus). The same impulse lay behind a new genre of popular literary works which were similarly centred on close attention to nature, with mankind removed from centre stage or even absent altogether. Gilbert White's *Natural History of Selborne* is the classic work of this kind. Second, people began to sense that nature had been brought under effective human control. Nature could accordingly be seen in less utilitarian terms: as humanity became emancipated from nature, and it became less dangerous, so it could be admired and cherished rather than simply used or feared.[5]

Both these tendencies were much enhanced by economic growth, and in particular by the development of industry and the expansion of towns in the seventeenth and eighteenth centuries. Although on a small scale compared with what was to come, these processes meant that a growing number of people no longer had such direct contact with nature as their forebears had had. Nature was no longer experienced as the immediate means of subsistence, nor was its destructive power as frequently and obviously manifested.

Agriculture of course remained the largest component of Britain's economy throughout the eighteenth century, and it was in agriculture that the confrontation between human endeavour and the recalcitrant or hostile power of nature was at its most inescapable. Even here, the seventeenth and eighteenth centuries witnessed an extension of human control. A pivotal concept was the notion of 'improvement', which in the agricultural context essentially meant the transformation of a landscape in the interests of enhancing agricultural output through subduing or controlling nature. A major form of agricultural improvement, for example, was drainage, whereby the natural tendency of a piece of land to flood or become waterlogged was overcome in order to improve crop yields. Another characteristic example of agricultural improvement was the 'reclamation' (from nature) of moorland. But perhaps the central element of the agricultural revolution was the enclosure of the commons and open fields, in order to allow these to be divided up and farmed individually rather than in common. Advocates of enclosure argued that this would lead to more efficient farming and raise output. Enclosure transformed the landscape, replacing the wide open sweeps of the fields and commons with the regimented, segmented landscape of small fields – the characteristic patchwork landscape of modern rural England. While, ironically, this patchwork landscape is now celebrated as exemplifying the harmony of time and nature which has gone into the making of the English landscape, at the time of its creation the landscape of enclosure was raw and oppressive.[6]

Seventeenth- and eighteenth-century landowners therefore had great success in 'improving' rural landscapes, but the success with which nature had been bridled and controlled led, in some minds, to a countervailing wish to let nature back in – under controlled conditions, of course. This fostered a taste among the early modern gentry for wild, romantic landscapes, exemplified by the paintings of Claude, and by his less celebrated English followers. A greater degree of self-consciousness about natural beauty developed, strongly influenced by painting. Theories of natural beauty were adumbrated, drawing on distinctions such as that between the 'sublime' (majestic, awe-inspiring landscape) and the 'beautiful' (which might be variously defined but usually involved a softer, more rounded landscape than the sublime). The notion of the picturesque, in which a scene possessed varied characteristics giving beauty through diversity and contrast, acquired general currency among the landed elite. Literary responsiveness to landscapes as objects of beauty in their own right appears to some degree to have followed in the wake of these painting-derived ideas.[7]

One of the most notable manifestations of the growing sensitivity to and interest in the beauty of nature in the seventeenth and eighteenth centuries was the English landscape garden. The history of landscape garden styles in eighteenth-century England is a complex subject, but in broad terms it can be said that the line of development was towards a more 'natural' look. Initially this emphasized smooth curves (serpentine lakes and rolling grassy parkland, as perfected by 'Capability' Brown), while later more emphasis was placed on the rougher qualities associated with the aesthetics of the picturesque. The evolution was strongly away from utility and artificiality towards beauty and naturalness. Landscape gardens served many purposes beyond the purely aesthetic, however. They indicated the wealth of the landowner, in that they suggested that he could afford to leave a large area of land devoted to ostensibly 'unproductive' purposes, hence insulating him from the economic foundations on which his wealth rested and distinguishing him sharply from those whose incomes derived from trade.[8] It was also the case, paradoxically, that the seemingly natural landscape garden acted to reinforce the mastery over nature which mankind (or at least the English gentry) had achieved: re-creating and indeed even improving upon nature under controlled conditions could be considered the ultimate evidence of successful domination. So nature – codified as landscape – became an object of aesthetic, especially visual, appreciation, rather than being experienced directly as part of the lived and worked-in world. With this, the concept of 'the countryside' came into being: rural landscape as an object of consumption, rather than as a means of production. The division between the two was written into the landscape in the contrast between the country house garden, with its naturalness, its curves and its irregularity, and the utilitarian landscape of enclosure (created at the behest of the same landowners): managed, controlled, often rectilinear, and self-evidently 'man-made'.

It was only as a result of the industrial revolution, and the massive urbaniza-tion which was its concomitant, that a wide enough gap opened up between most ordinary people and rural life for the countryside as an object of consumption to become a widespread experience, rather than being confined to an elite of landowners. Furthermore, not only were urbanization and industrialization the substrate from which attitudes to the countryside grew up, but the particular character of the urban experience in the nineteenth and, to a lesser extent, in the twentieth centuries had a decisive influence on the content of attitudes towards the countryside. If we are to understand attitudes to the countryside in England since 1800, we need, therefore, to appreciate both the scale and the nature of the transformation wrought by the industrial revolution on England's economy and society. This is the subject of the first chapter of this book.

Urban and industrial growth in the first half of the nineteenth century was, by historical standards, startlingly rapid. One of the first indications of the effects of the transformation of the social environment brought about by the growth of towns and of industrial employment was the response to this by writers, especially poets and novelists – the subject of Chapter 2. Literary attitudes to the countryside cannot be reduced to mere 'reflections' of wider social changes – they are mediated through the experiences and literary persona of the author. Nevertheless, attitudes to the countryside as expressed in literature in the first half of the nineteenth century bear the imprint of the industrial revolution very clearly. The countryside was increasingly used as a yardstick of the new society and environment of the industrial towns which were coming into being. This represented a more serious-minded, more socially critical deployment of the town/country contrast than had previously been usual; but the very seriousness of the critique of the industrial towns militated towards an increasingly idealized portrayal of rural life and of the countryside. This is especially apparent in the works of novelists who had only a limited knowledge of the countryside, such as Dickens, but it also affected some writers who had much greater familiarity with rural England than Dickens had – in particular Elizabeth Gaskell and George Eliot.

This literary response to the industrial revolution represented an essentially upper- and middle-class outlook. For the working class, or at least for many within it, an escape to a 'countryside in the mind' reached through delving into a volume of poetry or a novel was of limited appeal. Many working-class people were still illiterate in the first half of the nineteenth century and in any case the practical exigencies of working-class life demanded more concrete and less escapist solutions to the problems of urban living than could be offered by literature. Nevertheless, an important element of the working-class response to industrialization was also formulated in ruralist terms. Chapter 3 seeks to demonstrate this by considering the most striking manifestation of early nineteenth-century working-class ruralism: the political tradition of radical agrarianism. As we shall see, the aspects of the countryside which were cherished by the urban working class were different from those valued by people more removed from the struggle to earn a living. It was the countryside as a place in which an independent living could be made from the land, free of any employer's domination, that resonated with the working class, and which found expression in a remarkable succession of working-class political movements from Spenceanism to the Chartist Land Plan.

These working-class political movements shared grand ambitions, but partly because of the intransigent opposition of the state, and partly because of their own internal weaknesses, they made little progress in translating their agrarian programmes into practice. If we accept that it was in literature on the one hand and popular politics on the other that the most important middle- and working-class expressions of the impact of industrialization on attitudes to the countryside were respectively expressed, it would be easy to conclude that, at least in the early and mid-nineteenth century, attitudes to the countryside generated few important social changes. But this would be to overlook another strand of development, one which drew both on middle-class idealization of the countryside and on working-class agrarianism. This was the movement to provide the poor with gardens, allotments and parks, described and analysed in Chapter 4. The elite's conviction that having access to land, whether in order to work it or simply to walk over it, was morally and physically beneficial for the poor was one which had been fostered by literary enthusiasm for rural tranquillity and beauty; but at the same time, gardens, allotments and, to a lesser extent, parks ministered at a more modest level to the aspirations towards land which radical agrarianism had impressively expressed but failed to satisfy.

While gardens, allotments and parks could all be thought of as attempts to introduce elements of the countryside into the urban landscape, even the largest parks remained enclaves within an uncompromisingly urban residuum. In Chapter 5, a progression of influences is traced which ultimately led to a more ambitious attempt to introduce rural features into towns. This was the mid- and late nineteenth-century series of model village suburbs, which culminated in the garden cities of Ebenezer Howard. The garden city represented the most comprehensive and radical attempt to ruralize urban life, in that Howard's 'town-country' was intended to overcome the dichotomy between the two altogether.

In following the line of development from industrialization and the pro-ruralist response to it through to parks and garden cities, Chapters 4 and 5 move into the second half of the nineteenth century and even the early twentieth century. Important changes in the balance between town and country had taken place in the meantime, largely as a result of the progressive urbanization of Britain, which meant that by the 1860s a majority of the population lived in towns and cities. The countryside became increasingly marginal to the national economy, and as world agricultural output increased and transport networks improved, agricultural prosperity in Britain was sacrificed to cheap food for urban consumers. The countryside was therefore threatened both from within, through the decline in food prices, and from without, through the increasing political and cultural domination and physical intrusion of towns and of industry. In Chapter 6, literary attitudes to the countryside are again reviewed in order to chart the effect of these developments. It is argued that poets and novelists in the late nineteenth century demonstrated a greater intensity of engagement with the countryside than had been the case in the previous fifty years. The emphasis shifted from using the countryside as a device for criticizing the towns to an anxious concern about or pessimistic awareness of the threatened status of the former. In many respects the effects of the First World War reinforced this literary awareness of the fragility of rural England; more than ever, the countryside became a place to retreat to (often in the imagination) from an unacceptable or unbearable contemporary world.

Chapter 7 continues the theme of working-class politics and attitudes to the countryside into the second half of the nineteenth and the early twentieth centuries. Although the agrarian tradition and the ideal of independence on the land continued to attract a notable working-class following in these years, especially when, as by Lloyd George, it was deployed in opposition to a still-powerful aristocratic oligarchy, in the late nineteenth and early twentieth centuries it was increasingly for its aesthetic and spiritual rather than its political possibilities that land was valued, even among the working class. Perhaps the most important manifestation of this was the rise of preservationist organizations such as the Commons Preservation Society, the National Trust and the Council for the Preservation of Rural England (Chapter 8). To some extent, these organizations grew out of the same social milieu and the same set of moral and social assumptions that had informed the movement to provide urban parks: it was believed that the experience of nature and of the countryside was morally and physically improving and purifying. But the new element in preservationism, one which relates it closely to the changes in literary attitudes to the countryside described in Chapter 6, was the sense of the countryside as threatened and in need of protection.

The sense of the countryside as on the one hand threatened and on the other as an essential antidote to an urban-dominated world intensified during the interwar years, partly in response to the experiences of the war and partly because of the economic and social difficulties of the 1920s and 1930s. The high place which had been accorded to the countryside in national life by the 1920s created the opportunity for political exploitation, which the Conservative Party was particularly well placed to practise. Stanley Baldwin, prime minster for much of the interwar period, cultivated a close personal identification between himself and the countryside (despite his family's urban roots). It has sometimes been argued that the strength of the relationship between the countryside and British national identity inhibited the development of a modernized, maximally efficient urban-based capitalism in Britain, with correspondingly damaging consequences for rates of economic growth. This view is assessed in Chapter 9.

Whether or not ruralism harmed Britain's economic prospects, there can be little doubt that in the period after the First World War popular interest in the countryside was greater than ever before. The most impressive evidence of the rising enthusiasm of the working class for the aesthetic pleasures of the countryside in the interwar years was the growth in the popularity of rambling. This, and the conflicts it entailed between northern ramblers and aristocratic landowners, is examined in Chapter 10. Two further manifestations of the strength and diversity of pro-rural attitudes between the wars, organicism on the one hand and rural reconstruction on the other, are considered in Chapters 11 and 12 respectively. Rural reconstruction was based on the same nexus of ideas about the special status of the countryside that infused so much of the interwar relationship between countryside and nation. But to this it added an emphasis on the alleged value of the countryside, and especially of villages, in generating community. Rural reconstruction was not merely an outlook; its adherents, mostly in the voluntary sector, sought to put it into practice through a web of community-building activities such as the formation of Women's Institutes and the building of village halls. Organicism remained a rather more rarefied and esoteric outlook than reconstructionism, but was important in that it heralded a cast of mind which, if scarcely influential in the interwar period, was to have a dominant effect on attitudes, policy and social change in the countryside in the late twentieth century.

One of the results of the strength of pro-countryside feeling in the interwar period, and especially of the pressure placed on government by the preservationist organizations, was a gradual evolution between the wars towards a coherent system of urban and rural planning. This came fully into its own after the war with the election of the pro-planning Labour government of 1945. But there was an unresolved contradiction in public and political expectations of the countryside, one which was to be embodied in the Labour government's legislative programme, causing increasing problems in the next half century. This was the tension between the demand that the countryside should retain its traditional, unmodernized appearance on the one hand, as against the insistence on the maximum output of cheap food, produced by methods as ruthlessly modern as was necessary, on the other. Chapter 13 assesses the important countryside legislation of this first postwar Labour government, and the difficulties inherent in it.

Perhaps the respect in which these difficulties were to be most comprehensively and damagingly exposed in the years that followed was with regard to the relationship between agriculture and the environment. As technological change and the unrelenting price squeeze imposed on British agriculture drove farmers to adopt capital-intensive methods on an unprecedented scale, the fiction that agriculture and the environment were essentially in harmony was increasingly exposed for what it was. Late twentieth-century rural environmentalism can, therefore, be seen as in part derived from the elevation of the countryside into the wellspring of national identity and refuge from the modern urban world which had arisen since the industrial revolution, especially during the interwar years. The fraught postwar relationship between agriculture and the environment is considered in Chapter 14.

Perhaps the most important shift in the relationship between urban England and the countryside as an object of consumption in the postwar years occurred, however, not as a result of alterations in attitudes, but more because of the lifting of a material constraint which had previously inhibited enjoyment of the countryside. This constraint was the relative inaccessibility of most of rural England, a situation transformed by the postwar era of mass car owner-ship. Once most families had cars, it became possible to travel into the countryside for leisure purposes (Chapter 15) on an unprecedented scale. Rambling, which had already been popular among some groups in some areas in the interwar years, became a leisure activity enjoyed by tens of millions of people every year, and more varied forms of rural leisure, such as pony-trekking, rock-climbing, bird-watching and cycling developed too. Equally, improved mobility made it possible for large numbers of people, for the first time, to live in the countryside while working in a town or city. Chapter 16 assesses this 'counterurbanization' and its consequences for social relationships in rural communities. The arguments put forward in Chapter 14 about the increasing tension between farmers and environmentalists are deployed to explore how the influx of middle-class newcomers into traditionally agricultural villages led to conflicts between incompatible definitions of what the country-side was and what it should be.

These tensions, and others relating to the continuing contradiction between urban demands for both unspoiled beauty and cheap food from the country-side, contributed to the formation of a 'countryside movement' in Britain in the late 1990s. This movement claimed that the countryside had suffered unfair discrimination at the hands of an 'urban establishment', and that as a result a precious 'rural way of life' was under threat. The concluding chapter of the book examines the validity and origins of these fears by drawing on the account of changing attitudes to the countryside offered in the previous chapters. It argues that the rural crisis at the beginning of the twenty-first century is comprehensible only in the light of the development over the last two hundred years of a powerful nexus of ideas, values and aspirations centred on the countryside, which far exceeded its weight considered purely from the point of view of food production. An understanding of the evolution of attitudes to the countryside in England in the past is, therefore, an essential precondition for clarifying the troubled relationship between town and country in the present and future.

CHAPTER I

. . . .

Industrialization and Urbanization

§ ATTITUDES to the countryside since 1800 have been overwhelmingly conditioned by the transformation of Britain from a rural, agricultural country into an urban and industrial one. The most dramatic phase of this transformation took place in the first fifty years of the period covered by this book. Rather than begin with the countryside, therefore, it is in fact with the rise of urban, industrial Britain that a history of attitudes to the countryside since 1800 should start.

The immediate effects of the shift from a rural to an urban nation can be analysed under three headings: economic, environmental and social.

Economic

The most influential early formulation of the concept of an 'industrial revolution' was made by Arnold Toynbee in a series of lectures given in the late nineteenth century.[1] However, although Toynbee and the economic historians who followed him emphasized that the industrial revolution represented a more-or-less sharp break with the past and a marked acceleration of industrial output, this did not clearly differentiate it from previous episodes of economic growth such as that which occurred in fourteenth-century Italy or seventeenth-century Holland. It was only in the mid-twentieth century that a more precise concept was developed. W. W. Rostow argued that what was distinctive about the industrial revolution was not the increased rate of growth per se, but that this increased rate of growth was sustained.[2] Rostow's concept was summed up in the phrase that the industrial revolution was characterized by a 'take-off into self-sustained growth'.

Rostow's view of the industrial revolution had a decisive influence on the succeeding generation of economic historians. The characterization of the industrial revolution that emerged was that it had been a rapid, dramatic process which began in the late eighteenth century with a succession of inventions and innovations in the textile (especially cotton) industry. Two linked developments were seen as driving economic change forwards: the steam engine and the factory. The first made available a cheap form of energy which was more reliable, flexible and powerful than anything which had hitherto existed. The second provided a form of organization within which the potential of steam power could be fully exploited and putatively unlimited economies of scale achieved. This consensus of an industrial revolution which dramatically reshaped the British economy in the years from 1760 onwards, and was largely mature by about 1830, was given statistical underpinning by the pioneering research of W. Deane and P. Cole. Deane and Cole's output statistics appeared to imply that the rate of growth of the British economy had reached a peak prior to 1830, after which growth slackened until picking up again towards the end of the century.[3]

The broad consensus on the nature of the industrial revolution established by the theoretical work of Rostow and the empirical research of Deane and Cole was amplified by the research of other scholars in the 1960s and early 1970s, but in the late 1970s and 1980s this picture was challenged and undermined by a generation of economic historians, foremost among whom was N. F. R. Crafts, using the sophisticated econometric techniques developed by American historians to study the history of slavery. The attack began with a revision of Deane and Cole's output statistics. One of the most difficult problems besetting the compilation of economic statistics is how to ensure comparability between prices at different years. Clearly, 'raw' price statistics reveal little about actual output because they do not take the effects of inflation into account. In order to eliminate this unwanted distortion, it is necessary to choose a 'base year' and recalculate prices for other years so that they are comparable with prices in the base year. But this so-called 'index number problem' is crucially sensitive to the particular base year selected. Crafts argued that Deane and Cole had chosen an inappropriate base year, resulting in an overestimation of the rate of economic growth in the late eighteenth and early nineteenth centuries. Furthermore, their statistics were inaccurate or incomplete for certain important sectors of the economy, and they had given an excessive weighting to some of the more advanced industrial sectors, notably cotton. The net result was, Crafts argued, a large overestimation of the rate of economic growth in the late eighteenth and early nineteenth centuries. Crafts drew attention to the fact that the technological and organizational advances which were at the centre of the Rostow/Deane and Cole view of the industrial revolution – notably the steam engine and the factory – were confined to a relatively small 'modernized' sector of the economy. This modernized sector was important in the Lancashire cotton district; but outside Lancashire, factories and steam engines were few and far between. Most industries, and the vast majority of enterprises, remained unmodernized, characterized by a small unit size, allowing for few economies of scale, and traditional technology which was not susceptible of rapid improvement. While the Lancashire cotton factories did indeed achieve impressive output and productivity growth, this was swamped in the national statistics by the drag of the much larger unmodernized sector.[4]

Since Crafts published his initial revised output statistics, several further revisions to them have been made both by Crafts himself and by other economic historians. These modifications have not significantly weakened the original claim made by Crafts, that Deane and Cole had considerably over-estimated the rate of economic growth in Britain prior to the mid-nineteenth century. This has led some historians to invert what was previously seen as the determining characteristic of the industrial revolution, i.e. the rapidity of economic growth, and to emphasize instead how slow economic growth was in Britain in the late eighteenth and early nineteenth centuries. It has even been suggested that the term 'industrial revolution' should be abandoned altogether as a misnomer, at least for the British case.[5] These claims, however, are surely exaggerated. While output and productivity growth may have been slower than was previously believed, the relevant standard of comparison must be with British growth rates prior to the late eighteenth century.[6] While the quality of the statistical evidence for this period leaves much to be desired, it seems clear that there was a marked, if not necessarily dramatic, acceleration of output growth in the second half of the eighteenth century. In any case, it has rightly been pointed out that the rate of growth of national output and productivity are far from being the only or even necessarily the most important dimensions of an industrial revolution. Two other aspects of economic change also require consideration: regional patterns of development, and change in the structure of the economy.

It was clear to contemporaries and has been clear ever since that the industrial revolution had an important regional dimension. The contrast drawn by Crafts and other 'new economic historians' between the modernized and traditional sectors of the economy has served to highlight this aspect. In many respects, the more the slowness of economic and technological change in the traditional sectors is emphasized, the sharper the contrast between the traditional and modernized sectors becomes. Since the modernized sector was concentrated in a few regions, notably south-east Lancashire, the contrast between traditional and modern sectors is also a contrast between regions. Rather than being seen as 'first among equals', the eighteenth-century Lancashire cotton industry stands out as a startlingly new and different phenomenon, representing a sharp break with the past and even with the surrounding present.

The second dimension of economic change which is inadequately reflected in output and productivity figures is change in the *structure* of the economy. This aspect is something which Crafts himself has been at pains to emphasize. A relatively undramatic rate of economic growth may be accompanied by a highly dramatic change in the pattern of economic activity. Even if the classic years of the industrial revolution between 1760 and 1830 did not see as rapid a growth in output as was once believed, there is little doubt that the balance between different sectors of the economy shifted radically. In particular, the proportion of the population employed in agriculture fell sharply, while the proportion employed in industry rose correspondingly. There was a similar shift in the pattern of investment. This shift in employment and investment from agriculture to industry was highly visible to contemporaries and made a deep impression on them. It was hard not to notice the many new buildings – workshops, warehouses, cottages for industrial workers – being put up in most parts of the country. By contrast, the total value of national output – and still more so the rate of national productivity increase – is an abstraction which cannot be grasped visually. The dramatic transformation of the structure of the economy during the years of the industrial revolution was therefore far more obvious to contemporaries than the perhaps rather slow rate at which total output and productivity were increasing.

Environmental

The structural shift from a predominantly agricultural to a predominantly industrial economy was accompanied by a corresponding shift in population from rural to urban areas, in large part because industries increasingly tended to be located in towns. As a result, the population of most towns grew rapidly and in some cases extremely rapidly. Many towns and cities trebled their population in the first half of the nineteenth century. Such growth was particularly impressive in the areas where factory industry developed – initially south-east Lancashire and later the West Riding and other parts of the north and Midlands – but even towns in the less industrialized south of England increased their populations.

This rapid growth created major environmental problems, foremost among which were those related to working-class housing. The two main deficiencies of the working-class housing of British towns in the first half of the nineteenth century were overcrowding and low building standards. Overcrowding occurred for a number of reasons. The most important of these was that, in an era before effective planning legislation, high demand for housing provided landowners and speculative builders with an opportunity to make large profits on houses. The more houses that could be packed into a small area, the more profit could be made from it. In other circumstances, market forces might have reduced housing density as those looking for accommodation turned to better-quality housing at a greater distance from the town centre, but the limited availability of transport and the nature of the labour market in the early and mid-nineteenth century combined to prevent this. Before the introduction of trams and motor buses in the late nineteenth and early twentieth centuries, most working-class people had perforce to walk to work. This of itself set a limit on how far away from the workplace it was possible to live. Labour market conditions narrowed this limit still further. One of the main characteristics of employment in the first half of the nineteenth century was that it was unstable and frequently interrupted. Many workers were hired by the day, and in these circumstances it was essential for workers to be able to arrive early at the place of hiring to maximize their chances of obtaining work. Even for workers in more stable employment there were significant advantages to living close to work, such as being able to save money by eating lunch at home. So locations close to town centres or to major employers continued to command a premium. Such locations were inevitably in short supply, and landowners and builders were not in general self-sacrificing enough to forgo the gains they could make by building at very high densities. Herein were the origins of back-to-back housing laid out in confined courts.

The high rental value of urban land resulted not only in houses with far too little space around them, but also in overcrowding of people within houses. This was because houses were too small to fit large families adequately, and rents too high for the poorest families to be able to afford to occupy more than one or two rooms. In the most deprived areas, such as the Irish quarters of Liverpool, a high proportion of families lived entirely in cellars.

Back-to-back houses, and still more cellars, provided a very unhealthy living environment. Two out of four rooms in the typical back-to-back had no natural light or ventilation, and of course none of the rooms could be through-ventilated. Back-to-backs were often shoddily constructed at maximum speed and minimum cost. They had thin walls and were frequently subject to damp. Cellars were almost invariably damp and cold and extremely vulnerable to flooding.

These conditions led to ill health for three main reasons. First, because the quality of the housing was so poor and internal overcrowding so prevalent, working-class houses were difficult to keep clean. Dirty houses provided breeding grounds for rats and flies. Second, overcrowding within the house and the close proximity of a large number of other families living in similarly bad and overcrowded conditions meant that air-borne contagious diseases, such as tuberculosis, one of the nineteenth century's major killers, spread easily. Third, because working-class housing was rarely proof against leaking and flooding, water-borne diseases like cholera and typhoid also spread easily.

However, it was not only because of the inadequacy of working-class housing that early nineteenth-century towns were such unhealthy places. Equally significant was pollution, from both inorganic and organic processes. The most blatant source of inorganic pollution was industry. Almost any print of a nineteenth-century industrial town shows chimneys spewing forth smoke. Smoke, and the soot and ashes it deposited, was the most important atmospheric pollutant, responsible for aggravating respiratory disease (which was often fatal) on a colossal scale. But other industrial pollutants, even if not generated in such quantities, were even more damaging to those affected. Many industries released noxious gases into the atmosphere. The most notorious offenders in this respect were the alkali works. These emitted gases so harmful that they killed plants growing several miles away. The alkali works were eventually brought under at least partial control by legislation, but many other industries which polluted the atmosphere were still not effectively controlled even by the end of the nineteenth century.

Industrial pollution of watercourses was an equally serious problem. Virtually all rivers in industrial areas were heavily contaminated by industrial effluent, including toxic chemicals, mineral deposits and other waste products. In Manchester and many other industrial towns the rivers ran black with dyes and other chemicals. This not only endangered water supplies, but prevented the use of these rivers for bathing, a serious matter at a time when few working-class houses had running water and many did not even have a bathtub.

Besides polluting the air and water, industrial processes also contaminated the ground they used. Often land which had been used for industrial or extractive purposes remained unfit for any other use, due to toxic residues, for decades after the enterprise which had caused the damage had ceased to occupy the site. Arsenic pollution from copper-smelting, for example, turned virtually the entire Lower Swansea valley into wasteland by the end of the nineteenth century.[7]

Industrial processes were, however, not the only source of inorganic pollution. Domestic and commercial consumption of coal was in some areas a major cause of poor air quality. The infamous 'London smog', which could cause 5,000 excess deaths in a week, was largely the product of the hearths of London homes and offices, rather than industry.

Although some of the inorganic pollutants which billowed into the air, poured into rivers or were deposited on the ground were measure for measure more deadly than any of the organic pollutants, it was the latter which did the most damage because of the sheer quantity in which they were released. One major source of organic pollutants was animals. The number of horses used for urban transport increased throughout the nineteenth century, depositing an immense quantity of dung on the streets every day. Horses, though, were not the only animal offenders. While railways meant that not all cattle were now moved on the hoof to urban marketplaces and abattoirs, even those cattle which were moved by rail still had to be taken on the hoof from the railway termini to the slaughterhouses. In addition to this, some livestock was actually kept on a permanent basis within towns. Much of the urban milk supply came from cows kept in grossly unhealthy and disease-ridden conditions in urban dairies. Furthermore, some of the working class kept their own animals – usually pigs or poultry. These animals were often accommodated within the house (sometimes in the cellar).

Because early nineteenth-century sewerage systems were of very limited efficiency and extent, all this animal dung tended to accumulate in the streets rather than being removed. 'Crossing-sweepers' made a living by clearing a passage through the dung at places where pedestrians wanted to cross a road, but this literally only shifted the problem from one place to another. Many of the poor collected animal dung because of the profit to be made from selling it to farmers.[8] The result was that in working-class districts there were heaps of manure in most streets, in courtyards and outside the doors of houses. These were a breeding ground for rats, flies and bacteria and hence for disease.

It was human beings, however, who were the most dangerous source of organic pollution, because human excrement could carry infectious disease directly from one person to another. The main problem was again the deficiency or non-existence of sewers. Little if any profit could be made by providing sewers to working-class districts, and in the context of the limited administrative and interventionist capacity of local government until the last quarter of the century, few working-class areas had adequate sewers. Even where sewers were provided, their design was often poor, so they easily became blocked and then exacerbated rather than mitigated health risks. Frequently they were not connected to a main sewer. Even had better sewers existed, they would have been of limited value, since few working-class areas had proper water supplies. Water treatment was as yet a poorly developed science, and water supplies were often drawn directly from the same rivers into which industrial and domestic effluent was discharged. Furthermore, many working-class households were not able to obtain adequate quantities even of this polluted water, since they were reliant on pumps or wells which were often at some distance from the house. Personal and domestic hygiene was almost unattainable in these conditions.

Rapid urbanization and industrialization therefore placed a severe strain on the urban environment. Houses were too small, too close together, too poorly constructed, and had too many occupants. Air, water and land were polluted by industrial processes and domestic fuel consumption. Animal and human excrement accumulated in the streets. Early nineteenth-century cities were dirty, noisy, malodorous and unhealthy places in which to live.

Social

While there has been little dissent from the view that industrialization and urbanization had a deleterious effect on the environment of British towns, no such consensus exists with respect to the effects of the industrial revolution on working-class living standards (although clearly the unhealthiness of nineteenth-century towns has implications for this question). Indeed, the debate on the working-class standard of living during the industrial revolution has been one of the longest-running, most bitterly contested and most extensively researched questions of modern British history. Two main schools of thought exist. The so-called 'optimists' argue that although some groups of workers did experience a deterioration in their living standards, this was more than compensated for by a large rise in real incomes experienced by the majority of the working class. The 'pessimists' argue that average real incomes rose little if at all, and that any such rise was more than outweighed by a deterioration in the quality of life more broadly conceived. The early stages of the argument were inconclusive, mainly because both leading optimists such as R. M. Hartwell and leading pessimists such as E. J. Hobsbawm and E. P. Thompson drew on wage evidence which related to selected groups of workers.[9] However, in the 1970s and 1980s more painstaking statistical research and the techniques of the new economic history allowed comprehensive indexes of wages and consumer prices to be constructed. The index developed by P. Lindert and J. Williamson, published in the early 1980s, was generally regarded as substantially more authoritative than anything which either optimists or pessimists had produced before.[10] Lindert and Williamson's data appeared to demonstrate conclusively that real wages had increased rapidly during the classic period of the industrial revolution between 1760 and 1830; indeed, Lindert and Williamson claimed that they had 'nearly doubled'. This appeared to resolve the standard of living debate in favour of the optimists. Even allowing for margins of error it seemed inconceivable that so large an increase could be whittled away to anything less than a still-impressive rise in real incomes.

However, both optimists and pessimists had accepted in principle ever since the early exchanges between Hartwell and Hobsbawm that a true gauge of the standard of living would need to include not only real earnings but also less tangible elements such as health, amenities and the quality of the environment. Most contributors to the debate had focused primarily on real wages or earnings because the difficulty of quantifying the other dimensions of the standard of living, and hence of making non-subjective comparisons, appeared so intractable. In the 1980s, though, a new approach was developed. For some time historians had been interested in the possibility of using so-called 'anthropometric' data – especially human height – as a measure of living standards. The principal advantage of such data was thought to be that they would yield a 'net' measure of living standards – in other words that they would reflect all or at least most aspects of the standard of living, in contrast to the one-dimensional measure provided by real earnings. The first major dataset was that constructed by R. Floud, K. Wachter and A. Gregory, using records from the army and the Marine Society. This appeared to indicate that average height had increased significantly during the early years of the industrial revolution, but that after 1830 it had stagnated or even declined until the 1860s.[11] However, further research, and criticisms of the methods used by Floud, Wachter and Gregory, suggested that the apparent increase in average height during the early industrial revolution was a statistical artefact, but the fall in average height between the 1830s and the 1860s was confirmed.[12] The anthropometric studies therefore appeared to imply a diametrically opposed conclusion to the real earnings data so painstakingly and apparently conclusively assembled by Lindert and Williamson. The implication was that the disease environment of early Victorian cities must have been so hostile that any increase in real earnings was more than offset. Support for this view was provided by further statistical research on infant mortality and on life expectancy in Victorian urban areas, which confirmed that nineteenth-century British towns were markedly less healthy than the countryside, and that in general there was a positive correlation between the size of a town and its unhealthiness.[13] As the population moved from the countryside to the towns, and then became increasingly concentrated in the larger towns and cities, it would follow that working-class health would be put under pressure.

The most important recent contribution to the debate on living standards has been by C. Feinstein. Feinstein presents new data on wages and prices which suggest that Lindert and Williamson substantially overestimated gains in real earnings. Most groups of workers probably increased their real earnings in the late eighteenth and early nineteenth centuries, but only by about 30 per cent (less if making allowance for unemployment and if Ireland is included).[14] Feinstein's evidence fits better with the anthropometric data than Lindert and Williamson's, because height is closely related to nutrition, which in turn is heavily affected by income. At present, therefore, a moderate pessimist consensus appears to have been established, to the effect that while real earnings probably increased somewhat, this was more than counterbalanced by losses in other areas, notably nutrition and health.

The anthropometric studies represented a methodological advance on previous work because they aimed to capture a broader range of influences on living standards than income measures alone could do. However, even the anthropometric approach cannot capture non-material elements of the quality of life. Research on such non-material aspects remains poorly integrated with the mainstream debate on the standard of living because it has not proved possible to devise informative quantitative measures of these aspects, but the fact that there is no way of accurately measuring them does not, of course, imply that they were not important. One of the most important of these non-material aspects is how industrialization and urbanization affected the quality of family life. Contemporaries were deeply concerned about this and many believed that industrialization, and particularly factory industry, upset the balance between husbands and their wives and children. Industrialization often had the effect of displacing skilled male workers and making them unemployed, while women and children constituted an important part of the industrial (and especially factory) workforce. Historians have been more divided. Some have argued that the employment opportunities for women provided by industrialization gave women greater independence from often oppressive domestic relationships. Others, however, have emphasized that the increased industrial employment of women in the first half of the nineteenth century took place on unfavourable terms, in the context of a glut in the labour market. Wages were therefore very low. Women worked, by and large, because they had to in order to support their families; and rather than representing a release, industrial employment was more likely to mean subjection to the double tyranny of workplace as well as domestic exploitation.[15]

A second and related non-material dimension of the standard of living is the question of the nature of the work experience. In a celebrated essay E. P. Thompson argued that industrialization had brought about a marked intensification of work discipline. In the eighteenth century, most workers had been engaged in agricultural or artisanal production. Such work was largely dependent on human skill. Its pace could vary according to the worker's effort, and its timing was largely dictated by natural rhythms such as the length of daylight. Industrialization, especially in the form of factory production, permitted much less flexibility. Increasingly production was machine-dependent, and the pace of work was determined by the rate of the machine. Furthermore, as production became more capital-intensive, employers became increasingly concerned not to leave machinery standing idle. Regularity in working hours – clock-time rather than natural time – was therefore increasingly imposed on the workforce. The fact that a worker in a mechanized enterprise was likely to be performing a task which was closely interlocked with other parts of the production process pointed in the same direction: absenteeism was no longer tolerable.[16]

However, while Thompson's argument may be valid for the factory sector, as we have seen this was as yet relatively small. Research on other industrial areas, particularly that carried out by E. Hopkins on Birmingham, suggests that elsewhere industrialization may not have resulted in a comparable intensification of work discipline. In Birmingham, small workshops predominated. The number of workers per enterprise averaged fewer than twenty. Partly because of this, many workers progressed to become small masters themselves, and there were usually intermediate positions (for example through subcontracting) between employer and employee. Capitalization and the use of machinery was limited, artisanal modes of production continued to predominate well into the second half of the nineteenth century, and irregular working hours were the norm. The tradition of 'St Monday', whereby workers regularly took unauthorized leave from work on Monday, remained strong until the introduction of the Saturday half-holiday in the 1860s and 1870s.[17]

Whether an intensification of work discipline in the first half of the nineteenth century can be adduced as further grist to the pessimist mill therefore remains as open a question as whether industrialization adversely affected family life. Nevertheless, whatever the ultimate verdict on the standard of living question, few would dispute that industrialization and urbanization had an immense impact on those who lived through it, and that scarcely any aspect of their lives was untouched by it.

Recent scholarship has tended to downplay some of the larger claims that have been made about the industrial revolution. Nevertheless, even if we accept that the rate of economic growth was slower than was once believed and the level of real earnings higher, it is implausible to deny that the first half of the nineteenth century was a period of intense and, to contemporaries, startling change. The structure of the economy was radically transformed; by 1850 the typical British subject was an industrial worker in a town rather than a farmworker in the countryside. Even if we now know that traditional technology continued to predominate, to contemporaries it was the countless numbers of new industrial enterprises springing up across the country which were more obvious. Furthermore, the factories of the cotton districts represented a new form of industrial production which, because of its potential for productivity growth, had immense implications for future economic development. The environmental transformation wrought by urbanization and industrialization was equally dramatic, if almost wholly negative. The galloping expansion of the industrial towns and cities in the first half of the nineteenth century brought problems of disease and pollution on a scale previously unimagined. These problems were far beyond the capacity of the rudimentary structure of early nineteenth-century local government to resolve. The failure to regulate housing construction and pollution and to provide adequate clean water and sewerage facilities was a large part of the reason for the low life expectancy characteristic of nineteenth-century British towns and cities. As regards the working-class standard of living more broadly, it seems possible that there was a slow, if far from steady, rise in real earnings between the late eighteenth and the mid-nineteenth centuries. Many groups, such as certain categories of domestic outworkers, fell below the average and may have suffered an actual decline of real earnings. In any case, the limited rise in average real earnings was counterbalanced, and may have been more than outweighed, by the adverse environmental consequences of rapid urban growth, and perhaps by less tangible non-material factors such as the effects of industrialization on family life and on the experience of work.

In attempting to understand early nineteenth-century attitudes to the countryside, it is these disruptive and startling characteristics of urbanization and industrialization, rather than the continuities which have made more impression on some modern scholars, that we need to keep to the forefront of our minds. As we shall see in the following chapters, attitudes to the countryside in the first half of the nineteenth century were shaped primarily by urban and industrial change rather than by autonomous developments in the countryside. Only if we register the profound impact of the industrial revolution on the lives of contemporaries are the corresponding shifts which occurred in thinking and feeling about the countryside comprehensible.

· ·

CHAPTER 2

Literature and the Countryside, c.1800 to c.1870

§ WE saw in the last chapter that urbanization and industrialization had a dramatic and transformative effect not only on the economy but also on the urban environment, and on working-class living standards. Such marked social change in urban England inevitably also had profound effects on attitudes to the countryside, although, as we will see in subsequent chapters, attitudes to the countryside in turn affected the further development of urban and industrial society. The next two chapters attempt to assess the interaction of urbanization and industrialization with attitudes to the countryside in the context of two different traditions: first, the largely middle-class tradition of 'high' literature; and second, the largely working-class tradition of political radicalism. In subsequent chapters, we will see how viewing urban and industrial problems through a rural prism led to attempts to solve these difficulties through the application of selected aspects of rural life to urban settings.

One of the most strongly marked features of 'high' literature in the first half of the nineteenth century is the strong contrast often drawn in it between urban experience on the one hand, and rural on the other (with the latter strongly favoured). At first sight, it is tempting to attribute the development of this contrast to a direct and straightforward response to the socio-economic changes described in the previous chapter. The rapid pace of urban expansion, the ugliness, dirtiness and unhealthiness of the growing towns and the scale of the challenge posed by the latent radicalism of the industrial working class seem quite sufficient to account for a widespread literary reaction in favour of the countryside as the precursor of, and most readily available contrast to, industrial and urban England. However, although as we shall see there were important connections between social conditions and literary attitudes in the first half of the nineteenth century, writers never react in a direct and un-mediated way to social change because they are virtually always working in a literary tradition as well as being participants in and observers of society more broadly. So if we are to understand the way in which the writers of this period contrasted the countryside with the towns and cities, we need to be aware not only of the contemporary social context but also of the literary contexts within which these writers were working. The two most important literary contexts we need to consider are, first, the pastoral tradition, and, second, the influence of Romanticism.

The pastoral tradition is one of the earliest and most enduring literary genres. Its essential characteristics are that it describes an idyllic rural life in stylized terms. This idyllic life is often located in a 'golden age' set in the near or remote past in which men are at peace with one another, amply provided with food, shelter and any other essentials for a happy life by a generous nature, and free from the necessity for any onerous work. The idea of a rural golden age of this kind can be traced back to Hesiod, writing in the ninth century BC at the beginnings of the European literary tradition. However, a stricter definition of pastoral includes a second element not found in Hesiod: the rural way of life described should be concerned with animal husbandry and herding, not with the cultivation of crops. The force of this contrast is that animal husbandry is, at least under favourable circumstances, compatible with a leisurely and unexacting existence, whereas arable cultivation – at least before mechanization – was invariably physically arduous. Pastoral in this stricter sense first emerged in Greek literary culture in the third century BC; the poet Theocritus is often considered as the original source of the genre, but it was the Roman poet Virgil who had the greatest influence in the development and transmission of the pastoral tradition. Virgil wrote two major groups of rural poems, the *Georgics* and the *Eclogues*. The *Georgics* were concerned with practical instruction in primarily arable agriculture. The *Eclogues*, set in the mythical landscape of Arcadia (Greece), were by contrast paeans to the alleged simplicity and innocent pleasures of the shepherd's life. In this respect the *Eclogues* represent a retreat from the unpolished and earthy shepherds found in Theocritus, an important shift because Virgil's Eclogues were much imitated both in classical times and subsequently, and came to be regarded as the epitome of the pastoral as a genre.[1]

In the middle ages, little poetry was written in the classical tradition, but the revival of interest in Latin and Greek literature in renaissance Italy and France led to the revival of the pastoral. In the sixteenth century, the revived pastoral spread to England, notable Elizabethan examples including Sir Philip Sidney's *Arcadia* and Edmund Spenser's *The Shepherd's Calendar*. Variations on the pastoral persisted through the seventeenth century and, although often in modified or ironic forms, into the eighteenth century. Frequently the emphasis in these derived pastoral poems was on the contrast between rural simplicity and innocence, and urban degeneracy and vice. However, the early eighteenth-century poets Alexander Pope and James Thomson were the last major practitioners of pastoral in the renaissance tradition, partly because the eighteenth-century preference for poems which were useful or instructive as well as ornamental led to a shift within rural poetry towards the previously neglected georgic tradition.[2]

The development of the pastoral tradition had by this time created a firmly established poetic convention, in which very positive values were accorded to the countryside, in implicit or often indeed explicit contrast to the negative values attributed to urban life. However, although the pastoral tradition established the country/town contrast as one of the major genres of European literature, pastoral was in many ways a limited and unsatisfactory literary form. Built into it was the assumption that rural life was pleasant and easy; furthermore, from Virgil onwards the effect of the pastoral depended increasingly on the contrast between simple matter and elaborate style. Although pastoral was ostensibly about humble country people, it became the characteristic poetry of sophisticated courts. Hence its capacity for incorporated real rural experience was negligible; it could scarcely be considered as a mode of serious social criticism.[3]

The most influential rural poem of the mid-eighteenth century was Thomas Gray's *Elegy Written in a Country Churchyard* (1751). This departed from pastoral conventions in various ways, for example in describing rural work as exhausting rather than as easy and pleasant, but in its gentle melancholy tended strongly to reinforce the pastoral stereotype of the countryside as a peaceful retreat from the travails of urban life. Subsequent eighteenth-century poets habitually adopted a similar stance, with an idealized countryside serving as a foil to the decadent town – a contrast epitomized in William Cowper's line 'God made the country, and man made the town' (*The Task*, I, 749). In poems like Cowper's, the terms and values deployed in the town/country contrast were recognizably congruent with those which had been developed in the pastoral tradition. Some later eighteenth-century poets, it is true, did react against the mismatch between idealized poetic evocations of rural life and the often less agreeable realities of the latter, a mismatch that became increasingly blatant in the late eighteenth century as rural living standards deteriorated. Oliver Goldsmith's *The Deserted Village* lambasted the social consequences of enclosure, while George Crabbe's *The Village* sought to undermine pastoral by offering an account of a village community entirely dominated by selfish, sordid motives, mutual exploitation and unrelieved suffering. In their different ways both Goldsmith and Crabbe nevertheless remained caught in the constraints of pastoral. Goldsmith was able to articulate his anger at the effects of enclosure only by setting these off against a sentimentalized and unrealistic description of pre-enclosure village life, while Crabbe, who wrote *The Village* explicitly as a reaction against Goldsmith's idealizations, tarred both rich and poor with the same brush in his withering portrait, leaving no material from which a better future could be imagined and so ultimately neutralizing the implications of his social criticism.

The limited range and depth of responses to the countryside and to nature contained within the pastoral tradition and its derivatives were, however, radically transcended by the rise of Romanticism in the late eighteenth century. Romanticism, like the pastoral, has an almost infinite range of meanings, but in the context of literary attitudes to rural England it is the poetry of Wordsworth, Coleridge, Shelley, Keats, Clare and Blake that is most significant. A full discussion of the genesis of English Romanticism is beyond the scope of this chapter, but one of the crucial developments was the changing social basis of the audience for poetry. Prior to the eighteenth century, poets had in general been dependent on court or aristocratic patronage; only monarchs and noblemen combined financial resources with literary interests, so poets had little choice but to address themselves to this highly restricted elite audience. The growth in eighteenth-century England of a large and prosperous middle class, supporting an increasingly independent, self-confident and sophisticated culture, created for the first time a market for poetry (and indeed for other forms of imaginative literature). Writers were therefore by the same process freed from dependence on an aristocratic patron, and subjected to the apparently arbitrary caprices of the market. This permitted and encouraged a greater range of individuality, yet created a correspondingly intense sense of insecurity and isolation. Cut off from humanity in this way, writers might turn to nature for companionship and consolation. It was characteristic of Romanticism, and especially of the English Romantic poets, that they found in nature the revelation of true feeling and, hence poetic inspiration. The uncorrupted emotions which could be discovered or rediscovered through the encounter with nature were in turn potentially the source of a vision of restored unity between the poet and mankind, since they were free from the taint of selfishness and false values which otherwise set men apart from each other.

The Romantic attitude to nature contrasts with the characteristic eighteenth-century 'Augustan' attitude (although any such contrast tends to underplay the elements of transition between the two). Typically, early and mid-eighteenth-century poets had invoked nature in generalized and timeless ways. Woods, rivers or mountains might prompt reflections but were rarely described in a way which sharply identified them as one rather than another of their kind. The reflections induced were also likely to be generalized and only loosely associated with the natural feature which ostensibly gave rise to them. In the poetry of William Wordsworth, the first and most influential of the English Romantic poets, nature manifested itself far more actively and intensely. Wordsworth described particular moments of experience in precise and emphatic detail. These moments were highly individualized, both in that they were specific to Wordsworth himself, and in that they were direct products of the particular situation rather than being reflections hung on to a situation. Earlier poets often approached nature in a calm and detached spirit; for Wordsworth, nature was a ceaselessly active and transforming force, which fused itself with his poetic being. In this, Wordsworth was to prove a powerful influence not only on other poets of his generation but in forming the minds of later nineteenth-century writers and thinkers. J. S. Mill wrote movingly in his autobiography of how the descriptions of rural beauty 'and of thought coloured by feeling, under the excitement of beauty' in Wordsworth's poetry had provided him with a 'culture of the feelings' to supplement the dry and rationalistic cast of mind his education had implanted in him. Mark Rutherford wrote of his first reading of Wordsworth's poems in *Lyrical Ballads* that 'the change it wrought in me could only be compared with that which is said to have been wrought on Paul himself by the divine apparition'.[4] By the mid-nineteenth century, Wordsworth's once quite unusual reverence for nature had become part of the cultural atmosphere in which educated English people moved: most of the major Victorian poets, including Tennyson, Browning, Matthew Arnold and Gerard Manley Hopkins, took the profound importance of nature for granted.

The intensified and elevated awareness of nature popularized by Wordsworth led directly to a privileging of the countryside over the city, in a far more serious way than the pastoral tradition had ever aspired to. At the same time, another consequence of the Romantic infusion of individual moral meaning into nature was even more significant for the evolution of nineteenth-century literary attitudes to the countryside. This was that it made available to writers of the next generation a powerful vocabulary with which they could criticize urban growth and industrial expansion. The central word in this vocabulary was 'unnatural' (and its associated concepts). Since the natural was the touchstone of goodness, of pure feeling and of poetry itself, to label something as 'unnatural' was to deplore it in the strongest possible way.

The Romantics and their followers encountered urbanization before they encountered industrialization. As we saw in the last chapter, industrial growth was relatively limited in the eighteenth and early nineteenth centuries; it was only after 1830 that it became markedly more rapid. Urban growth, however, was quite considerable in the eighteenth century, above all in the case of London. It is unsurprising, therefore, that it was London which was initially most criticized as unnatural, and only subsequently that the industrial cities of the north began to be condemned by writers in the same terms.

While the influence of Romantic attitudes to nature, and behind them the long tradition of the pastoral, can be seen as forming the broad literary context within which early nineteenth-century writers responded to urbanization and industrialization, writers also brought their own individual experiences and perceptions to their writing. So even a brief assessment of literary attitudes to the countryside and to the industrial revolution must pay some attention to the differences of emphasis between some of the leading writers of this period.

Wordsworth himself left his readers in little doubt about his preference for the countryside over the city. In his *Lines Written a Few Miles Above Tintern Abbey*, one of his best-known and most influential poems, he records that memories of the River Wye gave him comfort when he lived 'in lonely rooms, and 'mid the din / Of towns and cities' (lines 27–8). Even more striking is his description of London's Bartholomew Fair in Book VII of his autobiographical poem *The Prelude* (completed 1805). Here Wordsworth denounces the fair at length and in violent terms:

> What a hell
> For eyes and ears, what anarchy and din,
> Barbarian and infernal – 'tis a dream
> Monstrous in colour, motion, shape, sight, sound.[5]

This is an extreme example of Wordsworth's hostility to the city, but in common with other passages in *The Prelude* it powerfully articulates what has become a central modern response to the city: the sense of the individual observer lost and isolated in an anonymous crowd. The contrast is of course with nature in the countryside, in which, rather than losing himself, the individual or poet can most fully realize his inmost being. However, although Wordsworth's elevation of nature and of the countryside is beyond dispute, his attitude to cities and particularly to London was capable of more variation than the lines quoted above may suggest. Williams, for example, argues that although one of Wordsworth's responses to London was a reactionary fear of the crowd, other passages in *The Prelude* indicate that he could at least envisage the possibility of a new form of human unity which would be facilitated rather than excluded by the city.[6]

William Cobbett, working in the quite different literary tradition of political journalism, also castigated London as 'unnatural'. Indeed, Cobbett developed the concept of London's unnaturalness into the cornerstone of a comprehensive indictment of the political system of his day. For Cobbett, London's unnaturalness consisted in it being (in his view) the 'artificial' consequence of government taxation. According to Cobbett, a corrupt government representing a self-interested elite imposed taxes on the largely rural population in order to fund war abroad and repression at home. Wealth was channelled away from the countryside to the seat of government in London, and there expended. As a result, prosperity and people were sucked out of the countryside and drawn into London, which Cobbett referred to as 'the Great Wen' in order to indicate that it was a deviation from nature:[7]

The dispersion of the wen is the only real difficulty that I see in settling the affairs of the nation and restoring it to a happy state. But dispersed it *must* be; and if there be half a million, or more, of people to suffer, the consolation is, that the suffering will be divided into half a million of parts.[8]

Cobbett's radicalism limited his influence on other contemporary writers, although his following among agricultural labourers and farmers was un-matched. A far more important influence on the intellectual and cultural life of the first half of the nineteenth century, however, was the historian and essayist Thomas Carlyle. Although working in a different idiom and addressing a different audience, Carlyle too used the concept of nature and naturalness as his crucial test of social organization and institutions. Carlyle's significance in formulating attitudes to the countryside is that he was one of the first writers to engage seriously with industrialization as opposed merely to urban-ization. Unlike Cobbett, Carlyle was capable of appreciating the potential grandeur of industrial production. But in his *Past and Present*, perhaps his most extended and widely respected meditation on industrialism, the ideal he contrasts with modern urban industrial conditions is medieval monasticism in the setting of a small country town.[9]

Disraeli, whose industrial novel *Sybil* popularized the phrase 'the two nations', was, like Carlyle, able to see some potential benefits in industry. His attitude to the countryside as compared to towns might seem therefore to be more neutral than that of Wordsworth or Cobbett, especially as a notable passage in *Sybil* exposes the poor drainage and inadequate maintenance behind the picturesque exterior of a country village. However, the 'solution' Disraeli offers at the end of *Sybil* to the social problems he identifies at the outset of the novel indicates that even in his case the latent preference was strongly for the countryside. Sybil, the 'daughter of the people', is married to a rural aristocrat, and the future of manufacturing is seen to lie in a new 'aristocracy of industry' which will build spacious and well-appointed factories in attrac-tively rural settings:

The vast form of the spreading factory, the roofs and gardens of the village, the Tudor chimneys of the house of Trafford, the spire of the gothic church, with the sparkling river and the sylvan background, came rather suddenly on the sight of Egremont. They were indeed in the pretty village street before he was aware he was about to enter it.[10]

Disraeli's primary interest was in politics rather than in novel-writing, and it is perhaps not surprising that for a more thorough-going analysis of in-dustrialism we have to turn elsewhere, for example to Charles Dickens. Dickens's *Hard Times*, his most sustained inquiry into life in an industrial town, was published in 1854. *Hard Times* was dedicated to Thomas Carlyle, and once again the crucial indicator of the human inadequacy of 'Coketown', Dickens's representative industrial city, is the term 'unnatural':

> It was a town of red brick, or of brick that would have been red if the smoke and ashes had allowed it; but as matters stood it was a town of unnatural red and black like the painted face of a savage. It was a town of machinery and tall chimneys, out of which interminable serpents of smoke trailed themselves for ever and ever, and never got uncoiled. It had a black canal in it, and a river that ran purple with ill-smelling dye, and vast piles of building full of windows where there was a rattling and a trembling all day long, and where the piston of the steam-engine worked monotonously up and down, like the head of an elephant in a state of melancholy madness. It contained several large streets all very like one another, and many small streets still more like one another, inhabited by people equally like one another, who all went in and out at the same hours, with the same sound upon the same pavements, to do the same work, and to whom every day was the same as yesterday and tomorrow, and every year the counterpart of the last and the next.[11]

This artificiality, ugliness and numbing mechanicalism is contrasted with the spontaneity and life of the countryside:

> … no temperature made the melancholy mad elephants more mad or more sane. Their wearisome heads went up and down at the same rate, in hot weather and cold, wet weather and dry, fair weather and foul. The measured motion of their shadows on the wall, was the substitute Coketown had to show for the shadows of the rustling woods; while, for the summer hum of insects, it could offer, all the year round, from the dawn of Monday to the night of Saturday, the whirr of shafts and wheels.[12]

Against the rigidity and regulation of Coketown, which stifles 'fancy' or the freedom of the imagination, Dickens sets the unregulated and natural world of the countryside.

In other works, however, Dickens adopted a more nuanced attitude, if not to industry then at least to the possibilities of the city. Significantly, his portrayal of urban life offers more dynamic elements when it is set in his home town of London. In novels such as *Dombey and Son* and *Bleak House*, Dickens develops Wordsworth's perception of the alienating anonymity of the urban experience, but seeks to demonstrate that the apparently impersonal and random forces governing this experience are in fact based on human choices and are therefore potentially amenable to human control. If some of Dickens's London novels are therefore more open to positive interpretations of the city, or at least of the city's potential, than *Hard Times*, it remains the case that the 'natural' (and what for Dickens is its correlative, the childlike) are crucial valuing measures for him. It is, in the last analysis, the absence of the natural in cities which obscures the human relationship between those who live within them.

Elizabeth Gaskell shared Dickens's admiration for Carlyle; the title page of *Mary Barton*, her novel of industrial working-class life in Manchester, includes a quotation from the latter. Gaskell's view of the industrial city in some respects recalls that put forward by Dickens in *Hard Times*. The first glimpse of Manchester ('Milton Northern') in *North and South* is as follows:

> For several miles before they reached Milton, they saw a deep lead-coloured cloud hanging over the horizon in the direction in which it lay. It was all the darker from contrast with the pale grey-blue of the wintry sky; for in Heston there had been the earliest signs of frost. Nearer to the town, the air had a faint taste and smell of smoke; perhaps, after all, more a loss of the fragrance of grass and herbage than any positive taste or smell. Quick they were whirled over long, straight, hopeless streets of regularly-built houses, all small and of brick. Here and there a great oblong many-windowed factory stood up, like a hen among her chickens, puffing out black 'unparliamentary' smoke, and sufficiently accounting for the cloud which Margaret had taken to foretell rain.[13]

Although her assessment of the aesthetic and environmental quality of Milton Northern remains bleak, Gaskell does show an admiration for some aspects of the society created by the cotton masters. In particular she seems to appreciate the emphasis on individual responsibility and the achievement of the factory owner who is the hero of the novel, Mr Thornton. Gaskell's contrast between industrial North and rural South is carefully balanced, but perhaps more significant is the fact that she makes it quite clear that if the North is to develop into a humane and truly civilized society, it will have to incorporate many of the distinctively rural qualities of the agricultural South.

By the middle years of the nineteenth century, therefore, writers had developed a powerful critique of the social and environmental conditions produced by urbanization and industrialization, a critique which was characteristically made in the form of the contrast between town and country. The countryside had in the hands of these writers become a measure of value of the new industrial towns and cities, in a way that was much more serious and searching than the essentially individual and moral (as opposed to social) opposition between urban decadence and rural innocence typical of the pastoral tradition.

In this way the countryside had become a means of assessing and potentially improving the quality of urban and industrial life, but one of the consequences of this particular critical strategy was that, intentionally or otherwise, the countryside was progressively idealized. While Cobbett had been fully alive to, and indeed angry about, the poverty and oppression so widespread in rural southern England, rural poverty is essentially invisible in the works of Dickens,

Gaskell, and even George Eliot. In the case of Dickens this may be partially excusable since Dickens was an urban novelist who rarely made use of rural settings. The same cannot be said of either Gaskell or Eliot, both of whom grew up in rural areas and set several of their novels at least partly in the countryside. Both the Helstone of *North and South* and the Loamshire of *Adam Bede* are presented in decidedly comfortable terms; the hardship, discontent and occasional violent protests of actual mid-nineteenth-century southern English agricultural labourers seem to belong to a different world to that portrayed in these novels. It has been argued that the effect of this suppression is not merely to disguise the bleak social conditions in the countryside at this time, but to mystify the real causes of misery operative in both town and country, such as the cyclical slumps caused by the trade cycle in a developing market economy. The effect is then to indicate, explicitly in the case of Elizabeth Gaskell and implicitly as regards George Eliot, that what needs to be done to make things better in the towns is to make them more like the countryside.

A telling indicator that writers were increasingly succumbing to an ever more idealized view of country life is that by the mid-nineteenth century rural novels were in most cases no longer being set in the present, but were displaced to the past, where the fiction of a well-functioning, integrated and on the whole contented society was easier to maintain.

In subsequent chapters we shall see both how this was the origin of a long and highly influential cultural tradition which diagnosed the social ills of Britain's industrialism through the prism of an idealized (and mostly just vanished) rural past, and how this idealization of the countryside also affected rural England itself – mostly deleteriously. First, however, we need to examine a second major response to urbanization and industrialization in which attitudes to the countryside played a major part: working-class political radicalism.

CHAPTER 3

. . . .

Radicalism and the Land, c.1790 to c.1850

§ ENGLISH radicalism in the first half of the nineteenth century displayed a persistent and often intense interest in land and in the countryside. However, early nineteenth-century radicalism was a multi-faceted phenomenon, and different varieties of radicalism construed the relationship between land and popular emancipation in complex and at times contradictory ways. This chapter attempts to elucidate the various strands of radical thinking about the land between the French Revolution and the 1840s, to account for the centrality of land to radicalism in this period, and to indicate some of the ways in which radical attitudes to the land had practical consequences both in the first half of the nineteenth century and thereafter.

The association between land and radicalism in England can be traced back at least as far as the civil war, when several political groups, notably the Diggers, argued for or even attempted to put into practice greater popular use-rights over land. Although attempts have been made to demonstrate links between mid-seventeenth-century political and religious groups and nineteenth-century radicalism, it was only in the wake of the French Revolution that a powerful challenge to the existing English political elite was mounted from within the excluded social strata. The immediate objective, and unifying goal, of the radicalism of the 1790s and the first half of the nineteenth century was political liberty, most often expressed in the form of a demand for universal adult male suffrage, and although almost all radicals believed that the aristocratic 'monopoly' on land ownership was the means by which the aristocracy had succeeded in establishing its political monopoly, not all radicals saw land reform as an immediate objective.[1]

The most systematic and influential of the radical thinkers who did see land as central not only to the explanation of political injustice but to its elimination was Thomas Spence.[2] Spence's arguments attracted a band of loyal followers, who themselves did much to disseminate his ideas within radicalism more broadly. Although there were also other sources for agrarian ideas within radicalism, Spenceanism was clearly the most fertile. The origins and nature of Spence's thought are therefore an essential context for understanding the relationship between early nineteenth-century radicalism and attitudes towards the land.

Spence was born in Newcastle in 1750, of Scottish Calvinist parents. He became a schoolmaster, and throughout his life education remained of great importance to him. There were three main influences on his early intellectual development. The first of these was his Newcastle background. Although a flourishing commercial town and port, Newcastle in the second half of the eighteenth century was not the major city and hub of industrial activity which it was to become in the nineteenth. Indeed, the countryside penetrated right into the heart of the town (a vestige of this can still be seen in the form of the 'Town Moor', a large tract of open country close to the centre of the city which has never been enclosed). To Spence, therefore, town and country did not present themselves as polar opposites; on the contrary, it was natural to see solutions to the problems of one in relation to those of the other. The second major formative influence on Spence was the lively intellectual culture found among Newcastle's artisans. Many of the rationalist ideas of the Enlightenment penetrated, often in popularized forms, to this cultural level. Spence's involvement in the Newcastle Philosophical Society appears to have underpinned his lifelong faith in and commitment to reason and progress, one of the more bizarre manifestations of which was the phonetic alphabet he developed. The third influence was religion. While Spence's rationalism meant that he necessarily looked to non-mystical, human processes to achieve political justice, his early exposure to the Old Testament appears to have provided him with a model for a more just society based on equal rights over land. The idea of the jubilee, found in Leviticus 25, was especially important to him. As expounded in Leviticus, the jubilee was an institution occurring every fifty years whereby land was redistributed to ensure that all members of the community remained equally well provided for. At the same time, debts would be cancelled and slaves and bond-servants freed, while the land would be left fallow for a year and no work would be done.[3] Spence interpreted the biblical jubilee as providing the scriptural basis for a general redistribution of the land on egalitarian principles; in his mind, the concept of the jubilee became synonymous with that of peaceful agrarian revolution.

In about 1787 Spence moved to London. This added two further important elements to his thinking. The first of these was the conviction that the agrarian transformation he looked for was imminent, or at least potentially so. This millenarian belief probably derived in part from the vigour of the often millenarian nonconformist sects which permeated the capital's artisan culture, and in part from the deep impression made on English radicals by the French

Revolution. The latter made what had seemed utopian or at least long-term hopes appear grounded in reality in a way they had not done before. The second element which London added to Spence's thought was a shift away from a belief that all that was required to bring about the jubilee was education, which would result in the general appreciation of the 'truths' which Spence advocated, to a position which explicitly accepted that physical force might be needed to bring the jubilee about. Probably it was the experience of government repression (Spence was imprisoned several times before his death in 1814) that was responsible for this second shift in Spence's ideas.

The foundation of Spence's political thought was the proposition that private ownership of land was the root of all social evil. It was this that allowed men to have power over each other, and so to abuse and exploit each other. Spence argued that land was the collective inheritance of all and should be taken back into public ownership, although on a parochial rather than a national basis. This argument rested on two theoretical premises. First, Spence adopted Locke's view that human beings had originally existed in a property-less 'state of nature', in which all were equal. Spence inferred from this that no generation had the right to appropriate the means of life from a subsequent generation. Since food was the primary means of life, and land was essential for food production, this implied that private appropriation of land was wrong. Second, Spence drew on the seventeenth-century political thinker James Harrington, who argued that agrarian equality was the guarantee of political liberty. If each member of the political community stood independently on the basis of his own land, political intimidation and corruption would be eliminated. An important consequence of the intellectual foundations on which Spence built his argument for public ownership of land was that he did not advocate public ownership of other forms of (movable) property. Just as life was an inalienable property, so movables were rightly private, because they derived from labour, which was an extension of the self.

Spence's political influence was slight until he came to London. Even after his arrival in the late 1780s he initially attracted few followers, perhaps partly because he saw himself as an educator first and foremost rather than as a political leader. Nevertheless, he did slowly seek out political associates. He was active in the London Corresponding Society, the leading metropolitan plebeian radical organization in the 1790s, and allowed a local revolutionary group, the Lambeth Loyalist Association, to practise armed drill in his room. From about 1800 onwards, his ideas became increasingly influential. The Society of Spencean Philanthropists was formed in 1811 or 1812, several of whose members became leading figures in metropolitan radicalism over the next two decades, among them Dr James Watson, Thomas Evans and Allen Davenport. A distinguishing feature of Spence's followers was their revolutionary zeal, perhaps partly attributable to a conviction that the jubilee was imminent. Thomas Evans and Alexander Galloway had been members of the secret revolutionary organization the United Englishmen in 1798; Thomas Pemberton and Charles Penderill were linked to Colonel Despard's conspiracy; and Arthur Thistlewood was executed for his part in the Cato Street conspiracy. Furthermore, in the years immediately after the end of the Napoleonic wars, between 1816 and 1820, when London radicalism was at its height, the Spenceans appear to have been instrumental in precipitating most of the attempts at insurrection. The three Spa Fields demonstrations of the winter of 1816–17, which attracted huge crowds, appear to have been planned as attempts at a Spencean jubilee.

It was partly their leading role in revolutionary activity which gave the Spenceans prestige and helped to promulgate Spence's ideas. In consequence, Spence and his plan were well known to all the leading radical figures of the 1820s and 1830s. Richard Carlile, the leading radical publisher and free-thinking journalist, proclaimed himself a follower of Spence, although he departed from Spence's plan by advocating that popular ownership of land should be achieved by means of an 'equitable tax' rather than through direct confiscation. Other leading radicals who acknowledged Spence's influence included Henry Hetherington and Francis Place.

Spence probably contributed more than any other thinker to the strength of agrarianism within radical circles in the 1820s and 1830s. Increasingly, though, his specific proposals became merged with other radical agendas. They were also given a new twist, and renewed vigour, through cross-fertilization with the ideas of the radical thinker, communitarian and philanthropist Robert Owen (1771–1858), the dominant intellectual influence on English plebeian radicalism in the late 1820s and early 1830s. In theory, Owen was not an out-and-out agrarian; at least in his early writings he advocated model communities based equally on manufacturing and agriculture. But in practice none of the communities established under Owen's aegis after his departure from the cotton mills of New Lanark succeeded in developing a viable industrial element, beyond that which was required to serve the needs of the community itself. Furthermore, as memories of New Lanark were overlaid by the experience of community-formation, the agrarian element in Owen's thinking increasingly predominated. By 1842 he was able to write that Britain 'must now become essentially agricultural' and that he would be 'very sorry ever to have a cotton factory again, for the substantial wealth of the world is only obtained from the land'.[4]

Owen's emphasis on co-operation and community formation, and his confidence that it was actually possible to begin making the 'new society' even before the old unjust society had been overcome, proved inspiring for thousands of radicals and provided a framework within which agrarian ideas could be put into practice even before any Spencean jubilee had been achieved.

Dozens of working-class co-operative associations sprang up across the country, influenced by Owen's ideas. While many of these initially confined themselves to trading, most of them seem to have cherished the ultimate ambition of setting some or all of their members on the land – in some cases in Owenite communities and in other as independent smallholders. Several of these associations, and some other groups of would-be agriculturalists, did succeed in obtaining land, and although in most cases the communities established were short-lived, this should not necessarily be taken as an indication of failure. One of the best known was Ralahine in County Clare, Ireland. Ralahine lasted for more than two years (1831–33), longer than most of the Owenite communities. Furthermore, the community was eventually disbanded for reasons which had little to do with its intrinsic viability. Ralahine was established by John Scott Vandeleur, and he retained ownership of the land throughout. Unfortunately, Vandeleur, as well as being a follower of Owen's, was addicted to gambling. He reached a point of crisis in November 1833, having lost all his possessions, and fled the country. Ralahine passed to his creditors, and the community was evicted. Prior to this point, it had functioned effectively and showed few signs of the weaknesses which had led to the collapse of most of the other Owenite communities within a short time of their formation. However, it has been pointed out that Ralahine differed from the Owenite communties in Britain in important respects. The Irish peasants of whom the community consisted were more used to agricultural work, had lower expectations and were socially and culturally more homogeneous than the diverse array of artisans, factory workers, farmers, clerks and others who entered English and Scottish Owenite communities. The relative success of Ralahine does not therefore necessarily indicate that similar results could have been obtained in Britain.[5]

Some of the Owenite-inspired agrarian ventures were eventually absorbed by the most impressive manifestation of working-class commitment to radical agrarianism – the Chartist Land Plan. The Chartist Land Plan was the outcome, in the first place, of the impasse in which Chartism found itself after the rejection by the House of Commons of the second national petition in 1842. The Chartists had tried all the political strategies in the repertoire of radicalism, from constitutional lobbying to alternative assemblies, general strikes and armed uprisings, and none had succeeded. O'Connor, the most influential Chartist leader, developed the idea of a land reform scheme as a way out of this strategic dead-end. He proposed that individual Chartists should subscribe a small sum to a fund which would eventually accumulate to a sufficient amount to allow the purchase of a small estate. This would then be divided up into smallholdings. A ballot would be held, and in accordance with this the smallholdings would be allocated to subscribers. However, while we can see O'Connor's adoption of the Land Plan as being an ad hoc way out of an otherwise insoluble dilemma, this does nothing to explain the success of his proposal. Only if we see the Land Plan in the context of the long-standing agrarian tradition within radicalism does its popularity make sense. While Spence had established the theoretical framework within which radicals could see land as the ultimate solution to political and social injustice, and Owenism had led many radical working men to hope that Spence's agrarian jubilee might be immediately achievable, the Chartist Land Plan offered a direct mechanism by which this could be accomplished.[6]

Agrarian aspirations were therefore centrally intertwined with radical ideology between the 1790s and 1840s, but it will already be apparent that, while most radicals agreed that land was important, they differed in their prescriptions for land reform. Spence, as we have seen, wanted public owner-ship of land which would be individually cultivated. Spence's followers did not always adhere to this; when O'Connor launched the Chartist Land Plan, which since it was based on the principle of rented smallholdings rather than collective parochial ownership might have seemed anathema to Spenceans, Spence's leading disciple Allen Davenport welcomed it by pronouncing that 'the jubilee is come at last'. Between Spence's parochial public ownership and O'Connor's rented smallholdings lay a wide range of ideas and proposals. Owenites argued for co-operative ownership and cultivation, but thought that this could take place in a piecemeal way rather than requiring any general change or 'jubilee'. Carlile wanted to achieve similar goals to Spence by means of his 'single equitable tax' on land. William Cobbett, perhaps the most influential radical of his day, was fully in agreement that land was central to political well-being, but offered no clear prescription for land reform. In so far as Cobbett had a coherent political position on landownership, he believed in the existing structure implemented in such a way that labourers would be guaranteed a decent living income.

Radical attitudes to land therefore varied markedly. Even more striking than this divergence is the fact that land occupied a central place in so much radical political analysis. This is puzzling for two major reasons. In the first place, as we saw in the first chapter, the early nineteenth century witnessed a drastic and in certain respects even cataclysmic process of industrialization and urbanization. The world, or at least Britain, was being transformed before the eyes of contemporary radical political leaders. With the benefit of hind-sight we know that the transformation was to continue and that agriculture and the countryside were to become, by the end of the nineteenth century, vestigial in demographic and economic terms. How was it possible that the early nineteenth-century radicals failed to discern what may present itself to us as an inevitable development? To place land and the countryside rather than industry and the city at the centre of a political system at this date would appear to be wilfully flying in the face of socio-economic reality. This might be more easily understood if agrarianism had been a rural ideology. But the second puzzling aspect of early nineteenth-century agrarian radicalism is that it was overwhelmingly an urban and industrial movement; indeed, agrarianism attracted strikingly few rural supporters. In attempting to understand agrarian radicalism, therefore, we need to find an explanation not only for how an ideology apparently so out of step with its times could gain so many adherents, but also for how it could attract the very group of workers to whom its analysis might seem least suited.

An obvious starting point is recent work in econometric history, some of which we considered in the first chapter of this book. By revising the chronology of the industrial revolution, econometric historians have (among other things) made agrarianism seem distinctly less inappropriate to its times. While according to the traditional chronology of the industrial revolution, industrialization was firmly established by the 1840s and entrenched even by the 1810s, the revised chronology suggests that it was only *after* 1830 that the industrial revolution really became a dominant experience. There are three important consequences for our understanding of agrarian radicalism. First, it is easier to accept that even in the 1830s industrialism might *not* have seemed to be a monolithic, irreversible fact. Second, the downwards revision for rates of growth re-emphasizes that economic, and still more so political, power remained firmly with the aristocracy – that is to say, based on land ownership – rather than with the middle class and industry. Third, emphasis on the very limited extent to which factories had spread before 1830 draws attention to the fact that the great majority of workers at that date were not factory workers, but artisans. Each of these points deserves consideration in a little more detail.

First, then, even as late as the 1840s it was far from clear that industrialization was an irreversible process. On the contrary, discerning contemporaries were often very doubtful about whether industrialism would have the strength to weather the severe difficulties in which it was enmeshed. Deep economic recessions in the postwar period and in the late 1830s and early 1840s seemed to indicate that if industrialism was a new form of society, it was a form which might well prove socially and even economically unsustainable. The ultimate effect of mechanization, it was feared, might simply be to displace labour, as a result of which workers' living standards would fall inexorably to subsistence level. Furthermore, because industrial development at least on a large scale was so recent in origin and had sprung up so suddenly, many contemporaries suspected that the industrial tide might ebb as quickly and as far as it had flowed in. Many were inclined to accept the claims of Cobbett and others that the rapid expansion of London and other towns was an 'artificial' creation of the Napoleonic wars and of the government borrowing which had paid for them. As such, it was easy to see industrialism as a temporary aberration from the natural order of things rather than as a new, potentially lasting form of social order.[7]

Whether industry was an aberration or not, it was in any case clear that economic and political power still rested largely with landowners rather than with industrialists. The combined wealth of Britain's landowners still far outstripped that of any other social group (as it continued to do in fact throughout the century). It was these landowners also who controlled the political system at both national and local levels. Nationally, it was not so much that the entire House of Lords consisted of landowners and that the Lords were at this date capable of blocking House of Commons legislation; more significant was the direct and indirect influence of the landowners on the composition of the lower house. At the local level, the dominant institutions were quarter sessions, petty sessions and the magistracy, all of which consisted very largely of landowners. But the most important point to which the recent emphasis on the slowness of economic growth in the first half of the nineteenth century draws attention is that even by the mid-nineteenth century most industrial workers were artisans rather than factory employees. If we approach agrarian radicalism as an ideology of artisans rather than of factory workers, its rationality becomes clearer. As small producers, artisans were under threat in the early stages of the industrial revolution from the development of new technology. This was not necessarily full-scale steam-powered technology harnessed in factories; most technological transformation was on a more limited scale, but even apparently minor changes in manufacturing processes, such as a new method for knitting stockings ('cut-up' stockings), could reduce wages and throw many out of work.[8]

The threat offered by industrialization to artisans was of a four-fold nature. In the first place, industrialization undermined the security of artisans by exposing them to competition from cheaper modes of production. Short time or even a complete loss of work might result. For British workers in the first half of the nineteenth century the experience of dearth or even famine was not remote: as recently as 1794–96 and 1799–1801 there had been a significant rise in mortality due to high food prices; and Ireland presented a constant warning of how far living standards could fall under adverse circumstances. Second, industrialization threatened to destroy the independence of artisan production. Artisans characteristically saw themselves not as employees but as independent producers; but as industrialization weakened their bargaining position they were frequently forced into more proletarian and hence dependent forms of work. In some cases, outworkers were forced to enter small workshops; in others, ownership of materials passed from the worker to the putter-out. Third, industrialization undermined skill, perhaps the most hard-won and intensely cherished possession of many artisans. Rapid technological change quickly made often painfully acquired skills redundant; or at least forced the worker to accept much lower wages than those to which he or she had been accustomed. Fourth, and as a consequence of the previous three tendencies, industrialization reduced the status of artisans.[9]

Land was germane to all these aspects. It offered a means whereby artisans could regain a measure of control over the work process. Rather than being forced to accept miserably low wages from an employer, an artisan with land could choose instead to spend the day cultivating his land. He thus re-established some independence and, in so far as the land would feed his family however low his income fell, some security. Status was also enhanced by becoming a landholder, and skill protected at least in so far as an artisan with land might well be able to continue to use his skill without this entailing dire poverty.

Nor was land provision necessarily relevant only to those artisans who were able to obtain land. If enough workers were able to withdraw from the labour market on to their land in times of glut, then the supply of labour would contract sharply, and for those remaining in the labour market, wages would correspondingly rise to more acceptable levels. Land was in this sense a 'safety-valve' which would release pressure on wages and employment. If workers were provided with land, industrialization could be redirected to labour's advantage, rather than imposing immiseration. Seen from this perspective, far from being a denial of or refusal to acknowledge industrialization, agrarian radicalism was a direct response to it.[10]

Furthermore, land was not something remote from most artisans' experience; in many parts of the country dual occupationism remained a significant presence, with artisans combining a trade with an agricultural occupation. This was so, for example, among the Gloucestershire weavers and the Swaledale lead miners. Even for city dwellers, the countryside was unlikely to be remote from experience. We have seen how Thomas Spence was influenced by the interpenetration of town and country in his native Newcastle. The survival of large commons adjacent to many other major towns and cities gave a significant rural flavour to the lives of many urban dwellers. Not only could these commons be used for the same purposes of gathering food and fuel as commons were in the countryside; they were also vital for popular recreation. Urban popular culture therefore remained strongly rural in content; animal fighting (such as ratting or cock-fighting), for example, retained great popularity. The countryside was not physically remote from the homes of most English workers in the early nineteenth century; most urban development was through infilling or ribbon development. The first kept the urban area compact, so the countryside was likely to be close at hand; the second ensured that the countryside reached far into the interior of the city. Further contact with the countryside resulted from temporary migrations in search of work, which took artisans into the harvest fields, or through the countryside when 'tramping' in pursuit of their trade.[11]

The commitment and faith of many radical artisans to agrarianism was sustained partly by this direct experience, but also through reading and discussion. Many of the books with which artisans were often most familiar were suffused with powerful ruralist imagery, whereby a return or journey to a 'promised land' of some sort resulted in permanent happiness. Particularly important influences in this respect were the Bible, the Book of Common Prayer, and Bunyan's *Pilgrim's Progress*. Such attitudes were reinforced by radical newspapers and pamphlets explicitly endorsing agrarianism. Although the most coherent theory of land came from Spence, and the strongest stimulus to co-operation from Owen, it was probably Cobbett's prose which did more than anything else to fix in the minds of many urban artisans the notion of rural life as intrinsically superior to urban existence, albeit oppressed by the injustice of a self-seeking aristocracy. Cobbett's portrayal of enclosure as a process by which the rural poor were cheated out of their rights resonated powerfully with agrarian radicalism: enclosure seemed a clear-cut case of aristocratic usurpation of popular rights; all the more so as enclosure was validated and enforced by an excluding parliament of landowners. Still more, the struggle over common rights highlighted the fact that popular access to and use-rights over land were a real, if vestigial, survival in the English countryside. This provided practical evidence for the historical existence of a 'state of nature' as posited by Locke (and then assumed by Spence, Tom Paine and other agrarian theorists) in which agrarian equality existed.[12]

By approaching agrarian radicalism as an essentially artisan ideology, we can better understand its diverse stance on the question of public versus private ownership. Looked at from a property-rights perspective, the very wide variety of positions adopted by agrarian radicals on this question (sometimes even by the same individual) appears to indicate confusion and incoherence. If, rather than trying to measure agrarian radicalism against the implicit standard of Marxian socialism, we see it in its own terms as a contemporary ideology of small producers, then it is easy to see that what mattered to the artisans who adhered to agrarian radicalism was not ownership of the means of production, but control over them. Even rented land like that offered by the Chartist Land Plan could provide this, so long as the conditions of tenure were stable and benign. The question was more how land could be made available to the working people on a large scale and on favourable terms, rather than whether public or private ownership was intrinsically preferable.[13]

The attitude of working-class radicals to the countryside differed sharply from that apparent in the largely middle-class novels and poetry examined in the previous chapter. Agrarian radicals saw land in predominantly instrumental terms: land, with labour applied to it, was the means of production, and once rightly distributed also the guarantee of independent subsistence. From this point of view, uncultivated or unused land was in the most literal sense a waste, and mirrored the unproductive class of landowners whose usurpation of such land prevented it from being properly cultivated. By contrast, the middle-class literary tradition had in the main little interest in land as a means of production, seeing it largely in visual and aesthetic terms as a place to which the sensitive individual could retreat to experience his true self through communion with nature. From this point of view, the wild, uncultivated landscape was preferable to an obviously controlled, managed, farmed landscape. What the two traditions had in common, of course, was that both endowed the countryside with powerful positive attributes, and both contrasted the presence of these attributes in the countryside with their alleged absence in the towns. In subsequent chapters we shall see how, in differing but related ways, attempts were made to translate these two traditions into practice through the provision of gardens, allotments, parks, model villages and, ultimately, garden cities.

CHAPTER 4

Gardens, Allotments and Parks

§ THE 'greening of the city' – the process whereby the densely built-up 'Coketowns' of the industrial revolution were modified so as to reintroduce some elements of nature – is one of the most striking aspects of the socio-economic history of urban England in the second half of the nineteenth century. However, it would be inaccurate to see this process as a simple one-way development from 'built-up' to 'green'. More useful is the idea of an equilibrium between town and country, which was upset by the rise of a market economy in the eighteenth century and by urbanization and industrial-ization in the nineteenth, but partially restored on a new basis in the later nineteenth and twentieth centuries.

The accelerating rise of the market economy in the eighteenth century led to a more emphatic and sharply defined assertion of exclusive private property rights at the expense of collective customary use-rights. One of the consequences of this was an increasing tendency to the privatization of previously public space, most notably through enclosure by Act of Parliament. While parliamentary enclosure is usually thought of in a rural context, its effects in restricting the access of the urban poor to land were almost equally important. In London, for example, St James's Square was enclosed in 1726, Lincoln's Inn Fields in 1735, Red Lion Square in 1736, Golden Square in 1750, Berkeley Square in 1766 and Grosvenor Square in 1774. In all these cases the result was the exclusion of the urban poor from what had previously been public space.[1]

The transformation of property relations was not alone in being responsible for the erosion of public space in cities. Urbanization massively accelerated the shift from public to private by multiplying land values; and it was also urbanization that intensified the pressure not merely to privatize formerly public open space, but to build over it.

As a result of these forces, provision of green space was at a low ebb in early nineteenth-century English towns, but from the fourth decade of the century onwards a strong resurgence occurred. It is with this resurgence and its causes – a complex mix of aesthetic, social, political and economic impulses – that this chapter is largely concerned.

The aesthetic impulse towards greening the city derived in large part from the literary tradition which we examined in Chapter 2, and in particular from the conception of nature formulated by the Romantic poets. While many of the great Romantic poets lived in the countryside during the most productive periods of their lives, their audience was largely urban and middle class. Wordsworth's conviction that nature was the gateway to spiritual truth fostered an enthusiasm for nature which occasional excursions into the countryside or holidays to the Lakes could not adequately satiate. Increasingly, the middle and upper ranks of the middle class sought to make their environs more rural, or moved to suburban locations where nature was more visibly present. Nor were literary conceptions of the relationship between human feeling and nature regarded by the middle class as relevant only to themselves. On the contrary, it was almost universally assumed that exposure to nature would affect the working class in the same way. Nature could therefore be an antidote to the supposed vices of working-class people: it would make them morally better, less base and ignoble in their aspirations, more refined and respectable. This had implications which went beyond the moral and even religious welfare of the working class. A prevalent view was that the perceived materialism, coarseness and lack of individual refinement of the working class would lead them to wish to expropriate the middle class's wealth if the political opportunity ever arose. In so far as exposure to nature would lead to a more refined sensibility, it could also be hoped that it would lead the working class away from political egalitarianism.[2]

Aesthetic considerations were therefore not always as disinterested as they might appear. However, restoring some element of rurality to the urban environment was also advocated for more directly social, political and economic reasons. From a social point of view, the main argument deployed was the sanitary one. For most of the nineteenth century, doctors were strongly committed to a belief in the virtues of fresh air, partly because of the predominance of the 'miasma' theory of disease transmission (which held that disease was spread through noxious vapours that could be dispersed by fresh air). Working-class health had direct and grim implications for middle-class health, as Victorian novelists relished pointing out and as the cholera epidemics of 1832 and 1848 made acutely apparent. The equation between unnatural living conditions and physical disease was amplified by a powerful current of anti-industrialism and fear of the city which was at its height in the 1840s but persisted throughout the nineteenth century. This fear was largely the fear of the landowners of a radically new phenomenon which was alien to their experience and which alarmingly failed to conform to their model of natural social relationships. To landowners the impersonality and lack of fixed hierarchical relationships characteristic of the emergent urban-industrial world indicated that this new world lacked the stabilizing mechanisms of their own rural social structures, and was therefore socially and politically dangerous. The familiar Victorian analogy between physical disease and moral corruption in the context of urban squalor was in part a reflection of this fear of the city. One conclusion was that the physical and moral dangers of urbanism needed to be tempered by rural elements. Providing rural 'lungs' in which city dwellers could breathe the restorative fresh air of the countryside was therefore the means to ensure not only public health but also social order.[3]

Political fears about the unpredictability and potential radicalism of the urban working class, or even of the deeply impoverished rural proletariat, could also be assuaged by using land as a means of altering the relationship between labour and property. By providing workers with entitlements to land, for example in the form of allotments, it might be possible to persuade them to regard themselves as small property holders rather than as the oppressed victims of property. It could be hoped, then, that workers with a patch of land might become anxious to defend the 'rights of property' against socialist threats. This was therefore another means by which the political threat of the new social formations of the industrial city could be averted or tamed by the reintroduction of elements drawn from the countryside.

Direct economic gains from reinserting rurality into the urban landscape were less widely anticipated, partly because almost by definition green space offered lower economic returns than commercial or industrial uses – this after all was one of the main reasons why market processes were not adequate for the task. However, in some contexts green space would more than pay for itself. Perhaps the most important in the nineteenth century was the middle-class housing development, which increasingly required acceptable garden provision if it was to be financially successful. Also of some importance, especially at the end of the century, was the municipal development of parks by resort towns such as Weston-super-Mare, which hoped thereby to attract more visitors and boost collective revenue.[4]

At this point distinctions must be made between different kinds of green space. The first is between the cultivated and the uncultivated. The most important cultivated urban green space of the nineteenth century was the allotment. Gardens represent an intermediate case, in that they were some-times cultivated, in whole or in part, and sometimes based on lawns and trees. Urban parks represent the least cultivated form of urban green space. However, parks themselves differed of course very considerably in the degree to which they approached 'wild' landscape. A second distinction is between private and public urban green space. Here the extreme form of private green space is of course the garden, and it is the allotment which plays an intermediate role, since although each plot was let individually the site as a whole was nevertheless bounded by a single external fence and shared many attributes in common. The park was the most fully public form. Partly because of these differences, the three major forms of urban green space had largely separate trajectories of development, and should be analysed in their own terms.

The origins of allotments are debatable. Small patches of land detached from houses have probably existed since the beginnings of agriculture, so in this very loose sense allotments date back to prehistoric times. But if we define allotments more narrowly as individual plots let under a collective arrangement for purposes which are partly social (rather than purely economic), a more precise, and far more recent, point of origin can be identified. It was in the mid-1790s, probably in 1795, that Sir Thomas Estcourt of Shipton Moyne first let allotments to his estate labourers. Estcourt was concerned to find ways of increasing food security during a period of dearth, while also aiming to relieve the poor rates. Although Estcourt wrote an account of what he had done which appeared in the *Reports* of the Society for Bettering the Conditions and Increasing the Comforts of the Poor, and which attracted a certain amount of attention, he had few immediate imitators. It was only the 'Captain Swing' riots of 1830 which induced landowners to provide allotments on a large scale (although several Acts of Parliament permitting public provision of allotments were on the statute books by the mid-nineteenth century, none was effective). As a result, the number of allotment sites increased from about 100 in 1830 to about 2,000 in the mid-1840s. The latter figure represents about 100,000 plots. By 1873 there were about 273,000 plots in existence, and perhaps as many as 600,000 by 1914.[5]

Until the last two or three decades of the nineteenth century the overwhelming majority of allotments were in the countryside rather than the towns; and it appears that the idea of allotments was taken from the former to the latter. However, urban allotments have some interesting precursors. It is not so much the market gardens shown on the outskirts of towns on many medieval and early-modern maps which are of interest, since these seem mostly to have had commercial functions. More relevant are the so-called 'Guinea gardens' which existed in the west Midlands (and possibly other parts of the country) in the eighteenth and early nineteenth centuries. These small gardens were common around the outskirts of Birmingham, Coventry and Warwick. They were like allotments in that they were detached from houses, but unlike them in that they were separated from each other by hedges. They also served a rather different function, in that food production seems to have been secondary to recreational purposes: flowers, trees and lawns took precedence over vegetables. Guinea gardens were, it seems, rented mainly by relatively prosperous artisans as a place to which they could take their families on Sundays and holidays. They are of considerable interest in that, although they died out in the first half of the nineteenth century because of the pressure of urban expansion in Birmingham, functionally they relate more closely to the continental tradition of summer-house allotments than to the British tradition of food-producing plots.[6]

The first city allotments that can be properly so called seem to have developed in about 1840 as a direct response to rural allotments. What is striking, however, is how limited was the response of the urban wealthy to the landowners' allotment movement. While it could be plausibly maintained that there were as many allotments as there were rural labouring families who wanted them by the mid-1880s, the great era of the urban allotment had to wait until legislation made public provision effective in the early twentieth century. Why rural landowners were so much more interested in promoting allotment provision remains unclear, because no detailed study of urban allotments in the second half of the nineteenth century has yet been written. Part of the explanation is probably that the high rental value of land in cities made it difficult for individuals to let allotments. It is also possible that the middle class preferred more passive and pastoral rather than active and agrarian forms of urban working-class relationship to the land. Interestingly, it seems mainly to have been large paternalistic employers, who to a certain extent were able to re-create something of the total social environment of a rural landed estate, who provided allotments (to their own workers). Among the most prominent early urban allotment landlords were the well-known Leeds textile manufacturers Marshalls. Subsequently it was notably paternalistic categories of employer such as the railway and the mining companies who became the most important providers of urban allotments. In the case of the miners, it seems likely that their marked enthusiasm for allotments is largely attributable to the extreme absence of the experience of nature in their employment. But the differences between the extent of allotment provision to different groups of urban workers is more to be explained by differences in allotment availability than by variations in demand for plots. It seems fairly clear from the high rents which urban workers were prepared to pay for allotments when they could get them, and from the rate at which urban allotment provision expanded after legislation became effective, that it was not lack of demand which limited the numbers of allotments being cultivated.[7]

One of the reasons why there was a need for an allotment movement in the countryside was that, contrary to what might have been expected, garden provision was grossly inadequate in rural areas by the early nineteenth century. This was partly because the same circumstances which had stimulated en-closure – primarily, high food prices – also encouraged landowners and farmers to deprive the poor of gardens, where these could be reabsorbed into the adjacent fields. It is true that the availability of gardens remained quite good in a few, mainly pastoral or fruit-producing counties such as Herefordshire and Kent. But in many others, and generally throughout the Midlands and southern and eastern England, gardens were small and few. It was often difficult to add to gardens, or to create new gardens for cottages which lacked them, because there was no space for this to be done (which was a large part of the reason why there could be an allotment movement but no gardens movement). The situation was further exacerbated by the population increase of the first half of the nineteenth century, which led to extensive infilling (many villages were artificially constrained in physical size because landowners did not want to surrender good agricultural land to building). Despite these difficulties, the popularity of and even devotion to gardening among the rural labourers and their families are well attested. The stereotypical image of the Victorian cottage garden is not wholly mythical; many villagers grew flowers with loving care, and in the second half of the century horticultural societies and shows proliferated. Garden provision in Victorian villages was therefore far from adequate, but the countryside nevertheless supported an active popular gardening culture.[8]

If villages lost gardens because of overcrowding, the situation in most towns was inevitably much worse, especially in the north where the rate of urban expansion was at its greatest and the pressure on space correspondingly most intense. The classic form of housing in the industrial revolution was the 'back-to-back', which by definition could have no garden attached to the house. Other prominent dwelling forms included courts and cellars, the first of which was unlikely to and the second of which could not provide gardens. In most of the larger towns and cities in the first half of the nineteenth century, therefore, gardens were largely confined to the middle class, although by the end of the century many of the better-paid artisans and some factory workers had at least a very small garden.

Despite the restricted supply of gardens to the urban working class in the nineteenth century, the English housing tradition was nevertheless at least potentially more compatible with gardening than either the continental or the Scottish traditions. On the continent, the predominant form of urban working-class housing was a flat in an apartment block, while in Scotland it was a flat in a tenement. In England, workers almost always lived in their own individual cottages, which made the provision of individual gardens directly linked to the home much easier. Some of the more advanced working-class housing developments did make provision for gardens. While evidence for popular attitudes to gardening among the urban working class is not so clear as for rural workers, some cities (Nottingham and Birmingham, for example) certainly supported a thriving working-class gardening culture. Where working-class families could obtain neither gardens nor allotments, as in central London, window-boxes were sometimes popular as a substitute.[9]

Gardens and allotments were a practical (if modest) realization of the deep-seated working-class demand for land whose political expression was radical agrarianism. Parks were often seen as a corollary of gardens and allotments, if on a grander scale and public rather than private in form. However, parks in fact differed substantially in their origins, subsequent development and effects from either gardens or allotments.

The earliest English parks were established in the middle ages by the monarchy and the nobility as reserves for hunting deer. They were of course private rather than public; indeed, so much private that to hunt in someone else's deer park was regarded as one of the most serious insults possible. One of the crucial features of the park, essential to its function as a reserve for deer, was that it should be enclosed by a fence or wall.

While there were always some tensions and disputes centring on parks (most frequently over poaching), it was only with the growth of cities and with the intensified attempts to maintain or assert exclusive rights over park-land that confrontation became large-scale and persistent. London, because it was a large city both in terms of physical size and population at least a century before anywhere else, was the first place in England where this confrontation between public demands for access and private assertions of exclusive right became a major issue. As London expanded, several large royal hunting parks became swallowed up in its growth. The history of the royal parks in the eighteenth and nineteenth centuries is largely one of royalty being forced to capitulate to popular demands for access to the parks both for recreation and as thoroughfares. It is alleged, for example, that when the Princess Amelia, ranger of the royal park of Richmond, asked Sir Robert Walpole how much it would cost to stop up the footpaths through the park, Walpole replied, 'Only a crown, madam.' It is because of the success of this popular struggle against the monarchy that the royal parks of London were (and have remained) opened to the people without fee or restriction of class.[10]

Just as the ever-expanding population of London, and later of other large cities, created a demand for public access to land from the propertyless, it also created a countervailing force; the desire for privacy and, especially, for the private enjoyment of green space began to command a high price from the increasingly prosperous upper middle class. This can be seen in the transformation of two of London's most important forms of open space: the residential square and the commercial pleasure gardens. The residential square developed in London in the mid-seventeenth century in imitation of the French *place* (the first London example was Covent Garden). Originally, London's residential squares were entirely open, with cobbles or paving extending from one side to the other. This enhanced the sense of the square as a unified architectural composition, and placed the emphasis on its public and urban character. In the late eighteenth century, however, the character of residential squares began to change. The central area of many of the squares was fenced, and only residents provided with keys. Trees were planted and the cobbles were replaced by turf. Initially, something of the formal architectural character of the squares was retained: small species of tree such as hornbeam were chosen, and they were ornamentally clipped, so that the view of the buildings was not drastically impaired. By the early nineteenth century, though, large species of tree such as the plane and the sycamore were favoured, and the trees were allowed to grow unchecked to their full height. The view from the street, or from the window of a house, was now not of houses but of trees and grass – of nature, in short. The causes of this shift appear to have been three-fold. First, the growth of a more private, familial sensibility stimulated the desire to convert the square from a place where residents mixed promiscuously with the crowd to one in which they could walk in seclusion, sheltered by the trees from prying eyes and by the fencing from intruding bodies. Second, the shift from an urban and architectural emphasis to a rural and natural one seems to have reflected the aspirations of the upper middle class to genteel status, the ultimate marker of which was the gentleman's rural park. If a private park was beyond the financial means of all but a tiny minority of the urban upper middle class, at least a gesture towards it could be obtained through the privatized and planted residential park. Third, the prominence of tall trees allowed to grow in their natural forms reflected the Romantic cult of nature so enthusiastically promulgated by the poets and novelists whose works were eagerly read by many of London's bourgeoisie.[11]

In a less dramatic way the commercial pleasure gardens of London also manifest the increasing desire of the wealthy to enjoy their walks free from the press of the multitude. Commercial pleasure gardens had developed in London in the seventeenth century. The proprietors initially made their money through the sale of food, drink and other commodities, without charging an admission fee. Since the main aim was to accommodate as many stalls and entertainments as possible, and to allow the free circulation of people, such gardens tended to be extremely formal in layout – gravel walks in parallel lines were characteristic. In the course of the eighteenth century, however, commercial pleasure gardens became increasingly socially exclusive: most began to charge admissions fees, with the explicit aim of keeping out those who were considered undesirable.[12]

The creation of Regent's Park from the former Marylebone Park in 1811 marks a significant development in the history of parks for three reasons: first because the model pioneered at Regent's Park was to be the basis for most of the important urban parks established over the next half century, second because it presages the major form which urban middle-class aspirations for quasi-rural surroundings were to take in the nineteenth century, and third because it reveals particularly clearly the tensions between residential exclusivity and public access. The essential idea informing the development of Regent's Park was that the upper-middle-class residents whom it was hoped to attract would be willing to pay a significant premium for the enjoyment of green space adjacent to their homes. The green space offered would be on a much grander scale than in the confined residential squares; indeed, the view from the windows of one of the houses around the perimeter of the park would not be dissimilar to that from a house genuinely set in its own grounds (if the viewer could forget the adjacent terrace for a moment). As such, Regent's Park offered the closest that a member of the bourgeoisie could hope to get to a real gentleman's park short of actually paying for one. This perception, that the upper middle class would pay an enhanced rent for the privilege of living in a rural-seeming environment with some of the trappings of gentlemanly life, was to provide the financial basis for the funding of dozens of parks later in the nineteenth century.

The emphasis in Regent's Park was initially not only on a quasi-rural setting but also on seclusion. The general public were not admitted. While most of the houses were arranged in a terrace around the rim of the park, there were also a few houses hidden away in the park itself. The advance both in natural surroundings and in seclusion over the residential squares pointed the way ahead to what was to be the major upper-middle-class housing form of the mid- and late nineteenth century – the suburban villa. Interestingly, however, the attempt to make Regent's Park exclusive failed, at least as far as access to the park itself is concerned. Public protests and persistent, large-scale non-compliance by ordinary Londoners eventually forced the crown to give way, and the entire park was open to the public by 1840.[13]

Probably the most significant park to follow Regent's Park was at Birkenhead. The importance of Birkenhead Park is that it took the principle of Regent's Park (the willingness of the upper middle class to pay large sums to obtain houses fronting on to green space) and used it as a means of funding, or at least part-funding, a park which was intended to serve for the enjoyment (and improvement) of the working class.[14] A further important and innovative feature of Birkenhead was its use of funding from the rates to develop and maintain the park. Birkenhead therefore inaugurates the era of the park as a social good. However, pioneering as Birkenhead was in many ways, the path indicated was not an easy one for other municipalities to follow. In order to permit the corporation to apply income from the rates to the park, a special Act of Parliament had had to be obtained, at great expense (partly because of the difficulties created by the Municipal Corporations Act of 1835, which restricted the objects on which corporations could spend money). Furthermore, while the combination of middle-class housing with public access was neat and, within its limits, effective, it was also restrictive: visitors to the park had to be forced to behave in ways which would not offend or upset the residents.

Despite these drawbacks, the pattern developed at Birkenhead was followed in subsequent years by several other northern municipalities, notably Manchester, where Philip's, Queen's and Peel parks were all financed using a combination of the income from associated middle-class housing developments and from the rates.[15]

It was no accident that most of the municipal parks which aimed to allow public access constructed in the mid-nineteenth century were in the northern industrial districts. These parks were a direct reaction to the appalling social and environmental conditions of the early industrial revolution outlined in Chapter 1, and to contemporary criticism of these conditions by writers such as Carlyle, Dickens, Disraeli and Gaskell, as described in Chapter 2. However, for all that was done by the northern municipalities, at the national level progress was slower. Despite the forceful advocacy of parks by the 1833 Select Committee on Public Walks and the 1840 Health of Towns Committee, little legislative action followed (although in 1837 provision was made for a parliamentary standing order to secure small 'exercise grounds' under future enclosure acts). It was only the Public Health Acts of 1848 and, especially, 1875 that marked a significant easing of the conditions on which local authorities could provide parks. The latter in particular provided the conditions which allowed the last quarter of the nineteenth century to be the golden age of public park provision in England, at least if measured by the number of parks opened.

In the mid-Victorian period, however, a rather different form of park was at least as common as the purely municipal park: the park provided by a wealthy philanthropist (often, inevitably, with mixed motives which included self-advertisement as much as benevolence). A good example is Joseph Strutt's Arboretum at Derby. This was one of the earliest parks opened with the aim of providing free access to all citizens. The drawback was that in order to fund the park it was free only on two days of the week – charges had to be levied on the other days to cover maintenance costs. The Arboretum was characteristic of mid-Victorian parks in its moral prescriptiveness. By-laws prohibited drunkenness and other 'immoral' forms of behaviour, and there was a strict ban on Sunday sports and amusements. The positive counterpart of this was the powerful educational thrust. All 802 specimen trees at the Arboretum were labelled in the conviction that this would encourage self-education among the working class. In this respect the Arboretum shared a common purpose with the botanic gardens which were opened in several British cities in the mid- and late nineteenth century. Most botanic gardens were established in the first instance for the pleasure and edification of their middle-class subscribers, but many of them subsequently developed a secondary aim: to civilize the working class through exposure to nature interpreted by science (a mission which, interestingly, was propagated across the globe through botanic gardens established in cities throughout the British empire).[16]

Unsurprisingly in view of the restrictive regulations under which many mid-Victorian parks were governed, and the often heavy-handed determination to 'improve' the working class, the establishment of parks was not always greeted with as much enthusiasm as might have been expected by those for whose benefit they were ostensibly intended. Grievances were likely to run particularly high when, as was sometimes the case, the 'new' park was not actually a new piece of open space, but simply a formalization of a hitherto less regulated space. Equally unsurprisingly, the actual behaviour of the working class in parks did not necessarily conform to the anticipated pattern. Not only were rules prohibiting the playing of games persistently flouted, but, more significantly, some of the larger parks (most famously Victoria Park in the East End of London) became venues for demonstrations and working-class political activism.[17]

At the core of the ethos of the park lay the conviction of the restorative and purifying influence of nature, and most nineteenth-century parks were designed to achieve as 'natural' an appearance as possible. Paths, streams and belts of trees were laid out in curves; trees were distributed irregularly; and care was taken to screen factory buildings or other unwanted reminders of the nearness of the urban from those walking in the park. By contrast, if there were any lines of sight to distant countryside features such as crags or woods, these were kept open so that the illusion of being in the midst of nature would be enhanced. When, as was sometimes the case, a corporation obtained control over a tract of countryside outside the city which subsequently, through urban growth, became incorporated into it, care was taken to preserve the rural features of the landscape. Even when in the late nineteenth century the increasing emphasis on physical fitness and hence athleticism required large flat sports grounds to be laid out in parks, park designers went to lengths to accommodate this without destroying the natural impression of the park. A new 'formal-informal' style was devised, in which the necessarily formal elements of the playing fields, tennis courts and the like were contrasted with 'wild' elements such as extensive rockeries, groves, streams or lakes and other putatively unregulated natural features.[18]

Allotments, gardens and parks differed in many respects, but they had one thing in common: all three provided a rural refuge from the city around them (the first two on an individual and the latter on a collective basis). Valuable as this was, it still left the surrounding city uncompromisingly urban which, even by the late nineteenth century, after decades of not wholly ineffective sanitary reform, still meant dirty, polluted and overcrowded.

The upper middle class might, and as transport improved increasingly often did, escape to the suburbs, or even in a few cases to the countryside itself. This still left the great mass of the people, lower middle class as well as working class, to endure the foul conditions described by Dickens and Disraeli, with allotments, gardens and parks as no more than a temporary escape. The next chapter describes a tradition which ultimately proposed, and attempted to implement, a more radical solution: to supersede the city with a new form of settlement that would build the essential characteristics of the countryside into its very principles – the Garden City.

. . . .

CHAPTER 5

Model Villages and Garden Cities

§ IN the last chapter we saw how the quality of urban life was improved during the nineteenth century by the development of oases of greenery within industrial towns and cities. Valuable though these gardens, allotments and parks were as places of escape from the ugliness and dirtiness of the surrounding urban environment, they remained separate from it rather than interpenetrating and transforming it. This chapter examines the origins, characteristics and influence of a more ambitious attempt to introduce rural elements into the urban landscape: the garden city.

The garden city derived from many influences, among them the political tradition of agrarian radicalism and the literary tradition descending from Wordsworth to Ruskin and William Morris. But perhaps the most important influence was the tradition of model village building in England, of which the garden city can in many respects be seen as the culmination.

Model villages, as their name implies, were rural in origin, and can be traced back to the eighteenth century (although the phrase itself was a Victorian coinage, reflecting the mid-nineteenth-century emphasis on the model village as an example set to other builders, architects and landlords). Initially the main impetus to model village building came from the desire of landowners to improve and embellish their estates. The fundamental aim was aesthetic; social considerations were marginal or even absent.

In the early and mid-eighteenth century most landowners saw the cottages of the poor as impairing the quality of the landscape in which they appeared. Cottages lacked aesthetic distinction and detracted from the unimpeded wide sweep of landscape that most estate owners wished to create. The poor and their homes were regarded as at best unworthy to form part of a fine 'prospect', and at worst as a social embarrassment detracting from the balanced harmony of ordered nature which Brown and Kent regarded as desirable. When a landowner decided to re-landscape a park, therefore, any cottages marring the view from the main house were liable to be demolished and removed to a part of the estate where they would be less obtrusive. This was done most famously at Nuneham Courtenay near Oxford, where the ramshackle old village in the park was rebuilt as identical brick boxes arranged in parallel lines along one of the main roads between Oxford and London, set some way away from the mansion. Another notable eighteenth-century example was Milton Abbas in Dorset. Here again an entire village was transplanted to improve the quality of the view from the main house. The style of housing adopted at Milton Abbas was more rustic than at Nuneham Courtenay, featuring whitewashed thatched rather than brick-built tiled cottages, but again the houses were aligned in regular lines either side of a road.[1]

Partly because of its prominent position on the Oxford to London road, Nuneham Courtenay attracted much attention, not all of it favourable. Oliver Goldsmith criticized it as an example of the ruthless imposition of aristocratic whim over social happiness on the one hand and nature on the other. However, it was aesthetic rather than social criticism which had the greater influence on the evolution of model village building in England. Particularly important was the rise of the taste for the picturesque in landscape design. The theoretical writing of Uvedale Price and the descriptions of the Wye valley and the Lake District by William Gilpin stimulated a turn away from the smooth contours of Brown's landscapes towards a landscape style which more self-consciously sought to compose the landscape in the same way a painter would compose a scene. The picturesque aesthetic admired diversity in scale and subject; buildings and other evidence of man's shaping hand were valued if they carried rich associations. From being seen as a blot on a grand sweep of landscape, cottages came to be seen as potentially enhancing the attractiveness of a landscape through adding to its picturesque qualities.[2]

Perhaps the finest and certainly the most noted example of a picturesque village was Blaise Hamlet, near Bath. Here all the cottages were newly built, each to a different design. Some were thatched, with long eaves overhanging the walls. Blaise Hamlet was much visited and imitated, but by the third decade of the nineteenth century another influence was beginning to make itself felt.[3] While many eighteenth-century landowners had felt little interest in or responsibility for the poor living in their cottages on their estates, by the second quarter of the nineteenth century such complacency was more difficult to sustain. A number of factors had come together to intensify rural poverty and to impose a severe strain on rural social relations. Perhaps the most fundamental was the rise in the rural population. In the absence of a commensurate growth in demand for rural labour, this resulted in rising unemployment, falling real wages and rising poor rates in many parts of rural England. At the same time, competition with more highly mechanized urban-based industry affected many long-standing rural industries, such as textile production in the south-west of England, while the enclosure of commons further undermined the household economies of the rural poor. The introduction of agricultural machinery, such as threshing machines and mole ploughs, threatened winter employment, while at the same time successive local and national reforms to the poor laws eroded relief scales and entitlements. This experience of poverty, exacerbated by the highly visible hand of the state and of the rural elite, generated social tensions which were released in a series of protests and riots between 1816 and the climax of the Captain Swing riots in 1830. The best-known response of landed society was the reform of the poor laws in 1834; it was believed that population growth and poverty were largely the con-sequences of a bad system of poor relief, and that reforming that system would remove the underlying causes of rural discontent. But a second and very different response was in many ways as important. This was the revival of the traditions of aristocratic paternalism. A catch-phrase among rural landowners in the 1830s and 1840s was 'property has its duties as well as its rights'. The housing problem was highlighted by the sanitary movement of the 1840s, which demonstrated compellingly the links between bad housing, ill health and immorality. Clearly, landowners, as the major landlords of rural cottage property, had a responsibility to ensure that their cottages met at least basic sanitary standards. Conscientious landowners saw model cottage building as a means by which they could put their religion into practice, improve the moral standards of the local poor and at the same time enhance the value and status of their estates. Furthermore, attempting to tackle the problem of rural poverty through attention to housing allowed landowners to avoid the question of wages, which although actually the most important element of the situation would have required fundamental change to address it effectively.[4]

Many mid- and late nineteenth-century landowners therefore constructed model cottages and villages which, while continuing the picturesque tradition in outward appearance, demonstrated the landowners' social concern and desire to improve the standard of rural housing. Such cottages were usually let at low or moderate rents that barely, if at all, paid for their construction. Landowners recognized that the poor could not afford to pay a rent high enough to allow a profit to be made from a cottage of good quality; this was, after all, why there was a rural housing problem in the first place. However, it is notable that a high proportion of model cottages and villages were in the vicinity of the seat of the landowner who built them; the sense of social responsibility was evidently strongest towards those whose connection with the owner was most obvious to the outside world.

The revival of paternalism among rural landowners had an ideological as well as a practical dimension. Paternalism was seen as offering an alternative to the hard selfishness often seen as characteristic of purely market-based social relations, as exemplified by the 'dismal science' of classical economics. In its emphasis on mutual responsibility and deferential hierarchy, paternalism permitted a reassertion of some of the older features of Anglican and landed social thinking against the new kind of society being brought into existence by industrialization. It was, however, not only rural landowners who were disturbed by the impersonal and potentially antagonistic relationships of urban and industrial society. Some of the wealthier industrialists of the mid-nineteenth century moved in the same social circles and were conscious of the same nexus of ideas as landowners. While they made their money from industry, these men were not necessarily hostile to aristocracy or hierarchy. They might look with envy at the apparent lack of interest in radical politics shown by rural labourers, and were as open to the promptings of religion towards social responsibility as landowners were. Furthermore, the rural setting of many of the early factories – which were often dependent on fast-flowing streams as a source of power – meant that the social situations confronting early industrialists were not necessarily as different from those facing aristocratic paternalists as might be imagined. Just as a great landowner might be able to dominate the social life of a village through owning all the land and cottages, so a factory owner who built a factory in a rural setting might own all the cottages and employ virtually all their inhabitants. If paternalism sought to create a total social world, a factory in the countryside might be at least as plausible a setting for it as a great estate.

Increasingly during the nineteenth century, of course, factories and other industrial concerns were set not in the countryside but in towns. Even here the opportunities for industrialists to create something approaching a total social environment were greater than might be supposed. In an era when almost all workers had perforce to walk to work on foot, the maximum distance at which it was practical to live from the workplace was small. Necessarily, most workers' houses were clustered round the place of employment. Factory owners were therefore in a good position to construct or buy this housing. As large and dominant local institutions, factories could be used as the focus for the provision of a network of paternalistic practices ranging from night classes to works trips to the seaside. Paternalism was therefore practicable for industrialists, and as relevant to the social problems they faced as it was for landowners. Under this influence, some industrialists looked to the example of model housing and village construction set by rural landowners, and attempted to apply it to housing their own workers.[5]

One of the earliest and best-known examples of model housing provided by a British industrialist was that built at New Lanark (1799–1829) in Scotland by Robert Owen. Owen's initial concerns with industrial efficiency and the humane treatment of his workers led him ultimately to a radical vision of a new form of communitarian society which reinvigorated the English radical agrarian tradition deriving from Thomas Spence. But while Owen's ideas had an immense influence on the development of socialism, their implications were too radical to make them attractive to other industrialists. New Lanark therefore stands outside the mainstream of industrial paternalism and industrial model housing construction in Britain.

A more important pioneer of industrial model housing, although an infinitely less fertile thinker, was Colonel Edward Akroyd, a West Riding textile manufacturer. Akroyd's most important model villages were Copley (built 1849–53) and Akroyden (1861–63). One of the important features of these villages was the employment of first-rate architects such as G. G. Scott. From the beginning, therefore, the aesthetic tradition which had informed rural model village construction was carried across into the industrial model village. Akroyd attempted to create a village-like style in the architecture of the houses, favouring features characteristic of the rural vernacular tradition such as steeply-pitched gables. Akroyden was built as a square of houses, looking inwards to emphasize the sense of an enclosed, village-like community. In the centre of the square was a large expanse of turf, while further rural features included large gardens and allotments at the rear of the houses.[6]

Shortly after Akroyd began the building of Copley, and also in the West Riding, a larger and grander model village was built (between 1850 and 1863) by Titus Salt. Salt named the new village Saltaire, after himself. Like Copley and Akroyden, Saltaire was in a rural setting, and the visual quality of the houses and the ensemble were as important as the comfort and convenience of the inhabitants. However, in being built in an impressive classical style Saltaire made little reference to the rural vernacular tradition or to the Anglican conservatism with which the latter was closely associated. More significant for the evolution of the industrial model village were probably several developments on Merseyside from the 1850s onwards. The first of the notable industrial model villages on Merseyside was Bromborough Pool, built by Price's Patent Candle Company in 1853. The instigators of the model housing, George and James Wilson, were from Lanark, and it is possible that they knew Robert Owen's housing at New Lanark. Bromborough Pool was followed by Aintree, built by Hartley's Jam Company in 1888. Neither Bromborough Pool nor Aintree was particularly notable in itself; their importance lies in the fact that they served as local precursors to the work of William Hesketh Lever. Lever, the owner of major chemical works on the Mersey and the founder of the company which later became Unilever, bought the rural estate of Thornton Manor in 1891. Here he constructed a classic example of a model village, replete with medieval symbolism and an idealized version of the rural vernacular (visible for example in the half-timbered cottages and the thatched shelter on the village green). At the same time – and in a similar style – Lever was building what was to become one of the most influential industrial model villages: Port Sunlight, close to Lever's factory on the River Mersey. Port Sunlight is significant as the first large-scale, consistent attempt to build an urban housing scheme in a rural idiom. The houses were gabled and tiled and provided with gardens. Trees and shrubs were planted extensively, to the point where they competed with the buildings for visual dominance. Port Sunlight demonstrated that it was possible to house workers for a large industrial concern in good-quality housing set in a quasi-rural environment.[7]

Several other model industrial 'villages' (perhaps model suburbs would be a more accurate term) were built shortly after Port Sunlight and under its direct influence. The two most notable, Bournville and New Earswick, were both built for Quaker employers and the characteristic combination of aesthetic and social priorities is again evident. Bournville was built at the behest of George Cadbury. The first phase took place between 1898 and 1905; and second phase followed from 1914 onwards. The houses at Bournville were less distinguished architecturally than those at Port Sunlight, but the emphasis on low density marked an advance on the latter. The low density of housing allowed a 20-feet setback from the road, permitting front gardens (which were lacking at Port Sunlight) as well as generous back gardens. Bournville successfully demonstrated that the high standards achieved at Port Sunlight could be replicated in economically viable low-cost housing.

New Earswick was begun in 1902 for another Quaker chocolate company, Rowntree. Tree planting and a vernacular style continued the rural emphasis of Port Sunlight and Bournville. Further steps away from the artificial, rectilinear and unnatural appearance of most contemporary urban working-class housing were taken by making the roads within New Earswick curve and by providing footpath access to many houses, thus allowing them to be set more completely amid natural vegetation (a design feature not feasible for later housing estates built in the era of the automobile). Many of the houses were built in culs-de-sac which were intended to increase the sense of community. The architects at New Earswick were Barry Parker and Raymond Unwin, who later worked for the Garden Cities Association at Letchworth and Hampstead Garden Suburb.

The tradition of model village and housing construction was vital for the development of the garden city. But the garden city did not develop in an unplanned and gradual way directly out of the model village tradition; it took a serious thinker to see in the example of the industrial model village the potential for a radically new way of approaching the problem of urban design. The thinker in question was Ebenezer Howard.

Howard published his *Tomorrow: a Peaceful Path to Real Reform* in 1898. It was perhaps the most influential work on urban planning ever published. Howard's central argument was a remarkably prescient one. He pointed out, for the first time, that the growth of cities not only brought with it a plethora of social problems, but was also ultimately self-defeating. The main advantages of gathering a population together in cities was to facilitate communications and provide a higher standard of collective services. Yet once a city grew beyond a certain point, its centre became ever more congested, while the suburbs on its perimeter were ever more remote from the collective services available at the hub. There was therefore a limit beyond which it was not desirable for a city's population to increase.

Howard's concern with effective communications and the provision of central services demonstrates that he was sensitive to the advantages of the city as a form of residential living, but he was equally conscious of the drawbacks which the typical late nineteenth-century industrial city possessed. While some of these drawbacks were the results of excessive size, not all were. The ugliness, pollution, high housing density and lack of natural vegetation in industrial cities were consequences not only of their size but also of the type of activities carried out in them and of their design and architecture. These harmful features were in direct contrast to the countryside, which was characteristically beautiful, relatively unpolluted and space-abundant, and in which nature was directly present.

What was needed was a new kind of settlement which would unite the advantages of town and country; which would indeed no longer be 'town' but 'town country'. Howard envisaged settlements of no more than about 32,000 people, which would consist of alternating belts of built-up areas and countryside, with extensive garden provision even in the built-up rings. This new kind of settlement would therefore thoroughly interfuse urban and rural, overcoming the ancient dichotomy between the two. In an echo of the Spencean proposal to take land into public ownership on a parochial basis, Howard suggested that the land on which the 'garden city' of his plan was built should be owned by the city administration itself. The rent from this land would then be applied to supporting social, educational and cultural services, so permitting a high level of communal provision. This suggestion reflected both Howard's knowledge of the intellectual tradition of English agrarian radicalism, particularly Spence, and also his interest in the land reform debates of his own times (examined in more detail in Chapter 7). Howard's conception of an ideal future city that would be free of the distorting ugliness characteristic of the late nineteenth-century industrial city was not entirely derived from English sources, however; he was also influenced by the utopian American novelist Edward Bellamy, author of the best-selling novel *Looking Backward*, and by the Russian anarchist Peter Kropotkin.[8]

Howard himself was instrumental in translating the ideal vision outlined in *Tomorrow* into concrete reality. In 1899 he founded the Garden Cities Association, and conferences were held at Bournville in 1901 and Port Sunlight in 1902. Shortly after the Port Sunlight conference, the Garden City Pioneer Company Limited was established, with the aim of building the first example of a garden city. A site was chosen in Hertfordshire, and construction began in 1903 at what was to become Letchworth. Letchworth incorporated most of the essential features of Howard's garden city ideal. A ring of agricultural land surrounded the new settlement, and there was extensive vegetation within the town itself, with an active ongoing planting policy. The housing was of good quality, but was designed as far as possible to realize Howard's aim of creating a community in which all classes rather than merely the wealthy would be able to benefit from an attractive living environment. The houses were built in a rural vernacular style, with red roofs, white rough-cast walls, gables, low eaves and arts and crafts details. Only light, non-polluting industry was permitted.[9]

Letchworth was the first of a long line of new settlements taking their inspiration from the garden city ideal. Within a very short time, however, some of the central features of Howard's vision were being modified or discarded in settlements which claimed to inherit the mantle of Letchworth. A pointer to the future was Hampstead Garden Suburb, begun only two years after Letchworth in 1905. This is often considered as the most successful of the garden cities from an aesthetic point of view and as one of the finest achievements of its architects, Barry Parker, Raymond Unwin and Edwin Lutyens. But for all its aesthetic merits, Hampstead Garden Suburb departed from Howard's ideals in two important respects, both deriving from the fact that it was indeed a suburb rather than a free-standing city. First, it was not surrounded by a belt of agricultural land but by other urban areas, and so was not set in the countryside in the way that Howard's plan indicated. Second, it was not an independent economic unit, but was integrated into the economy of the city which enveloped it. Even the Garden Cities Association itself departed to some degree from the ideals set out in *Tomorrow* when it came to build the second garden city, Welwyn Garden City. This again was not built as and was never intended to be a free-standing economic entity, but was a commuter settlement for London. As such, it scarcely addressed one of Howard's fundamental criticisms of the over-large city, that the greater the distance between place of residence and place of work, the more clogged with traffic the transport network becomes.[10]

Beyond Letchworth, Hampstead Garden Suburb and Welwyn Garden City, the garden city idea was extensively taken up, for example in the new towns (such as Harlow and Peterlee) built after the Second World War, and in innumerable largely middle-class suburbs throughout the country. In many ways, though, the countless progeny of the garden city are a testament to the betrayal or at least very partial application of the original idea. Some elements of garden city planning, particularly the large gardens, trees and shrubs, low housing density and a vernacular architectural idiom have been so generally incorporated into house building both in Britain and in several other countries (such as the USA) that most middle-class suburbs look to some extent like garden suburbs. But the almost universal adoption of the outward style of the garden city serves to disguise the equally universal abandonment of the principles which originally informed that style. It is difficult to see the modern middle-class suburb as representing a committed attempt to overcome the distinction between town and country. By a ironic inversion of Howard's aim of combining the best features of town and country, the suburbs have often been criticized for uniting some of the worst features of both: the suppression of nature characteristic of the town and the social narrowness allegedly characteristic of the countryside. Still less can the suburb be seen as embodying Howard's ideal of a new form of self-owning settlement, where rents from the land would be applied to social purposes. So while the garden city has been immensely influential with respect to the design of housing in Britain (and elsewhere), and has to a great extent shaped the visual appearance of the modern middle-class suburb, in some respects the history of the garden city since Letchworth has been one of retreat from the ambitions of the original ideal. Howard's vision of a comprehensively ruralized and self-contained city owning its own land and providing generous social services on that basis has yet to be fully achieved.

. . . .

CHAPTER 6

Literary Attitudes to the Countryside in the Later Nineteenth and Early Twentieth Centuries

§ LITERARY attitudes to the countryside in the second half of the nineteenth and the first half of the twentieth century demonstrate both continuity with and a development from those of the preceding fifty years assessed in Chapter 2. The theme of the contrast between town and country which was so marked a feature of the first half of the nineteenth century is equally in evidence after 1850, and with the same strong positive valuation attached to the countryside in contrast to a typically negative perception of urban life, but this theme is presented in new ways.

Perhaps the most notable contrast between literary attitudes to the countryside in the second as against the first half of the nineteenth century is the much greater verisimilitude of writing about the countryside in the latter period, especially after about 1870. Late Victorian writers often possessed a much more acute and closely focused awareness of the realities of rural life and of the countryside than had their early nineteenth-century forebears. Writers are of course in the first place individual creative agents and only in the second place components of general cultural trends, and few large generalizations can be made about them to which there are not more or less prominent individual exceptions. The suggestion that rural writing in the latter part of the nineteenth century was more realistic and specific could be countered by objecting that there is no writer after 1850 who can approach Cobbett in the immediacy and concreteness of his presentation of rural society. This may be true (although George Sturt and Flora Thompson could be counted on the other side), but Cobbett was writing in reaction to the tendencies of his own times and the dogged, down-to-earth realism of his prose was in part intended to embarrass and give the lie to the mainstream tendency to ignore or play down the reality of rural life. Other early and mid-nineteenth-century writers offered a much less sharply focused picture of the countryside. As we saw in Chapter 2, even writers who saw themselves as engaged in a project to describe society realistically, such as Elizabeth Gaskell and George Eliot, were generally unable to extend this realism to the rural poor. In contrast, late nineteenth-century writers such as Hardy, Jefferies and Sturt offered precise and careful accounts which sought to establish their authenticity through unprecedentedly detailed descriptions of the physical and social fabric of rural England.

A telling manifestation of the greater concern with verisimilitude of rural writers in the second half of the nineteenth century and the early twentieth century is the rise of regionalism in English rural writing. Regionalism testified to a felt need to achieve a more exact relationship between social experience and literary representation. By grounding writing in a specific, actually existent social milieu, tendencies towards abstraction and generalization could be undercut by a more vivid particularity. The impulse towards regionalism was apparent to a certain extent in the poetry of Barnes, Hardy and Housman and the prose of Jefferies, Sturt, Hudson and Massingham, but it was in the novel that regionalism developed most strongly and consistently.

The roots of regionalism in the English literary tradition lay in Sir Walter Scott's 'Waverley' novels, which were embedded in a specific geographical setting (the Scottish Borders) and depended on locally specific customs, social situations and landscape in a way no previous novel sequence had done. Although these novels of course described the Scottish rather than the English countryside, they were widely read south of the border. Scott's evocative descriptions of landscape, which he used to amplify the local distinctiveness of the places and characters he wrote about, had an influence on subsequent novelists which in some ways paralleled that of Wordsworth on nineteenth-century poets. Seen from the point of view of the evolution of the regional novel, it was probably Scott's influence on the Brontë sisters which was most important. Just as Scott had used the hills of the Scottish Borders, so Emily and Charlotte used the Yorkshire moors to provide the substrate for their writing. Emily's poetry and her single mature novel, *Wuthering Heights*, together constitute what most critics would agree is the most powerful literary realization of moorland scenery in the English language. In its approach to landscape *Wuthering Heights* transcends mere description – its characters seem to grow out of the landscape, to the point where some of them (the first Cathy and Heathcliff in particular) seem almost to be human extensions of it. But for all its vividness, *Wuthering Heights* remains an imaginary rather than a real landscape: the place-names are fictitious, and Wuthering Heights and Thrushcross Grange exist in a world which is only tenuously embedded in the geography of the actual Yorkshire moors. The moorland of Charlotte Brontë's novels – especially *Shirley* and *Jane Eyre* – is presented more concretely, though less vividly, but, as with *Wuthering Heights* but unlike later regional novels, it would be largely beside the point to attempt to map the events described in

Charlotte's novels on to the actual terrain of the Yorkshire moors. In terms of the evolution of the regional novel, therefore, Emily and Charlotte Brontë mark a development in that they were among the first writers to achieve an authentic English literary landscape comparable to that which Scott had created in the Waverley novels. Even so, their landscapes do not have the detailed, precise, one-to-one correspondence with real places that was to become characteristic of literary regionalism later in the nineteenth and in the early twentieth century.

Several of the other major mid-nineteenth-century novelists also displayed an interest in regional settings, but these were rarely fully realized. The 'Loamshire' of George Eliot's *Adam Bede* indicates an intention to ground the novel in a plausible geographical specificity, but ultimately serves as an abstract, generalized representation of the countryside, to be contrasted with a similarly generalized industrial region ('Stoneyshire') adjacent to it. Elizabeth Gaskell's contrast between 'North' and 'South' again betrays a generalizing intention, while Dickens establishes no consistent rural terrain to match his preoccupation with London, despite occasional forays into Kent and Lincolnshire. It is only with R. D. Blackmore, and especially his masterpiece *Lorna Doone*, that the English regional novel can be said to have come into its own. Unlike previous novelists, Blackmore took pains to ensure that his literary region could be mapped accurately on to the real geographical region which gave rise to it, in this case the West Country (especially north Devon). Most of the place-names of *Lorna Doone* are not fictionalized, and almost all the events described can be located on the ground. Furthermore, the distinctive landscape, traditions and social structure of north Devon are not only vividly evoked, but actually play an integral role in the action of the novel.

It was not, however, Blackmore's north Devon but Hardy's Wessex which became the classic and most influential example of regionalism. Hardy showed that a regional basis could be used to generate a novel series which explored rural life in greater depth and variety than Blackmore achieved. Almost all rural novelists of the next seventy years followed Hardy's example in basing their fiction in a carefully specified and evoked region. The Sussex of Rudyard Kipling and Sheila Kaye-Smith, the Dartmoor of Eden Philpotts, the Lancashire of Constance Holme and the Shropshire of Mary Webb were all descendants of Hardy's Wessex.[1]

The specificity and topographical accuracy of regional novels were part of the explanation for their popularity. More important was a general upsurge in the demand from the reading public for rural literature of all kinds that began in the last two decades of the nineteenth century and continued strongly into the post-First World War years.[2] It was not only rural novelists such as Hardy and Webb who were read avidly, but also essayists such as Jefferies and poets such as Brooke and Edward Thomas. Much of the rural writing produced in this boom period is marked by an intense sense of the countryside being under threat. The threat was perceived as coming both from within the countryside and from without.

The main perceived threat from within was the agricultural depression and its attendant consequences of rural depopulation and the decline and often sale of great estates. At its most sober, this is the guiding principle of Rider Haggard's *Rural England* (1902). A latter-day version of Cobbett's *Rural Rides*, it describes a countryside falling into dereliction through low farming incomes and lack of investment. The only salvation would be agricultural protection, but Haggard believes that in a political world dominated by an urban electorate wedded to free trade this is unobtainable. Similar accounts can be found in rural novels, especially in the interwar period (the depression of the 1920s and 1930s affected more farmers more damagingly than that of the late nineteenth century). In Winifred Holtby's *South Riding*, for example, the hero, Robert Carne, is a landowning farmer who, despite his generosity towards his neighbours and his deeply humane outlook, is ruined by low prices and forced to sell his land.

If rural writers were aware that the countryside was threatened from within by internal collapse, their sense of the threat to the countryside from without became increasingly vivid, especially in the early twentieth century. Urban England intruded into rural England in many ways. Most obvious of all was the physical intrusion. Much of the growth of towns and cities in the first half of the nineteenth century had been through infilling. The need for workers to live close to their places of work in a period when casual employment was the norm had limited the growth of working-class suburbs, while middle-class suburbs developed less rapidly than they might have done had adequate transport links been available. But improvements in urban transport, particularly through the development of trams and of suburban railways, allowed a rapid acceleration in the rate of suburb development in the last third of the nineteenth century. The classic literary denunciation of suburbanization, however, had to wait until *Howards End* (1910), in which E. M. Forster wrote of the 'red rust' of London spreading out into the Hertfordshire countryside, and asked of the station for Howards End, 'Into which country will it lead, England or Suburbia?'[3]

Many writers feared more subtle aspects of urban intrusion into the countryside than the merely physical spread of bricks and mortar. A powerful tradition lamented the invasion of the countryside by urban and industrial technology, and the transformation of agricultural and rural craft work this entailed. In *Tess of the D'Urbevilles*, Hardy made a noted contribution to this tradition in his description of a steam threshing machine: 'Close under the eaves of the stack ... was the red tyrant that the women had come to serve – a timber-framed construction, with straps and wheels appertaining –

the threshing-machine which, while it was kept going, kept up a despotic demand upon the endurance of their muscles and nerves.'[4]

The displacement of traditional rural handicrafts by mechanized production methods was equally decried by rural writers, receiving its most celebrated expression in George Sturt's *The Wheelwright's Shop* (1923). This describes in meticulous, reverent detail the stages involved in making a wooden wheel. Sturt's aim was to show that the unwritten, practical knowledge of a skilled rural craftsman embodied a kind of understanding, derived partly from experience and partly from traditional lore, for which the ease and speed of powered machinery was, at least in human terms, a poor substitute.

Many rural writers also saw a political threat to the countryside arising from urbanization. While in the first half of the nineteenth century the countryside had been substantially overrepresented in the House of Commons, after the Second Reform Act (1867) the balance tilted irrevocably towards the towns. The political marginalization of the countryside was symbolized by the failure of government to take any effective steps to mitigate the agricultural depression. Many rural writers, especially those with conservative sympathies who could more easily equate the previous political hegemony of the landed aristocracy with the interests of rural society as a whole, saw the dawn of urban democracy as antithetical to the interests of the countryside. Such a perception, for example, is fundamental to Constance Holme's best-known novel, *The Lonely Plough*, and forms a significant element even in more politically nuanced works such as Holtby's *South Riding*. More popular fiction, such as the romances of Daphne du Maurier or the detective novels of Agatha Christie and Dorothy L. Sayers, often invokes images of decaying country houses whose inhabitants are at risk of robbery and murder, which among other meanings may allude to a perceived democratic threat to the stable, elite-dominated rural way of life.

Finally, rural writers often saw the countryside as threatened by urbanization and industrialization in socio-cultural terms. Influences which were perceived as urban – education, mass-circulation newspapers, new styles of clothing, music and dancing – were thought by many writers to be eroding traditional rural popular culture. Hardy expressed his regret for the replacement of the old church band by the new harmonium in *Under the Greenwood Tree*, while Sturt's *Change in the Village* was a sustained account of the erosion and eventual destruction of rural customs by modernizing economic and social forces emanating from the towns.[5]

If the rural England of late nineteenth- and early twentieth-century writers was presented in greater detail and with greater knowledge than had been the case in the early or mid-nineteenth century, the picture offered was also in many ways therefore a darker one. Writing about urban and industrial England also took on a darker hue in this period. Broadly speaking, most writing about towns and industry in the first half of the nineteenth century had been critical of them, often harshly so, but in the main the criticism had been of specific social and environmental conditions rather than of industrialism as a way of life. Disraeli's horrifying description of the mining village Wodgate in *Sybil* is a denunciation of working, living and religious conditions in a mining village, not of industrial life per se. Nor does Elizabeth Gaskell intend the cotton industry criticized in *Mary Barton* to stand for all types of industry. The nearest mid-nineteenth-century writers came to a denunciation of industrialism as a general system was *Hard Times*, which as Raymond Williams noted was uncharacteristic within Dickens's *oeuvre* in its totalizing hostility to urban life. In the later nineteenth century, as industry made the transition from exceptional novelty to familiar norm, writers increasingly interpreted industrialism in the totalizing way of *Hard Times*, seeing it as a form of civilization that looked set to become universal in the future. This response to, and revulsion from, industrialism as a whole way of life is evident in Jefferies' *After London*, which describes a world in which nature has reasserted itself and cities have disappeared, in Morris's *News from Nowhere*, in which again London has been replaced by countryside, and in many lesser late nineteenth-century works. It persisted strongly into the interwar period and is present in a pure form in Aldous Huxley's *Brave New World*. Writers who were less apocalyptically minded, such as George Gissing, typically present an equally negative and unmitigated picture of urbanism as a way of life.[6]

A central element of literary attitudes to the relationship between town and country in this period was the sense that with the dominance of the urban-industrial world, nature was being ever more brought under the control of mechanical processes. This fear of the subordination of nature to mechanization can be related both to the new awareness of industrialism as the coming universal condition, and to the awareness of the threatened, vulnerable defencelessness of the countryside in the face of this mechanization. It was linked to an increasing responsiveness to the natural, instinctual and spontaneous in human beings. The alienation of modern humanity from nature was potentially a tragic vision, and is at times present in this way in Hardy, as for example in *The Return of the Native*, where Egdon Heath has become a dark and destructive force to those of its residents who have been educated out of their original customary harmony with their environment. A more positive sense of nature as the ever-fertile source of life can be found in D. H. Lawrence, for example in the opening chapters of *The Rainbow*. Here, untamed nature is celebrated as the antithesis of the etiolated, eviscerated anti-life of the urban industrial world. This sense of nature as the source of life often led, as in Lawrence, to a conflation of nature and sexuality, a link which was adopted and exploited by a generation of minor rural novelists in the 1920s mocked by Stella Gibbons in *Cold Comfort Farm*.

Less vulnerable to metropolitan satire, but equally a response to the sense that industrialism had alienated man from nature, was the reaffirmation of the restorative power of rural work as a means of establishing a direct connection between man and nature which many writers in this period extolled. One of the earliest and best-known examples is the sheep-shearing scene in *Far from the Madding Crowd*. Hardy made the same point at greater length in *The Woodlanders*, where the profound involvement of Giles Winterbourne and Marty South in tree planting is seen both as explanation for and symbol of their harmony within themselves and with nature, in contrast to the more superficial relationship between most of the other characters and their environment. Sturt's quiet, careful accounts of rural craftsmanship and of how it depended on custom and tradition rather than standardization and theory provided a non-fiction counterpart to Hardy's more lyrical presentation of rural work in his early novels.[7]

At the same time, then, that it was being seen as threatened, the countryside was also being seen as the essential antidote to the ills of urban civilization (a perception which was given its culminating expression in Leavis and Thompson's *Culture and Environment*, where Sturt was taken as the last witness of a rural 'organic community' based around work in harmony with nature, which had been eroded and destroyed by industrialization).[8] It is this dual perception of the countryside as at once under threat and yet embodying necessary or even eternal values that accounts for one of the characteristic features of writing about the countryside in the late nineteenth and early twentieth centuries: the paradoxical presentation of the countryside as at one and the same time eternal and unchanging, and yet undermined and receding into the past. Perhaps the clearest and most powerful expression of this characteristic contradiction is Hardy's poem 'In Time of "the Breaking of Nations"':

> Only a man harrowing clods
> In a slow silent walk
> With an old horse that stumbles and nods
> Half asleep as they stalk.
>
> Only thin smoke without flame
> From the heaps of couch-grass;
> Yet this will go onwards the same
> Though dynasties pass.
>
> Yonder a maid and her wight
> Come whispering by:
> War's annals will cloud into night
> Ere their story die.

Written during the First World War, when tractors were being introduced in large numbers to replace the horses lost to the army, the poem's assertion that 'this will go onwards the same' betrays its own wishful thinking. Hardy's use of the archaic term 'wight' suggests that, despite his desire to shore up the traditional rural way of life as a bulwark against change, he himself already locates the world he claims is eternal in the past. The increasingly desperate assertion that the countryside is 'unchanging' is the reverse side of the coin of the intense awareness of how threatened and fragile it in fact is.

Hardy was grappling with an intractable problem, aware of the need for rural values which were nevertheless incapable of surviving in a modern, urbanized world. Much of the power of his later novels, however, derives from the tension between these two positions. Other writers rid themselves of this painful tension by displacing their account of the countryside from the present into the future. Often, as in Jefferies' *After London* and Morris's *News from Nowhere*, this rural future was tinged with a distinctly medieval past. In both works, cities have been destroyed or superseded by a renewed country-side. This strategy permitted writers not only to indulge the satisfaction of demolishing the cities they hated, but also allowed them to escape the implausibility of seeing the actually existing countryside as securely embodying 'eternal values'. There are parallels here with the strategy adopted by some mid-Victorian writers, George Eliot and R. D. Blackmore for example, of setting their rural novels in the past so as to avoid the difficulties of engaging with the social conflict and poverty of mid-Victorian rural society. The important difference here is that this earlier displacement, arising out of a less acutely felt conflict and contradiction, offered only an escape in the mind, whereas in Morris's *News from Nowhere* the countryside has become a model for a real alternative future society.[9]

Hardy, Jefferies and Morris were all dismayed by the changes they saw taking place in the countryside, but, although in a complex and often contradictory way, all three were honest enough to acknowledge them. Many other writers attempted to steer a more circuitous route round the facts of rural change. An increasingly popular means of achieving this, which in part accounts for the mushrooming of regional fiction at this time, was to select a remote portion of the countryside which could, without too obviously violating the truth, be portrayed as untarnished by 'outside' influences. This was what Eden Philpotts did with Dartmoor, and to a certain extent Mary Webb with Shropshire. A perhaps more honourable alternative was to avoid the difficulty by presenting an essentially private rather than social version of the countryside. If the countryside was constituted by the individual's experience of nature rather than by the relationship between nature and the rural community, then a genuinely unchanging rural world of birdsong and trees could be substituted for the irredeemably undermined socialized countryside. Perhaps the purest example of this drastic narrowing of the scope of the literary countryside was the poetry of Edward Thomas. The compensation for the narrowing was that what remained afterwards could be described honestly and without evasion.[10]

The 'timeless' countryside offered both by idealizing rural novelists like Philpotts and Webb and by those who sought to retreat into their own private countryside like Thomas could all too easily be identified with an 'essential England'. This alignment of a countryside purged of conflict and change with national identity was in evidence from well before the First World War. Conservative poets such as W. E. Henley, Henry Newbolt, John Drinkwater and the poet laureate Alfred Austin purveyed a debased Wordsworthian romanticism epitomized by Austin's 1902 publication, *Haunts of Ancient Peace*. This took the form of a journey to find unspoilt countryside which was then seen as the essence of England. The identification of a highly selective version of the countryside with the essence of Englishness was not necessarily conservative and imperialist in its implications, as the example of Edward Thomas indicates, but the outbreak of war in 1914 demonstrated how easily the pastoral stance evident in Rupert Brooke's 'Grantchester' could slide across into the overtly patriotic and pro-war 'If I should die'.[11]

After the war, this identification of a speciously unchanging countryside with English national identity became in many ways still more attractive, but at the same time even less plausible. It became more attractive because a more honest view would have disclosed an England racked by unresolved conflicts. Urban England, where four-fifths of the population lived, was the setting for mass unemployment and the General Strike. But identifying England with the countryside was even less plausible than it had been before the war because it was even clearer that England's future was necessarily urban and industrial, and that in economic, social and even political terms the countryside had become not only marginal but negligible. This conjunction between an increasing temptation to identify the countryside with English national identity and the decreasing plausibility of such an identification accounts for one of the most striking patterns evident in literary attitudes to the countryside in the interwar period: that while there was an unprecedented volume of minor writing about the countryside, major writers increasingly turned their attention to other subjects. Characteristically the minor writing marks a retreat from the position of Hardy's mature novels in that it progressively eliminated conflict, modernity and tension from its field of vision (for example through a revival of a mystified version of the country house as an emblem of rural community, as in some of Constance Holmes's novels). By contrast, the major writers of the interwar period tended either to avoid the countryside as a subject altogether, or moved away from it. T. S. Eliot might at first sight appear to be a partial exception to this, in so far as his *Four Quartets* use rural place-names as reference points, but on further reflection it is clear that rurality and the countryside were very far from being at the centre of Eliot's preoccupations – as a comparison with Hardy's poetry vividly demonstrates. Other modernist poets such as Pound and Auden had even less to say about rural England. D. H. Lawrence, the major novelist of the period, is an interesting case since his early novels do address the rural–urban theme, but in *The Rainbow* he recognizes that, deficient as urban England is in the rootedness old rural England allegedly offered, his heroine Ursula Brangwen must nevertheless move through and beyond this in the 'widening circle' of her life. The limitations of the customary life of the land mean that a return to it cannot be a solution to the alienation of man from nature which Lawrence follows Hardy in diagnosing.[12]

The response of major writers such as Lawrence and Auden in turning away from or ignoring the countryside was honest and realistic, but at the time it was probably the minor writers of rural life (particularly Mary Webb and Sheila Kaye-Smith) who obtained the wider readership. The misleading identification of England with a timeless countryside was a deeply reassuring one. In popularizing among the middle class the idea of the English country-side as a refuge from modernity, the minor rural writers helped to foster the growth of preservationist sentiment in interwar England, and the formation or expansion of organizations such as the National Trust and the Council for the Preservation of Rural England. These developments will be assessed in Chapter 8. For some social groups, however, the 'country in the mind' offered by Mary Webb and her kind did not provide an adequate refuge from the powerful reshaping forces of industrialism and urbanization. This was generally true for the working class, which had pressing material concerns that a literary retreat could do little to assuage. Many within the late nineteenth- and early twentieth-century working class were as susceptible to the call of the country-side as were the readers of rural literature, but wanted a more substantial, material, actually existing rural retreat than literature could provide. It was this demand which underpinned the popularity of land reform within the working class in the period before the First World War, and it is this subject with which the next chapter is concerned.

CHAPTER 7

Land Reform After 1850

§ FOUR central questions need to be addressed when considering land reform in the second half of the nineteenth century and the early twentieth century. First, why did the idea of land reform, which appeared to have reached a political dead-end with the failure of the Chartist Land Plan, revive strongly in the 1880s – by which time land might have seemed largely irrelevant to a society now plainly committed to an urban and industrial future? Second, how did the ensuing land reform movement succeed in sustaining such a high level of political interest in its agenda for the next three decades? Third, why despite this sustained interest were the land reformers not more effective in achieving their political goals? Finally, what if anything was the long-term legacy of land reform in British politics?

The collapse of the Chartist Land Plan was a devastating blow to the tradition of agrarian radicalism. The failure of both 'physical' and 'moral' force (violent and non-violent protest respectively) to achieve the political aims of Chartism had, it seemed, left agrarian radicals with no alternative but to attempt to achieve a redistribution of landed property by non-political means. Yet the fiasco of the land colonies and of the select committee hearings into O'Connor and the Land Plan in 1847 seemed to demonstrate that agrarian reform was no more to be attained through attempting to work within the existing political system than through attempting to overthrow it. Agrarian radicalism was indeed so badly disrupted by the failure of O'Connor's scheme that at least in its working-class guise it disappeared as an organized political force for the next twenty years.

If agrarian radicalism had reached a dead-end politically by 1850, there nevertheless remained thousands of individual Chartists who had been influenced by the agrarian radical tradition handed down by the Spenceans, Owen and then through Chartism itself. Although these Chartists in many cases no longer saw any immediate prospect of accomplishing their larger goals, many remained committed to an agrarian viewpoint and to the moral ideals of political equality, mutual improvement and self-respect which had been common to radicalism in the first half of the century. These commitments found expression through more local, practical and piecemeal forms of activity, the most important of which were the freehold land societies. These shared much in common with the Chartist Land Plan and with the smaller radical organizations that had attempted to settle their members on their own property in the 1830s and 1840s. The aim of the freehold land societies, of which Malcolm Chase has identified 184 between 1847 and 1854, was to provide their members with land. While the intention was usually to build a house on this land, part of the plot was often reserved for a garden or smallholding. Initially at least the freehold land societies also preserved something of the political motivation of earlier manifestations of agrarian radicalism. Because of the survival of the 40-shilling freehold franchise in the counties under the 1832 Reform Act, by purchasing land through a freehold land society former Chartists (and others) could acquire the right to a vote (even if living within a borough, they were entitled to vote in elections for the relevant county). Some of the freehold land societies emphasized that in making property affordable to the working class they were striking a blow at aristocratic privilege and exclusion. It is true that the freehold land societies gradually lost their political edge and became more concerned with commercial gain and individual improvement as they mutated into the building societies which did so much to disperse real property among the lower middle class and 'respectable' working class, but they nevertheless indicate that agrarian impulses did not suddenly vanish from the working class as an immediate result of the failure of the Chartist Land Plan. It would indeed be extraordinary if impulses which had been so persistent and prominent in the radical tradition in the first half of the nineteenth century had not continued, albeit in a subdued form, after 1850.[1]

The freehold land societies became progressively less political as they merged into the wider current of lower-middle- and upper-working-class respectability. But in the late 1860s agrarianism resurfaced as a political movement with the formation of the Land and Labour League (c.1869) by socialists and former Chartists. Some uncertainty still surrounds the causes of this revival, but the trade depression of the late 1860s and the more general revival of radicalism in the agitation leading up to the Second Reform Act and its aftermath clearly contributed. The League argued for land nationalization and state provision of smallholdings, but organizational weaknesses and the revival of trade in the early 1870s brought about its effective demise.[2]

Although working-class agrarian radicalism was badly damaged by the failure of the Chartist Land Plan, a related middle-class movement emerged in the 1850s and 1860s as a by-product of the anti-corn law agitation and the repeal of the corn laws. The Anti-Corn Law League had been intended as much as an attack on the aristocracy as it had aimed to reform the structure of taxation, and one of the League's most successful strategies had been to encourage its supporters to purchase freeholds, and hence votes, thus transferring political influence away from landowners to the middle class. After the repeal of the corn laws, the leading figures within the League were faced with a tactical dilemma: their success had in fact removed their chief weapon against the aristocracy, and threatened to lead to a political accommodation between the middle and upper class. Yet since to Richard Cobden and John Bright the aristocracy represented the vestiges of feudalism, such an accommodation could only be inimical to political and economic progress. Cobden and Bright therefore began to develop a more comprehensive critique of the political role of the aristocracy. Most of their previous Anti-Corn Law League supporters were unwilling to follow them in this, but although radical Liberalism was never able to secure majority middle-class backing, what was lacking in quantity of support was at least partly compensated for by its quality. Especially important was the weight added by J. S. Mill to radical Liberalism. Mill was the foremost British economist and philosopher of his day and as such his views commanded respect well beyond the confines of radicalism. He argued that land law reform was a political and economic priority, and called for the abolition of primogeniture, the taxation of the so-called 'unearned increment' (any rise in value of a piece of land not attributable to the landowner's own improvements), and the transfer of Irish land from the landowners to the peasantry. On this basis, he founded the Land Tenure Reform Association, which campaigned for the abolition of primogeniture and of the entail, for easier land transfer and for the taxation of the unearned increment.[3]

The activities of the freehold land societies, of the Land and Labour League and of the Land Tenure Reform Association during the 1850s, 1860s and 1870s kept the tradition of land reform alive, but they were on a very small scale in comparison with the upsurge of land reform opinion and organizations which occurred from the 1880s onwards. The socio-economic background to this major revival of land reform was a conjunction of an economic downturn affecting agriculture and industry simultaneously, together with a political crisis over Irish landownership. Signs of agricultural depression were apparent from the mid-1870s, but it was only in the late 1870s and the 1880s that the combination of sharply rising tradable world food supplies with an unusual sequence of poor harvests became severe. One of the responses of farmers was to cut costs by introducing labour-saving machinery. This prompted an outflow of displaced agricultural labour from the land, aggravating the depressed conditions that were also affecting many urban-based industries in these years. Both urban workers and many politicians became increasingly interested in ways of encouraging agricultural labourers to stay on the land because of the damaging effects of this flow of rural migrants on employment and wages. At the same time, radicals argued that the cause of the agricultural depression was the inefficiency of landowners, who were shielded from the invigorating effects of competition by artificial barriers to land transfer such as entails and the legal costs of land transfer. The solution to agricultural depression was, from this perspective, to reform the land laws and to break the great estates up into smallholdings. For these reasons, land reform, particularly those varieties of it which either promised to provide labourers with access to their own land, or to revive the prosperity of agriculture, attracted increasing political attention from the late 1870s. Party politics tended to reinforce this. The agricultural depression allowed protectionists to obtain a political hearing, at least within the Conservative Party, for the first time since the early 1850s. Liberals had to find an alternative remedy for agricultural depression, and turned to land reform to do so. By adopting land reform arguments about the deleterious effects of the special legal status given to real property, Liberals could claim that what was needed was more, rather than less, free trade. Although Liberal attempts to equate restrictions on land transfer with tariff barriers might be dubious in economic terms, they had a powerful rhetorical potential. If further fuel to the land reform debate was required, it was provided by the gathering crisis in Irish tenurial relations precipitated by the Irish Land League and its campaign to withhold rent.[4]

The formation of the first of the two leading late nineteenth-century land reform organizations arose directly out of the controversy over Irish land. In November 1880, Alfred Russell Wallace wrote an article in the *Contemporary Review* arguing that after three generations all landed property in Ireland should be nationalized. This prompted the establishment of a new middle-class land reform organization, the Land Nationalization Society, in March 1881, with the aim of applying Wallace's proposed remedy for Irish land to the English situation. The Land Nationalization Society argued that land should be taken into public ownership, but that existing landowners should be compensated for this. It would be only the land itself, not the buildings which stood on it, that would be nationalized. Initially, the Land Nationalization Society sought a single enabling Act that would vest the nation's land in the state. Later, it developed an alternative policy which it came to prefer. This was the so-called 'tax or buy' principle, whereby landowners would be required to declare the value of their own land. The advantage of this was that if a landowner undervalued his land, the state would be able to buy it on attractive terms; but if he overvalued it, the state could benefit by taxing the land on this high valuation.[5]

An alternative approach to land reform was proposed in Henry George's *Progress and Poverty*, which was published in England in 1881 and attracted intense public interest. George based his argument for land reform partly on economic and partly on moral grounds. Land, he pointed out, was the only fixed factor of production. Because of this, landowners were in possession of a resource which necessarily became ever more scarce with respect to labour and capital, the other factors of production, both of which were flexible and tended to enlarge as economic development occurred. Economic development was, George argued, the result of the exertions of employers and employees; landowners were passive in this process and, at least in their role as land-owners, contributed nothing to it. Yet they were among the chief beneficiaries of economic growth, collecting their 'unearned increment' as a result of the efforts of others. Since the unearned increment was, at least in George's view, the cumulative result of society's industriousness, it should in justice be returned to society. The most effective way to do this was to tax all the unearned increment away, leaving landowners with just enough net income from land to induce them to continue collecting rent. Not only would this rectify an injustice, but the resulting tax income would be sufficient to allow other taxes (which fell on capital and enterprise and were therefore un-desirable) to be remitted. It was because of this last point that George's plan later became known as the 'Single Tax' proposal.[6]

There were two important differences between the Land Nationalization Society's programme and that projected by Henry George. In the first place, George did not propose nationalization, and from this point of view his position was less radical than that of the Land Nationalization Society; but, second, he did not propose to compensate landowners either, and in this respect he was more radical than the Land Nationalization Society. The latter argued that under the existing economic circumstances whereby land was 'mono-polized' by a small number of owners, George's tax on the unearned increment would simply be passed on by landowners to their tenants, and so would fail to tax land ownership to any significant degree. This was their main reason for arguing that, attractive as the arguments of *Progress and Poverty* might seem, their intention could in fact be achieved only by land nationalization.

The controversy between George and the Land Nationalization Society led to the establishment of a Georgeist rival to the latter in 1883. This was initially known as the Land Reform Union, but changed its name to the English Land Restoration League in 1884 (and eventually to the English League for the Taxation of Land Values in 1902).

Although the Land Nationalization Society and the English Land Restora-tion League differed substantially in their practical proposals, the underlying moral and philosophical premises informing these proposals were in fact similar. Both organizations argued that people had a 'natural right' to land, because land was necessary to the support of life, and was therefore inalienable (an argument with close affinities to that made by Thomas Spence in the late eighteenth century). To this was sometimes added a theological claim: that God had given land to mankind for its subsistence, and that 'monopoly in land' was therefore against the divine will. A historical justification for land reform was also ready to hand (and again directly echoed that advanced by agrarian radicals in the 1820s and 1830s): that at one point (perhaps before the Norman conquest), land had been widely distributed among the population, but that it had subsequently been appropriated by a greedy and self-interested class of landowners. The final argument was the economic one, that impediments to the development of an active market in land allowed landowners to charge excessive rents.[7]

Both the Land Nationalization Society and the English Land Restoration League propagandized for their views energetically in the early 1880s, but although they attracted much interest, especially from urban radicals, neither initially succeeded in gaining any substantial political influence at the parliamentary level. A handful of Liberals elected in 1885 were Georgeists, and subsequently the English Land Restoration League was able to penetrate municipal and, eventually, parliamentary Liberalism, but this was not until the early twentieth century. In the 1880s, land reform would have made little political progress had it depended solely on the influence of its two leading organizations. But in fact a more powerful political force attached itself to the cause in the early 1880s: the radical Liberal politician Joseph Chamberlain. Chamberlain had been a member of Mill's Land Tenure Reform Association, and land reform had been one of his political aims since the early 1870s, but it was only in the 1880s that it became his leading theme. Clearly, therefore, Chamberlain was reacting to the strong popular feeling in favour of land reform rather than creating it.[8]

Two further factors made land reform particularly attractive to Chamberlain in the early 1880s. First, the Liberal Party had reached a point of ideological crisis. By the mid-1880s all the major Liberal goals had already been accomplished. Free trade was virtually complete, taxation levels had been brought down, the efficiency of government had been improved and moderate franchise reform had brought the middle class and the 'respectable' working class within the constitution. The Liberal Party began increasingly to look like a party which had lost its *raison d'être* as Gladstone lurched from one apparently opportunistic campaign to the next. Land reform could restore a sense of purpose and direction to the party. Second, the Third Reform Act of 1884 had given most male agricultural labourers the vote. This opened up the possibility of a rural campaign which could serve Chamberlain as a vehicle for his own political advancement and at the same time revive Liberal energies.

It was these considerations which gave rise to Chamberlain's 'Unauthorized Programme' of 1885. This proposed to give local authorities greater powers to purchase land compulsorily in order to let out allotments and smallholdings. Land taxation would be increased by imposing graduated death and house duties and a levy on the unearned increment. More stringent valuations would be imposed on land selected for compulsory purchase so as to reduce the cost of land purchases by local authorities. Finally, there would be an inquiry into the effects of the Enclosure Acts, and commons which had been enclosed improperly would be restored to public use.

Chamberlain's land reform programme was in large part developed, and promoted, by his ally Jesse Collings. It is clear from the Unauthorized Programme that Chamberlain and Collings were not prepared to adopt in full the Georgeist programme, and still less that of the Land Nationalization Society. They had no intention of abolishing private property in land or of taxing landowners out of existence. Their interest in re-establishing peasant proprietorship was greater, as was indicated by their formation in 1883 of the Allotments Extension Association (which became the Allotments and Small-holdings Association in 1884). But even on this point the measures they proposed were relatively cautious and limited and could scarcely be considered as posing an important threat to the incomes of landowners.

The Liberal Party split over the issue of Irish Home Rule in 1886 might have been expected to destroy land reform as a parliamentary force, because as a result of it Chamberlain and Collings were forced into alliance with the Conservative Party. Most of the support for land reform had come from the radical wing of the Liberal Party, from which Chamberlain and Collings were now divorced. Worse still, even could they persuade their Liberal Unionist colleagues of the merits of land reform (which was unlikely because of the predominance of Whig landowners within Liberal Unionism), they could scarcely hope to influence the staunchly pro-landowner Conservative Party in the same direction. In fact, far from spelling the end of land reform, the events of 1886 stimulated it. Because the Liberals were freed of the restraining influence of the Whigs, they were able to pursue more radical policies. The Liberal Unionists had a desperate electoral need to demonstrate their radical credentials. A moderate version of land reform, shorn of its anti-landowner rhetoric, was one of the least destabilizing methods by which the Liberal Unionists could demonstrate that they had not forgone their Liberal principles.

Within the Liberal Party, the English Land Restoration League made increasing progress after 1886, especially in London where the very high level of ground rents made land taxation an irresistibly attractive means of financing social welfare. This ultimately brought official recognition from the party as a whole, when in 1889 the National Liberal Federation adopted resolutions in favour of the taxation of land values. Two years later the 'Newcastle Programme' of the National Liberal Federation advocated municipal letting of smallholdings and the taxation of ground values, as well as free land transfer and the reform of leasehold tenures.[9]

At the same time, Chamberlain and Collings continued to make progress within the Liberal Unionist/Conservative alliance. Collings had made repeated attempts to promote allotments and smallholdings bills in the early 1880s, but with very limited success. However, in 1887 the government passed the first comprehensive allotments legislation – the 1887 Allotments Act. This gave local authorities powers of compulsory purchase to create allotments. In 1892 the government passed the Smallholdings Act, thus acknowledging another of Collings's long-standing demands. However, the Smallholdings Act was weakened by offering only tenancies rather than outright ownership, and by failing to include compulsory purchase clauses. Partly because of the second omission, a mere 652 acres of land were acquired under the Act between 1892 and 1902.[10]

In the mid-1890s both the English Land Restoration League and the Land Nationalization Society made strenuous efforts to broaden their political constituencies to include rural labourers, to whom land reform was felt to offer particularly great advantages, but who had up to this point shown little interest in land reform except as it bore on the question of allotment provision. To bring their respective messages to the labourers, the two societies resorted to travelling lecturers, who moved from village to village in their campaign vans. The English Land Restoration League's vans were painted red, while those of the Land Nationalization Society were yellow, but the bright colours of the vans appear to have made a stronger impression than the words of the lecturers, because no powerful groundswell of support for land reform resulted. During the remainder of the 1890s, land reformers made only slight progress. The Liberal Government of 1892–95 was unable to carry out the Newcastle Programme because of opposition from the House of Lords, while the Conservative administration which succeeded it refused to support Collings's Purchase of Land (England and Wales) Bill. Chamberlain's increasing absorption in his duties as Colonial Secretary deprived Collings of effective political support.[11]

The return of the Liberal Party to government after the 1906 general election resulted in renewed progress on the less controversial aspects of land reform, particularly allotments and smallholdings. The main achievement was the 1907 Allotments and Smallholdings Act, which increased the maximum size of allotments and created smallholdings commissioners to ensure (by compulsory purchase if necessary) that enough rented smallholdings were provided. But the more controversial, and central, issue of land value taxation ran into predictably greater difficulties, because Conservative peers in the House of Lords voted down or mutilated the land reform bills put forward by the government in 1907 and 1908. These bills applied to the valuation of Scottish land; it could be anticipated that if the government attempted to legislate similarly for English land it would encounter even more determined resistance.[12]

Despite the bitter hostility within the Conservative Party to land taxation, Conservative policy on land reform was not wholly negative. On the contrary, after 1906 the party became increasingly committed to moderate land reform.

The main focus of policy was on fostering owner-occupied smallholdings. While this was to a certain extent a competitive reaction to the rising tempo of land reform within the Liberal Party, its origins predated the 1906 election. First, Conservative policy on smallholdings was closely related to the party's stance on tariff reform. Without tariff reform, it was argued, smallholdings would be economically non-viable. But similarly, tariff reform would be politically non-viable if the rural electorate (which meant above all the labourers) could not be persuaded that the linked benefits which enhanced access to land would bring outweighed the drawbacks of higher food prices from the consumer's point of view.[13]

The recently established Labour Party was also affected by the land reforming policies being promoted by the Liberals. Land reform was indeed an important bond between Liberalism and Labour. Liberal attacks on aristocratic land monopolists elided with Labour hostility to mine owners, who in the main were large landowners. Labour policy on land reform to a large extent mirrored Liberal policy, although with a stronger commitment to ultimate nationalization of the land.[14]

Varieties of land reform therefore enjoyed a significant measure of support across the political spectrum in the first decade of the twentieth century. Nevertheless, although it might seem to be an issue on which the three main political blocs could have agreed, the opposite in fact occurred. This was, at least in part, because of the highly divisive way in which land reform was promoted by the Liberal Chancellor of the Exchequer, Lloyd George. In his 1909 budget, Lloyd George proposed two new forms of land taxation: first a tax of one penny in the pound on the capital value of land, and second a tax of 20 per cent on the increment in the value of land subsequent to its official valuation. The budget also included higher income tax, new death duties and a supertax. The last two of these in fact would have burdened landowners more heavily than the land taxes. But it was the latter which landowners resented most bitterly. They regarded the land taxes as involving unwarranted government intrusion into their private affairs, and as unfairly singling out landowners for hostile treatment. Furthermore, they rightly saw the relatively moderate level of land taxes Lloyd George proposed as merely the beginning of what might ultimately become a major imposition. Finally, landowners reacted angrily to the 1909 budget because it came from Lloyd George, who had already established a reputation for inveterate hostility to the aristocracy.[15]

The rejection of Lloyd George's proposals by the House of Lords led the Liberal government to call a general election in January 1910, which resulted in a reduced Liberal majority. After this, the budget was passed. Due to the intransigence of the House of Lords towards Liberal legislation, the government decided to introduce legislation to curtail the powers of the Lords. This legislation – the Parliament Bill – was rejected by the Lords, resulting in a second general election in 1910, after which the bill was passed. With the Lords now effectively neutralized, Lloyd George planned to use land reform, and in particular the taxation of land values, as the central plank of a high-profile campaign intended to sweep the Liberals to victory in the election which Lloyd George anticipated would be called in 1915. The land campaign was accordingly initiated, and a committee of pro-government 'experts' established to explore the potential for a major reorganization of landholding and taxation. The Land Enquiry Committee issued its first report, on rural land, in 1913, and the second in 1914. The first report especially roused considerable public interest, but although the tide of public opinion seemed to be running in favour of land reform, Lloyd George was forced to abandon the land valuation clauses of his 1914 budget. This seems mainly to have been because of his inadequate preparation, which allowed Conservative critics to expose inconsistencies in the legislation. How serious this setback would have been had war not broken out is uncertain. But once war was declared, it was soon obvious that there was no possibility of making progress with such controversial legislation. The First World War therefore came at the worst possible time for land reformers: it froze all progress at the point when land reform had established an unprecedentedly high political profile and a seemingly irresistible momentum.[16]

By the time the war ended, memories of the prewar land campaign had long faded, driven out by the quite different and uniquely intense emotions of the war. Nevertheless, the mere fact that land reform had been cheated of its political moment would probably not of itself have been sufficient to prevent renewed progress after the war. Many within both the Liberal and Labour parties remained committed to land value taxation. What was more serious was the split in the Liberal Party. Lloyd George had formed a coalition with the Conservatives in 1916, and this coalition continued after the war, forming the first postwar government. It is true that Lloyd George and the Conservatives were able to co-operate to some degree on the less controversial aspects of land reform, notably in the Land Settlement Act of 1919, which aimed to provide ex-servicemen with smallholding tenancies. But even this limited measure was underfunded and in the event only 24,000 ex-servicemen, rather than the 750,000 originally intended, were settled on the land.[17] As for Lloyd George's more ambitious and anti-aristocratic prewar land reform proposals, it was quite clear that there was no question of reviving these while he remained tied politically to the Conservatives. The Asquith Liberals were of course still free to advocate land taxation, but the 1918 election reduced them to a rump, and the Liberal Party never again held office. The rise of the Labour Party meant that after 1918 the politics of labour against capital replaced those of people against aristocracy. Land permanently lost the political centrality it had had between 1880 and 1914.

There were intermittent attempts to revive land reform. Once Lloyd George had freed himself from coalition with the Conservative Party, he again set out an ambitious programme of land nationalization and smallholdings provision in his *Land and the Nation* manifesto of 1925. But by this time Liberalism had become permanently politically marginalized. There were still some land reformers within the Labour Party, however, and one of them, Philip Snowden, became chancellor in the 1929–31 Labour government. Snowden's 1931 budget included land valuation and taxation proposals, but these had not been implemented by the time the government fell from power. The National government which ensued, dominated by the Conservative Party as it was, first suspended and then repealed these measures. Snowden's budget represented the last gasp of the land reform tradition deriving from the campaigns of the 1880s, in that it was the last time that land reform was promoted as the central plank of a political platform by a major politician. Faint echoes of the land reform tradition were, it is true, apparent in some subsequent Labour legislation, such as the clauses in the 1947 Town and Country Planning Act which imposed charges on increases in land values arising out of development; but by this time land reform had long since ceased to possess a powerful political resonance, and it was never again to hold anything like the centrality it had for much of the period between 1880 and 1914.[18]

In the long term, the demise of land reform should not be attributed merely to the accident of the outbreak of war in 1914 or to the subsequent split in the Liberal Party. It is uncertain whether Lloyd George's plans for land valuation and taxation would have been legislatively or politically viable even had war not prevented their implementation. The process of valuing land proved to be immensely complex, time-consuming and expensive, and incurred high political costs because of its unpopularity with those whose land was valued.[19] Crucially, this included the small owners of urban property as well as the great aristocratic landowners. The underlying moral premise of Liberal land reform policy was that land represented a separate and morally inferior form of property from capital. Capital was acquired through skill and effort, land merely by inheritance. In practice, land and capital could not be neatly separated, at least in the English context. There were hundreds of thousands of middle-class property holders who owned both houses and the land on which they stood. To this large and electorally important group, an attack on landed property was an attack on their wealth, no matter that its prime target was the large landowner. The alternative policy, pursued by the Conservative Party, of trying to unite land and capital through dispersing land ownership as widely as possible (as in the smallholdings policy, or, subsequently, attempts to broaden home ownership) was in fact to prove more politically durable.[20]

If land reform subsided very rapidly as a political issue during and after the First World War, this did not imply any loss of public interest in the countryside more generally. On the contrary, public enthusiasm for and concern about the countryside had never been greater. The most striking manifestation of this was the rise of rural preservationism. Although the origins of preservationism can be traced back to the nineteenth century, the movement accelerated markedly in the period after 1918. The decline in practical interest in the politics of land was therefore paralleled by an equally striking increase in aesthetic interest in the appearance of the countryside. It is with the rise of rural preservationism and its relationship to English national identity that the next chapter is concerned.

CHAPTER 8

Preservationism, 'Englishness' and the Rise of Planning, c.1880–1939

§ IN the late nineteenth and early twentieth centuries the countryside was more obviously affected by urban influences than ever before. Perhaps the leading aspect of this was the physical expansion of towns into the country-side, through the development of suburbs. Suburbs had, of course, been features of some of the larger towns from long before the end of the nineteenth century. But the rate of expansion of suburbs, and the quantity of countryside 'lost' as a result of this, was higher during the late nineteenth and first half of the twentieth centuries than it had previously been. The most intense phase of suburban growth was during the interwar years. Suburban-ization was a characteristic of all Britain's largest cities at this time, but was especially notable around London. The new suburbs catered pre-eminently for the middle class, but many working-class people either moved voluntarily to suburbs, or were forcibly evicted in the course of slum clearance programmes. London's largest and best-known interwar suburb, for example, was the Becon-tree housing development, which was intended to accommodate 100,000 largely working-class families moved out from the East End.[1]

There were a number of reasons for the very active growth of suburbs in the interwar period. Part of the explanation lies in rising living standards, especially in the south and Midlands. While high unemployment in the tradi-tional heavy industries kept living standards low until the late 1930s in much of northern England, further south the economic situation was different. The south and Midlands benefited from the flow of industries and jobs away from the north. The net effects of the growth of new industries such as the electrical industries, car-making and chemical processing more than counterbalanced the loss to the national economy caused by the difficulties of heavy industry. For those in employment, living standards rose quite noticeably. This rise in living standards led to aspirations for better-quality housing in more attractive locations. The willingness of the middle class to pay more for good housing had been the basis from which many Victorian parks had been funded. The same impulse to escape from the dirty and socially undesirable surroundings of the central cities to a place where it would be possible to surround the home with trees, enjoy the pleasures and status of a large garden and live in greater seclusion is evident in the 'flight to the suburbs'.

The spread of suburbs, both before and after the First World War, was facilitated not only by rising living standards but also by improvements in transport. Much of the improvement in transport occurred at the end of the nineteenth century with the advent of trams and a more developed suburban railway network, but developments in the early twentieth century were important too. Motor bus services proved more flexible than trams had ever been. The network of intra-urban bus services was more dense than the tram and railway routes with which the buses competed, and bus routes could be more easily extended to new outlying suburbs than tram lines. But a more radical transport revolution was also beginning to make itself felt during the 1920s – the rise of the motor car. Ultimately, cars were to make possible a degree of separation between place of work and place of residence that was unimaginable at the start of the twentieth century. In the 1920s car ownership, although expanding rapidly, was confined to the relatively wealthy, so although it was important for this group it did less to promote suburbanization than the improvements in public transport.

The commitment of the architectural profession in Britain to low-density housing was another factor which contributed to the rapid pace at which suburbs extended into the countryside between the wars. The influence of the ideas of Ebenezer Howard and the garden city movement on British architects had been considerable, and although many aspects of Howard's thought were ignored or misunderstood, the emphasis which he and his colleagues Raymond Unwin and Barry Parker placed on ensuring that houses were set in sufficient space was widely accepted. Naturally, low-density housing occupied a larger area of land, and therefore of countryside, per family accommodated. However, even had the suburbs not been built at lower densities than nineteenth-century housing, much land would still have been required for housing in the interwar period. This was partly for demographic and partly for economic reasons. Demographically, household size was falling as the number of children per family declined and as older people lived longer. Since there was no corresponding fall in population, this meant a rise in the number of households. The main economic reason necessitating a larger stock of housing was the shift in economic activity from north to south, which resulted in population displacement towards the south and therefore a need for more houses in that region.

One of the forms of suburbanization which attracted particular hostility was ribbon development – houses extending out for miles into the countryside along the line of a major road. This often occurred when a new bypass had been constructed. Bypasses were attractive locations for new housing to be built, because of their high accessibility by car. Yet from the point of view of the local authority which had sponsored the bypass, ribbon development destroyed much of the value of the new road. A bypass was intended to be a fast through route which would keep traffic moving and avoid accidents between vehicles and between vehicles and other road users or pedestrians. But once houses lined both sides of a bypass, both advantages were undermined. Local traffic would manoeuvre in and out of the garages of the houses adjoining the bypass, or park on the bypass, thus replicating the congestion problem the bypass had been built to solve. This would also constitute a safety hazard. Ribbon development of any kind, whether on a bypass or not, had further drawbacks. The intrusion of 'urban' houses deep into the countryside was seen by many as a defacement of the landscape. Ribbon development also created problems of service supply, and hence of cost. Because ribbon development could extend for miles beyond what were otherwise the limits of a city, it was expensive to lay on services such as mains water, sewers and gas. Whether from an economic or an aesthetic point of view, therefore, ribbon development was condemned by many as the most damaging form of urban physical expansion into the countryside.[2]

Buying a house in the suburbs often, at least in part, reflected a desire to live in more rural surroundings. For some of Britain's wealthier citizens, a more complete escape was possible. Those who could afford a car were able to move right out of the towns and settle in rural villages. Because of the limited technical capabilities of cars in the 1920s and the poor quality of many rural roads, the maximum distance at which it was possible to live from the place of work was still quite low, even for those with cars. This, though, was the beginning of commuterization which, in the second half of the twentieth century, was to become the single most decisive force affecting the composition of rural communities (see Chapter 13).

If the bricks and mortar of new suburbs and commuter houses were the most obvious dimension of the increased visibility of urban intrusion into the countryside, almost equally important were the demands made on the countryside by towns for leisure purposes. The transport improvements of the late nineteenth and early twentieth centuries had not only facilitated suburbanization but also made the countryside much more accessible to visitors. Once again, the motor bus (both in its guise as a regular timetabled service and as an excursion coach) carried the largest numbers, while cars were significant for a small but rapidly growing group. Also important were the cheap train fares offered by many railway companies for weekend or bank holiday excursions. However, second only to the bus in terms of the number of people actually transported into the countryside was the bicycle. Bicycle ownership rose very rapidly in the early twentieth century, and cycling clubs such as the Clarion became immensely popular. Most of these cycling clubs chose to take their rides in the countryside.[3]

City dwellers therefore were more easily able to get to the countryside than they had been in the mid-nineteenth century. They also had more time in which they could do so. Hours of work fell progressively from the 1870s onwards, and holidays became more general. For those who could afford to make use of them, more hours of the week and days of the year were available for use in leisure activity than ever before. Many could afford to do so because of the rise in average incomes.

The results of a more accessible countryside, more leisure time and more disposable income were striking, especially from a visual point of view, and once again it was in the interwar years that trends which had been apparent from the late nineteenth century onwards developed most fully. A range of new facilities and features sprang up along the increasingly travelled rural roads to serve or exploit urban visitors to the countryside. Petrol stations catered for the rising volume of motor traffic, while a proliferation of tea shops offered to refresh weary tourists. Once out of the tea shop and back on the road, the tourist was likely to be bombarded with roadside advertisements which were to be found on almost all major roads in both town and country. Nor was it only the day-tripper whose presence and expenditure reshaped the visual appearance of the countryside. Holidaymakers and retirees wanted to experience the countryside too. Caravan and camp sites spread quickly, especially along the coasts and in the more scenic inland areas. 'Plotlands' were created by developers who appreciated the willingness of lower-middle-class and working-class city dwellers to buy a plot of land in a rural location – or what had been a rural location – even before they necessarily had the capital to construct a house on the site. The resulting amorphous agglomeration of shacks and bungalows manifested many of the most objectionable features of ribbon development, from their alleged aesthetic poverty to the difficulty of laying on services. The most notorious example of plotland was Peacehaven, near Brighton in Sussex. Peacehaven was sited on what was perhaps the finest section of chalk cliffs in Britain, where the South Downs meet the sea. Yet far from being carefully designed to harmonize with this distinctive landscape, Peacehaven was a sprawl of bungalows in varying stages of completion (many plots were left vacant for years and became overgrown), with no evidence of thought given to architectural or landscape considerations either in the design of the houses or the layout of the town.[4]

One of the most important responses to the increasing visibility of urban influences on the countryside in the late nineteenth and first half of the twentieth centuries was the formation of organizations dedicated to preserving a range of features of the landscape, including scenery, buildings and wildlife.

While these organizations did not restrict their operations to the countryside, in practice it was with the countryside that most of them were overwhelmingly concerned. A list of the more important pre-1914 preservationist societies gives some indication of the number and scope of preservationist organizations that had been established even before the First World War:

Commons Preservation Society (1865)
Kyrle Society (1876)
Society for the Preservation of Ancient Buildings (1877)
Derwentwater and Borrowdale Defence Committee (1882)
Lake District Defence Society (1883)
National Footpaths Preservation Society (1884)
Selborne League (1885)
Plumage League (1885)
Society for the Protection of Birds (1889)
Society for Checking the Abuses of Public Advertising (1893)
National Trust for Places of Historic Interest or Natural Beauty (1894)
Society for the Preservation of the Wild Fauna of the Empire (1903)
British Empire Naturalists' Association (1905)
Society for the Promotion of Nature Reserves (1912)

The aims of these societies varied widely. Some, such as the Society for Checking the Abuses of Public Advertising (SCAPA) and the Lake District Defence Society, were primarily concerned with protecting the rural landscape from unwelcome visual alteration. Others, like the Society for the Preservation of Ancient Buildings (SPAB), sought to maintain the fabric of valued buildings. The National Trust conflated these objectives. The Commons Preservation Society (CPS), the Kyrle Society and the National Footpaths Preservation Society were predominantly occupied with questions of public access, while for the Selborne League, the Society for the Protection of Birds and the Society for the Promotion of Nature Reserves, wildlife protection was central. However, despite their diverse goals, these societies had much in common beyond the simple fact that they were all committed to preservation in one form or another and that they all emerged in the late nineteenth or early twentieth centuries. In particular, there was a high degree of overlap in their membership. Octavia Hill, for example, was active in the Kyrle, Selborne and Commons Preservation societies and in the National Trust. Robert Hunter was a leading figure in all these organizations and was a member of SCAPA. James Bryce and Sir John Lubbock were members of the Selborne and Commons Preservation societies, of the SPAB and of the National Trust; Bryce was also a member of SCAPA. Hardwicke Rawnsley was a member of the Selborne Society, the Derwentwater and Borrowdale Defence Committee, SCAPA and the National Trust. George John Shaw-Lefevre (Lord Eversley) was a member of the CPS, SCAPA, the Selborne Society and the National Trust. William Morris was a member of the SPAB, the Kyrle Society, the Selborne Society and SCAPA. Most of the late nineteenth-century preservationist organizations were therefore closely linked through their leading members.[5]

The emergence of this interconnected group of preservationist organizations in the late nineteenth century raises an important question: was this a sign of a general turning away from the present towards the past in English national culture? Perhaps the most influential historical account to engage with this question has been Martin Wiener's *English Culture and the Decline of the Industrial Spirit* (1981). As his title implies, Wiener saw rural preservationism as part of a more general rejection of the entrepreneurial spirit which, he alleged, was essential to economic dynamism under industrial capitalism. Wiener claimed that Britain had made only an incomplete and imperfect transition to a bourgeois society. Unlike France or America, which both experienced democratizing revolutions informed at least to some extent by an anti-aristocratic ideology, Britain had no bourgeois revolution and remained politically and economically dominated by the landed aristocracy. While commerce and finance were acceptable forms of wealth generation to the aristocracy, industry was considered tainted. As a result, anti-industrial values remained ensconced at the heart of British culture, and through the medium of the public schools decisively affected the outlook even of the business class itself. For Wiener, rural preservationism was evidence of a nation which had lost confidence in its future and which sought to shore up a moribund social order through enshrining the relics of a pre-industrial past as the crown jewels of its culture.[6]

One of the difficulties of Wiener's account is that to portray nineteenth-century England as an unusually conservative society, hostile to innovation, seems to fly in the face of what is after all the single most startling feature of English nineteenth-century history: that England was the first country to undergo an industrial revolution. Wiener skirts round this difficulty by arguing that while in the early nineteenth century businessmen remained at least largely independent of and separate from the aristocratic elite, in the second half of the century the upper echelons of industry were progressively absorbed by landed society. A process of assimilation took place whereby industrialists became infused with the values of the aristocracy, including their pro-rural and anti-industrial assumptions. Wiener allocates a central role in this process to education, and in particular to the development of the great English public schools in the period after 1850. These public schools began to take an ever rising proportion of upper-middle-class boys, but the values which prevailed within these schools remained strongly those of the landed elite. Industrial occupations were looked down upon; money ought to be inherited or made at a seemly distance from its recipient, as was the case with finance and commerce (which Wiener argues were more readily accepted by the landed establishment). The curriculum of the public schools for a long time reflected this disdain for the 'dirty' business of making money by working for it; 'modern' subjects relevant to business needs such as the sciences were resisted, while subjects which had no business application but were identified with the leisured, exclusive way of life of the elite (notably Greek and Latin) were the bedrock of the curriculum. While Wiener saw the public schools as the most important site of class integration, he also regarded the universities (Oxford and Cambridge) as playing an analogous role, although less significantly because of the small numbers of middle-class undergraduates throughout the nineteenth century.[7]

Beyond boyhood and youth, the process of assimilation and absorption continued through the adult status system. A relatively limited number of the most successful industrialists were given titles, helping to tie the leading industrialists into a system which denigrated the significance of their occupation as against land and commerce. Many aristocrats themselves invested in shares and became company directors in the late nineteenth and twentieth centuries. In this way, the old elite maintained its domination of prestige. Industrialists were not excluded from the elite; on the contrary the most successful of them were cautiously welcomed into it. Largely for this reason, no final collision between the old elite of land and commerce and the newly wealthy men of business occurred, but in general the industrialists were a disparaged group who remained on the fringes of the elite.

In this view, the struggle over the repeal of the corn laws was the high-water mark of a radical bourgeois ethos in Britain. The vehement hostility to the aristocracy manifested by the Anti-Corn Law League was a reflection of a class critique of an 'idle' landed elite made by a rising and self-confident industrial middle class. The accommodation made by the elite, led by Peel and the Whigs and Liberal Tories who co-operated with him, as expressed in the repeal of the corn laws in 1846, served to head off what might have developed into a full-scale clash between classes and values. After 1846, the radical Liberals Richard Cobden and John Bright, who were both committed to a class-based attack on the aristocracy, repeatedly lamented how easily their followers had been bought off and how complacent towards aristocratic political, social and cultural domination the industrial bourgeoisie had become.

Wiener's argument has been amplified by other historians who have drawn attention to conservative or regressive features associated with ruralist attitudes and preservationist organizations. Alun Howkins, in an essay on perceptions of the English landscape in the late nineteenth century, argued that the landscape which came to be seen as 'characteristic' of English scenery, and therefore as most attractive, was in fact a highly artificial and regionally specific selection. In particular, Howkins argued, it was the landscape of the south of

England – especially the chalk downlands of Kent, Sussex, Surrey, Berkshire, Wiltshire and Dorset – that was favoured. Howkins claimed that preservationists shared this bias towards the southern English landscape, and that this was reflected in the early purchases of the National Trust. What was at stake, according to Howkins, was far more than simply a failure to offer an accurate or balanced reflection of the real landscape diversity of England or Britain. The landscape region favoured embodied social and cultural values which, Howkins argued, were intrinsically conservative in their implications. The south of England was a gentle landscape in which conflict and strife were largely invisible. The rolling hills, hedgerows, thatched cottages and elm trees spoke of rural peace, stability, changelessness, and the benign integration of history and landscape. Furthermore, this was a landscape of social hierarchy. Much of it had been created by the great landowners, and the relationship of church, manor house and cottages which could be found in an idealized southern English landscape was a landscape of enduring deferential hierarchy. The landscapes to which this was preferred would not necessarily have yielded such comforting and complacent social messages. The ruggedness of the northern hills, for example, would have conveyed a less benign impression of the countryside, and, furthermore, as a landscape in which the presence of small farmers was more obvious than that of large landowners, the form of society validated by a landscape aesthetic based on northern moorlands would have been less socially conservative.[8]

Another historian whose arguments reinforced Wiener's position was Georgina Boyes. Boyes examined the 'Folk revival' in early twentieth-century England. The traditional account of the revival was that a group of dedicated collectors, notably Cecil Sharp, had recorded the traditional songs and dances of rural England just in time to save them from the oblivion to which the increasing dominance of urban and commercial cultural influences would otherwise have doomed them. Boyes argued that this interpretation was seriously inadequate. She demonstrated that the concept of 'the folk', which underpinned the revival, was a contradictory and self-serving one. The assumption that rural popular culture was largely unchanging and that the village songs and dances had been transmitted in essentially the same form for centuries or even millennia was not supported by evidence and involved an artificial and arbitrary definition of 'uncorrupted' folk traditions as those which showed no signs of having been affected by 'alien' influences. This assumption legitimated the conclusion that 'the folk' was fundamentally uncreative, since its only acceptable cultural role was to transmit in unchanged form the customs it had inherited from preceding generations. This in turn allowed middle-class collectors like Sharp to pose as the sole authorities over what constituted 'genuine' folk songs and dances. Once the new category of 'the folk' had been defined in this way, it could be put to a variety of cultural uses. Perhaps the most important of these was that a folk culture which was safely located in the rural past, and which therefore excluded the potentially more challenging and politicized culture of the contemporary urban working class, could be used as the basis for the reconstruction of a consensual national culture with conflict written out of it. English national identity could be associated with the rediscovered traditions of 'the folk', and in this way a rural, backwards-looking and elitist version of Englishness reinforced.[9]

Boyes's suggestion that a conservative ideological slant could be grafted on to a pre-existing popular appetite for tradition parallels the argument put forward by Patrick Wright in *On Living in an Old Country* (1985). Wright argued that a nostalgic desire for connection with the past arises out of the circumstances of everyday life rather than being fostered artificially for ideological purposes by interests seeking political hegemony. Where Wright differs from Wiener and Boyes is in his suggestion that the roots of popular nostalgia, and of the preservationism which he sees as a derivative phenomenon, lie not in specifically English circumstances but are general to 'modernity', i.e. the cultural condition of the industrialized Western world. Wright sees modernity as being characterized by ceaseless and accelerating change, creating a generalized condition of anxiety, which leads to a hankering after the stability of the past. This yearning for a more stable, secure and comprehensible past provides fertile soil for historically based constructions of national identity, and results, among other consequences, in preservation of traces of the past being a universal feature of modern Western societies. However, Wright is not dismissive of a degree of English exceptionalism. He argues that because England experienced the traumas of modernity (especially industrialization) first and with particular intensity, English national identity became more strongly backwards-looking and constricted than was the case in other countries. Rural nostalgia and attendant preservationism are seen by Wright as component parts of this constricted national identity.[10]

Wright's observation that nostalgia and preservationism were general phenomena of Western modernity rather than being confined to England (albeit developed more acutely in England than elsewhere) raises two important questions: first, how central was preservationism to English culture?; and second, is it valid to see preservationism as a decisively conservative impulse within national culture? With respect to the first of these questions, an important position has been advanced by Peter Mandler. Mandler does not dispute that there was an anti-urban strain of ruralism within English culture during this period; but he does question its centrality. Where Wiener, Howkins and others see ruralism as representing the main line of development of English culture in this period, Mandler sees it as the limited reaction of a disaffected cultural and intellectual *'derrière-garde'*. He points out that the membership of the preservationist organizations remained tiny during the nineteenth century (the exponential growth in membership of organizations such as the National Trust and the RSPB dates from after the Second World War; before the First World War both societies numbered their membership in the hundreds rather than the thousands, and the total membership of all the preservationist societies combined was under ten thousand). The political impact of rural preservationism was, Mandler claims, correspondingly slight. He cites the failure of the preservationist societies to pass effective preservationist legislation as evidence of their political marginality and hence of their marginality within English elite culture as a whole.[11]

Mandler also points to continental examples to bolster his claim that English national identity in the late nineteenth and early twentieth centuries was not distinctively rural. In both Germany and France, he argues, rural, anti-urban values were more deeply entrenched than in England. The German political elite remained much more impermeable to businessmen, and much more dominated by aristocratic landowners, than the English elite was right down to 1918. In France the political importance of the peasantry, and the cultural significance of the rural *France profonde*, gave ruralism a power and political reality which it did not even begin to approach in England.

Does Mandler in his own turn overstate his case? There are two main respects in which his arguments are open to criticism. First, it is questionable whether the pro-rural individuals and movements he dismisses were really as marginal to the English cultural tradition as he maintains. It is true that the preservationist societies had few members prior to the Second World War, but they did not on the whole seek a mass membership. They were essentially elite organizations which sought an influential rather than a democratic membership.[12] Mandler's comment that the legislative achievements of the preservationist societies were negligible may also be somewhat wide of the mark. The National Trust Act of 1907, which allowed the Trust to declare land inalienable, was a crucial piece of legislation for the preservationist movement. More fundamentally, it needs to be borne in mind that legislative change was not the primary objective for most of the preservationist societies. The Commons Preservation Society was successful in its efforts to have the objectionable clauses of the Statute of Merton amended in 1893, for example, but its central strategy was to use the courts to enforce the law with regard to common land as it stood. In this the CPS had significant success. Similarly, the National Trust was conceived not as a campaigning organization, but as one which would operate privately through donations of land from landowners. To argue that the preservationist organizations cannot have been influential within national culture because they did not achieve greater legislative change is to miss the point that most of these organizations were not primarily trying to achieve legislative change. Equally open to dispute is Mandler's statement that a 'well-rounded' account of English culture at this time would not place the folk revival anywhere near its centre. This seems to ignore the fact that folk dancing became an important element of the curriculum of most English primary schools during the interwar years.[13] Nor does Mandler devote adequate attention to some figures of unquestionable cultural centrality, such as Hardy and Vaughan Williams, whose ruralism is indisputable.

Second, Mandler's claims are more valid for the pre-First World War period, to which three-quarters of his article is devoted, than to the period after 1918. The vast influx of townspeople into the countryside in the interwar years, for day-trips, holidays, or to live permanently, was in itself a sign that the countryside had become more central to national identity than it had been before 1914. This was partly because of the effects of the war. The English countryside was, of course, used as means of stirring up patriotic emotion during the war, but it seems that both during and after the war an equally important reaction was a more private one. Many, saddened, embittered or simply disillusioned by the experience of the war, turned away from public culture into private worlds of feeling and aesthetic response. This turning away towards private feeling easily found a mode of expression in the solitary communion with nature which had been a strand of English culture since Wordsworth. We have already seen in Chapter 6 how many writers sought a personal experience of nature in their post-First World War work. There were other reasons, too, for the larger role played by the countryside within English culture in the 1920s and 1930s. Not only did an idealized countryside provide an emotional refuge for those scarred by the war, it also offered similar relief to many for whom the present rather than the past was the main anxiety. Persistent high unemployment and the looming shadow of war made an imagined countryside an appealing alternative to grim urban reality. However, it should be pointed out that the more central role played by the countryside in English culture in the interwar period was not an entirely spontaneous development; as we shall see, politicians of various persuasions (pre-eminently the Conservative Prime Minister Stanley Baldwin) sought to promote ruralism for their own tactical ends.

A balanced conclusion would accept Mandler's fundamental point that preservationism, contrary to the claims put forward by Wiener, was not hegemonic within English culture in the late nineteenth and early twentieth centuries; but that, contrary to the implications of Mandler's argument, preservationism was nevertheless one among a number of important currents which contributed to the construction of national identity in this period. Perhaps a more forceful criticism of Wiener's position than that offered by Mandler is to argue, not that preservationism was uninfluential, but that it is misleading to characterize it as an intrinsically regressive force. The leading preservationists were not, as we might expect if preservationism were irredeemably backwards-looking, politically conservative. On the contrary, late Victorian preservationism was dominated to a remarkable extent by liberals and, to a lesser extent, socialists. Octavia Hill, Robert Hunter, Lord Eversley and James Bryce were all liberals, while William Morris became a Marxist, and John Ruskin, although politically unclassifiable, expressed values with marked socialist affinities and was to exercise a powerful and enduring influence on the socialist tradition. The connotations of preservationism as a political force were indeed potentially radical. At the heart of preservationism lay the concept that where private property rights threatened natural or man-made beauty, they should yield to the good of the community as a whole. Preservationists might not in practice seek out direct confrontations with private property rights (although the style of the CPS and of Canon Rawnsley's various Lake District organizations was at times demonstratively confrontational), but the theoretical premises of the movement were inescapably and fundamentally at odds with notions of absolute private property. Many Conservative MPs indeed opposed the preservationist organizations on precisely these grounds.

Few of the leading figures within preservationism would have accepted a description of their aims as a retreat into the past. On the contrary, most of the leading preservationists regarded their activities as being very much about improving the future rather than sanctifying the past. Preservationism did indeed draw on the values it perceived in the past to criticize the present, but it did so with the aim of fostering a better future. Significantly, many of the leading preservationists were, in other capacities, actively involved in attempting to improve the quality of the urban environment. Octavia Hill was a tireless campaigner for improved working-class housing, while Shaw-Lefevre and Robert Hunter were involved in sanitary reform. For both Ruskin and Morris, preservationism was only one part of the much broader social change they considered necessary. In looking to the past, preservationism sought not to escape from the present but to hold a mirror up to it in which its defects would become more apparent.

This characterization of preservationism as centrally concerned with human experience and with improving the future rather than retreating into the past is strengthened by a consideration of the importance of achieving public access within late Victorian and Edwardian preservationism. Maintaining access was the predominant concern of the CPS and, of course, of the National Footpaths Preservation Society, but it was also a major feature of the National Trust in its early days. Access was a cause with radical and anti-aristocratic connotations; indeed, campaigns against exclusion from open spaces had been a prominent element of radicalism since the 1790s. In this respect, preservationism can be seen to be related to other 'progressive' components of attitudes to the countryside in the late nineteenth and early twentieth centuries. There was, for example, some consonance between preservationist commitment to access, and the struggle against usurping landowners which this sometimes involved, and the efforts of land reformers to break down aristocratic 'monopoly' of land and gain rights for labourers to allotments and smallholdings. In this respect, preservationism, at least in its pre-First World War guise, can be seen as corrosive of aristocratic predominance and social conservatism rather than supportive of it. In view of the close association which was to develop between preservationism (especially the National Trust) and country house visiting in the second half of the twentieth century, it is noteworthy that in the late nineteenth and early twentieth centuries preservationism and the popular appeal of country houses were moving in opposite directions: the former was growing quickly while the latter was in steep decline.[14]

Nor was the England which the preservationists sought to preserve quite so socially and politically slanted as some historians have suggested. It was less the 'South Country' than the Lake District that played the decisive role in the formation of the National Trust, for example. Since Wordsworth had attacked the earliest proposals to build a railway into the Lake District, that area had been at the forefront of struggles to protect rural landscape against urban intrusion. Canon Rawnsley's Derwentwater and Borrowdale Defence Committee and his Lake District Defence Society were among the most important of the early regional preservationist associations, and it was no coincidence that so many of the National Trust's early properties were in the Lake District. Many of the leading figures within the preservationist movement in fact either lived in the Lake District (as did Ruskin and Rawnsley), or were closely associated with it. Yet if we are to accept that the implications of the landscape of southern England were politically conservative, because of the placid character of the landscape and the strongly hierarchical social relations which subsisted in it, we must presumably also accept that the very different landscape of the Lake District could have had quite contrasting socio-political implications. The abrupt crags and inhospitable fells of Westmoreland and Cumberland presumably imply restlessness and energy as much as the 'imagined village' of southern England implied the opposite; and the social structure of the Lake District, based around small, often owner-occupying farmers rather than large landed estates, tenant farmers and labourers, similarly had more egalitarian and less deferential overtones than the landscape of the chalk downs of the south.

Rather than accepting that the priorities of late Victorian preservationism were shaped by the dominance of the south of England in the perception of landscape, it may be more appropriate to emphasize that the landscape aesthetics of the early preservationist movement were to a remarkable extent dictated by literary influences. Several of the leading figures within the movement were themselves writers of stature, notably of course Ruskin and Morris. Ultimately the most important influences were the Romantic poets, above all

Wordsworth. The Lake District provided a literary landscape which was to a significant extent a refuge from, and could be deployed in opposition to, the 'establishment' landscape of the south. Wordsworth's *The Prelude*, for example, repeatedly linked the grandeur of the Cumbrian mountains with the independence and dignity of those who lived and worked among them. Seen in this light, the prominence of the Lake District in the formation of late Victorian preservationism suggests that preservationism may have contained a more critical and dynamic potential than Wiener and his followers have been willing to allow.

The suggestion that preservationism was not intrinsically anti-modern is endorsed by David Matless in his study of the relationship between ruralism and national identity in the interwar years, *Landscape and Englishness*. Matless argues that the equation between ruralist values and anti-modernism assumed by Wiener does not hold, at least after 1918. On the contrary, interwar rural preservationism was in large part a movement promoted by a group of town planners and architects who were self-consciously and systematically pro-modern in their values. The planning–preservationism axis was connected principally with left-wing political ideas which were in no way anti-urban and which regarded industrial technology – properly regulated and under public control – as an essential means of social advance. The most important planner-preservationist organization during the interwar years was the Council for the Preservation of Rural England (CPRE), formed in 1926. The CPRE was an umbrella organization consisting at the time of its first annual report in 1927 of representatives from twenty-two other organizations, including the Royal Institute of British Architects (RIBA), the County Councils Association, the National Trust, the Commons Preservation Society and the CLA. While the last three organizations, especially the CLA, were all conservatively orientated by the mid-1920s, it was the self-consciously 'progressive' RIBA which was initially the most influential element of the new organization. The architects who shaped CPRE policy in the early years of the organization were, in many cases, committed to a modernist aesthetic. Many, such as the CPRE's first chairman Patrick Abercrombie, were members of the Town Planning Association and had sympathy with garden city ideals.[15] This modernizing agenda was reflected in the nature of the ruralist values propagated by the CPRE. What the organization sought was a tidy, ordered countryside – not necessarily an old-fashioned, unchanging, traditional countryside. In *The Face of the Land*, a book produced under the aegis of the CPRE, the advent of pylons to the countryside was for example celebrated because of the clean modernist aesthetics of lines of pylons striding across the countryside. If Englishness became more closely aligned with rurality in the interwar years, therefore, this did not necessarily imply that anti-industrialism rose concomitantly.[16]

Some elements of rural preservationism, notably the CPRE, the architectural profession and the garden city movement, manifested left-wing, 'modernizing' characteristics in the interwar period, and were closely linked with the rise of town and country planning, but at the same time a shift towards the political right can be detected in the sympathies and leadership of many of the older preservationist organizations. Among the more influential organizations, this was most apparent in the case of the Commons Preservation Society and of the National Trust. The leading figure in the Commons Preservation Society in the 1930s was Sir Lawrence Chubb. While Chubb's Liberal predecessors Shaw-Lefevre, Robert Hunter and Octavia Hill had used both the law and direct action to enhance and maintain access to open space for urban dwellers, Chubb seemed more concerned about fostering good relations with the Central Landowners Association (CLA). This proclivity earned him mistrust from the more radical preservationist and access organizations such as the Ramblers Association. The latter held Chubb (who was acting as go-between for the Ramblers Association and the CLA) responsible for deceiving them about the trespass clauses of the 1939 Access to Mountains Act.[17]

The rightwards move of the National Trust was also evident both in personnel and in policies. Again, the Liberal leadership of the Trust's prewar years was replaced by figures with Conservative Party affiliations after the First World War. The implications of this became apparent in the 1930s. The Trust became less concerned about access than it had been and switched its attention away from landscape towards country houses, which had previously been a very minor aspect of the Trust's work, quite subordinate to preserving 'places of natural beauty'. A crucial development was the Country Houses Scheme, under which the Trust took over ownership and responsibility for country houses from their allegedly impoverished aristocratic owners, and then allowed the former owners to continue to live in the houses as the Trust's tenants. This was to become a major aspect of the Trust's work and, more than anything else, was responsible for establishing the conventional late twentieth-century perception of the Trust as a conservative and elitist body.[18]

Why was it that the National Trust and the Commons Preservation Society both became more conservative in the interwar years? One reason was that the political context which had sustained the Liberalism of the founders of each of the two organizations altered beyond recognition during and after the First World War. Not only did the Liberal Party itself split, and then collapse as an electoral force in the early 1920s, but the nexus of liberal and non-conformist voluntaryism which had been associated with the Gladstonian party also withered. In the interwar years voluntaryism remained an important strand of social life, but now in the main as a conservative rather than a radical force. Late nineteenth-century Liberal voluntaryism had often been a radical and disruptive force, challenging the state's jurisdiction and claiming independence from it. Interwar voluntaryism tended to complement the state's work instead of challenging it, allowing government to evade responsibilities and expenditure. The National Trust and the Commons Preservation Society were particularly vulnerable to a rightwards shift due to their unusually high degree of dependence on landowners. The National Trust existed to own land, but since it wished to maintain its independence from the state it could do so only through bequests and gifts from landowners. Furthermore, where it was unable to buy land it considered in need of protection it attempted to ensure its protection by arranging management agreements with the existing owners. Whether seeking to buy land or to make management agreements, the Trust's effectiveness was dependent on frequent and co-operative contact with landowners. To a certain extent the Commons Preservation Society was in a similar position, as it was easier to protect commons by establishing cordial relations with their owners than by recourse to expensive and uncertain legal methods. Daily contact with landowners led these two preservationist organizations insensibly towards sharing many of the political preconceptions common among landowners, chief among them the belief that the economic crisis of the great estates was synonymous with the socio-cultural crisis of the countryside. Having imbibed such influences, the leading figures within the Trust and the Commons Preservation Society could regard only with distaste the anti-aristocratic behaviour of some of the pro-access organizations, especially the ramblers' federations. Sir Lawrence Chubb's disgust at the Kinder Scout mass trespass, which he considered to have been funded by 'Russian money', was typical of this mindset.[19]

The increasingly right-wing and establishment stance of the older preservationist organizations between the wars was mirrored by the success with which the Conservative Party took advantage of the strong association which had developed between rurality and Englishness. The use made by the Conservative Party of ruralist rhetoric needs to be set in the context of the long-term shift in the relationship between Conservatism and nationality which had been underway since the mid-nineteenth century. In the late 1840s, in the wake of the repeal of the corn laws, the Conservatives were not seen as the party of the nation but, on the contrary, as a distinctively sectional party. Saddled with the ideological baggage of protectionism, the Conservatives were seen as the party of agriculture and of landed interests, which had put the narrow concerns of a small class of food producers above those of the nation (defined as consisting essentially of food consumers) as a whole. This identification between Conservatism and sectionalism persisted in the third quarter of the century, while the Liberal Party was seen as the natural party of government and also as the party of the nation, in so far as it embodied the principles of free trade, retrenchment and reform. However, partly through the guidance of

Disraeli, the Conservatives in this period began a long process of redefinition which by 1918 would lead them to displace the Liberals as the party most closely identified with the national interest. An early stage in this process was Disraeli's success in persuading the party to abandon agricultural protection. Subsequently the careful cultivation of links between the Conservative Party and the empire and monarchy powerfully assisted this redefinition. The success of the Conservative Party in identifying itself with a vague, emotive, traditional rurality in the interwar period was part of the process by which the party transformed itself from the rejected protectionist rump of 1846 to the core of the National government of 1931.[20]

The connection between Conservatism and rurality was forged by, and most powerfully concentrated in, the personality of Stanley Baldwin, who was prime minister for most of the 1920s and the early 1930s. Baldwin carefully cultivated an image of himself as a countryman (despite, or perhaps partly because of, the fact that his family's fortune was derived from the iron industry). He dressed in tweeds, was usually to be seen with a pipe, and made it plain that he preferred the countryside to towns. One of his favourite pastimes was bird-watching. His speeches often drew on rural imagery, including the famous and often quoted speech in which he evoked 'the sound of corncrakes calling on a dewy morning, the tinkle of the hammer on the anvil from the blacksmith's forge'. Ironically, many of Baldwin's ruralist speeches were delivered over the radio, and this use of modern technology to propagate a traditionalist message ensured that Baldwin's implicit equation between the countryside, himself and Conservatism reached the widest possible audience.[21]

Baldwin's deployment of ruralist imagery served important political purposes and was in many ways a vital underpinning for the ideological positioning of interwar Conservatism. By presenting himself as a simple, quiet-loving, unambitious man of the countryside, Baldwin projected an anti-ideological, almost non-political construction of himself. In this way he identified himself more closely with the nation, and implicitly accused his political opponents of being ideological and political where he was not. In clothing himself (literally as well as metaphorically) in rural style, Baldwin presented himself as homely, familiar, traditional and therefore safe. This complemented his political motto of 'safety first', as well as aligning him and Conservatism with other key features of interwar culture such as the retreat into privacy and domesticity, and the less aggressive and confrontational, more feminized public ethos of the middle class in the 1920s and 1930s as compared with the pre-First World War period.[22]

Baldwin's self-identification with rurality may have been sincere, although it was undoubtedly self-serving. In an interesting article in *Rural History*, Simon Miller questions the socio-economic consequences of this political idealization of the countryside. It is obvious that the deployment of ruralism as political propaganda can serve to distract attention from problems in the urban and industrial economy, and this was clearly the case in the 1920s and 1930s, but Miller argues that Baldwin's ruralist pose also went hand-in-hand with a turning away from the real problems of the countryside. The rurality which Baldwin evoked was, Miller argues, an emphatically non-agricultural country-side. It was the aesthetic countryside, not the working countryside, which Baldwin celebrated. One of Baldwin's favourite novelists, Mary Webb, explicitly contrasts the obsession with farming and agricultural profit of Gideon Sarn with the reverence for nature of her heroine Prue Sarn in her best-known novel, *Precious Bane*. Baldwin's lack of interest in or real concern for agriculture mirrors Webb's, in Miller's view. Miller argues that the real problems of the countryside were rooted in the difficulties of agriculture in a free trade environment, and that Baldwin's government did virtually nothing about this. From Miller's point of view the real stance of the Conservative Party towards farming was revealed by the 'Great Betrayal' of 1921, when, despite promises to the contrary, the government withdrew guaranteed prices for agricultural products. Miller notes the reintroduction of a measure of agricultural pro-tection in the wake of the crisis of 1931, but points out that tariffs were reintroduced as a general measure primarily in order to assist industrial output, not as part of a specifically agricultural policy. Tariffs did little to halt the flow of agricultural imports in the 1930s, most of which in any case came from empire countries.[23]

Miller's argument that a misty-eyed rural romanticism allowed the real socio-economic problems of the countryside to be overlooked is a powerful one. There is, indeed, no doubt that idealization of the countryside had entered the ideological armoury of the Conservative Party and has remained part of Conservatism's attempt to portray itself as the party of the nation since Baldwin's time. A startling repeat of Baldwin's stance on the countryside was offered by John Major in the early 1990s. Major, like Baldwin, presented himself as a plain and simple man with limited ambitions and rural tastes, evoking 'village cricket and warm beer' as representative of what was best, and what he most cherished, about Britain. Yet, like Baldwin, Major's govern-ment presided over a ruinous agricultural depression when farm product prices (partly as a result of the BSE crisis) plummeted and many farmers were forced to sell their land and give up farming.

Despite the plausibility of Miller's argument, however, it tends to overstate the extent to which the countryside was discriminated against by government. Miller's account of the 1921 'Great Betrayal' does not stand up to scrutiny; as subsequent research has demonstrated, the 'Betrayal' was nothing of the kind. Although it is true that government had offered farmers promises which it then broke, this was by agreement with farmers' leaders. Farmers' leaders were only too pleased at the time to accept the withdrawal of guaranteed prices because the 'quid pro quo' which the government offered them was the abolition of minimum wages. Farmers disliked government 'interference' with the setting of wage levels so intensely that they were content to accept the loss of minimum prices in exchange for the deregulation of wages.[24]

If the 'Great Betrayal' was more a betrayal of farmworkers than of farmers, other aspects of government policy in the 1920s and 1930s were perhaps not as antipathetic to agriculture as Miller suggests. In many ways the government treated agriculture much like other industries. With rare exceptions it did not offer subsidies to manufacturers who found themselves in difficulties, so failing to subsidize agriculture cannot easily be seen as representing a bias against farming.

It is therefore only partially accurate to suggest that political idealization of the countryside functioned to permit government neglect of agriculture during the interwar years. A better explanation of the contrast between rhetoric and political action with respect to the countryside at this time may lie in the exigencies faced by modern, market-orientated Conservatism at times of economic depression. By definition, a *laissez-faire* Conservatism is ideologically poorly placed to offer economic amelioration in a depression, because it is axiomatic to *laissez-faire* Conservative ideology that market-distorting government intervention will damage rather than assist economic growth. Conservative governments therefore have an imperative need to distract attention from their economic helplessness, and one way of doing this is by celebrating the beauties of the countryside and seeking to capitalize on an identification with the peace, stability, tradition and harmony imputed to the countryside. This is not as part of any plot to sacrifice the countryside to urban interests, but in order to distract both rural and urban voters from the government's powerlessness. The function of rural idealization is to evoke images of security and reassurance, thus channelling political support towards Conservatism and disguising the impotence of its economic policy.

Miller's emphasis on the way in which the countryside was disadvantaged in comparison to urban Britain by the political deployment of pro-rural imagery also tends to blur the very real distinctions in wealth and power which existed within the countryside in the 1920s and 1930s (and still in some degree persist today). Not all rural inhabitants lost equally from the failure of government to adopt policies which gave agriculture better support. While many landowners and some farmers remained wealthy individuals throughout the interwar years, hundreds of thousands of farmworkers and their families were forced off the land by farmers attempting to reduce costs by cutting back on labour.[25] Small farmers whose incomes were already low were similarly more vulnerable than larger farmers. At this point, Miller's exposure of the way in which the rural myth could serve to disadvantage agriculture politically needs to be linked to a wider critique of the social effects of rural aestheticism, made perhaps most powerfully by Raymond Williams in *The Country and the City* but also by other writers including Howard Newby and John Barrell. This critique has argued that aesthetic appreciation of the countryside has often served to gloss over inequities in rural society. In the landscape paintings of John Constable, for example, the poor at work are rarely visible; the idyllic countryside seems almost to produce itself, like nature, rather than being shaped and worked by human hands and effort.[26] We have already seen how many writers, especially in the mid-nineteenth century and again in the interwar years, offered an idealized version of the countryside in which the poverty and hardship of rural labouring life were invisible. The political functions which idealization of the countryside can provide are, therefore, not only to subordinate agricultural to urban interests, as Miller argues, but also to disguise injustice within the countryside.

Miller's argument tends to focus on the relationship between Conservatism and the rural idyll. This is understandable since Conservative governments were in power for almost the entire interwar period. But it is important to consider briefly the relationship between rural idealization and the political position of the other two main political parties as well, because in the case of both the Liberal and the Labour parties, rural idealization had a more progressive political function at this time. In the case of the Liberal Party, the nineteenth-century tradition of looking to land reform for political solutions continued into the 1920s. The emphasis on land rather than on aesthetics implied a more constructive and focused agricultural policy than that offered by the Conservatives. More important in view of the political eclipse of Liberalism in the 1920s and 1930s was Labour policy towards the countryside. In spite of its strongly urban roots, Labour was surprisingly favourable towards agricultural interests, or at least towards those of farmers. From Labour's point of view farmers did not fit easily into the schema of workers versus capitalists, since farmers worked with their hands but in some cases employed labour as well. Nevertheless, partly for electoral reasons and partly because of the strength of the pro-rural guild socialist tradition within the Labour movement, Labour tended to see farmers as workers and therefore as deserving of support. Labour policy advocated land nationalization with land re-let to farmers, and guaranteed prices. The full significance of Labour's rural myth was to become apparent only in the aftermath of the war, when it contributed to the momentous 1947 Agriculture Act. This, however, demonstrates powerfully that rural idealization does not always operate to the detriment of rural interests. Whether this is so or not depends crucially on the political context and rhetoric into which it is inserted.[27]

Other than its influence on the 1947 Agriculture Act, perhaps the most significant long-term consequence of interwar ruralism was its contribution to town and country planning. Again, it was only after the Second World War with the passing of the Town and Country Planning Act (also of 1947) that the strong hold which rural preservationism had established over public attitudes bore fruit in correspondingly effective legislation. Prior to this, planning regulations had been slow to develop. The first statutes which permitted local authorities to exercise some measure of planning control over rural areas were the Housing and Town Planning Acts of 1909 and 1919. These, though, gave only limited powers to certain local authorities, were permissive and were intended primarily for urban areas. The Conservative-dominated governments of the 1920s and 1930s fought shy of introducing any comprehensive national planning legislation. Nor, in the main, were they willing to contemplate either of the two leading alternative policies which might have afforded effective protection for threatened countryside of high scenic appeal. The first of these policies would have been a programme of land purchases by the state, but not only would this have been expensive, it would also have pointed the way towards the land nationalization that Conservative landowners had struggled against so successfully and for so long. The second policy would have been to fund the National Trust to take on the same role by proxy. As the Trust was a voluntary organization and owned its land in a private capacity, this solution might have been more ideologically acceptable to a Conservative government. But the cost and a fear of undermining the valuable independence of the National Trust from government proved sufficient deterrents.[28]

As a consequence of the inadequacy of the 1909 and 1919 Acts for rural planning purposes, the countryside was left virtually undefended against the pressures of suburbanization and urban leisure demands in the 1920s. Partly as a result of lobbying by preservationists, several ad hoc acts were passed relating to specific problems. Councils were given powers to control the siting of petrol stations by an Act of 1923, and to check roadside advertising under an Act passed two years later. Clearly this legislation was reactive and far too narrow in scope to allow local authorities to check all the harmful developments they might wish to prevent. A more ambitious approach was adopted by the Labour government of 1929–31, which promoted a town and country planning bill. This fell with the collapse of the government, but was revived in virtually identical form by the ensuing National government, and passed as the 1932 Town and Country Planning Act. As the first legislation which sought to establish a comprehensive framework for rural planning this Act was a milestone, and the direct precursor of the 1947 Town and Country Planning Act, the most decisive British planning legislation of the twentieth century. Nevertheless, it had damaging weaknesses. Most serious of these was the fact that it was, like previous planning legislation, a permissive Act, which could be expected to be implemented by the more active local authorities but not necessarily by less energetic councils. Also problematic was the inadequacy of the procedures regulating compensation for landowners, the value of whose holdings was reduced by planning restrictions. Under the 1932 Act landowners were able to claim very generous compensation. Nor was there any guarantee that a local authority would act with urgency to produce a planning scheme under the 1932 Act; indeed, on the outbreak of war seven years later most counties had still not finished their planning schemes. To some extent these shortcomings were mitigated by the successful use by local authorities of Interim Development Control, whereby the council concerned requested would-be developers to obtain guidance from the council about whether their development intentions were congruent with the council's projections for the area in its planning scheme. Since companies knew they risked having buildings demolished without compensation if, even after being informed, they put up buildings which infringed council recommendations, Interim Development Control could be quite a powerful weapon.[29]

Although recent research has emphasized the positive value of the 1932 Act, and of the permissive planning regime established in the 1920s and 1930s, it is noteworthy that two of the most important rural planning problems of the interwar years had to be addressed in separate legislation despite the existence of the 1932 Act. These were, in the first place, ribbon development (an Act to restrict this being passed in 1935) and, second, the London green belt Act (1938). Nor, despite the success with which some local authorities such as Surrey made use of the permissive planning legislation the government vouchsafed, can it be said that the practical effects of the 1932 Act were impressive. The interwar years probably witnessed the highest annual loss of rural land to development of any period of British history, much of it due to house building in the 1930s.[30]

The achievements of planning, and of preservationism in attempting to obtain effective planning legislation, were therefore quite limited in the interwar period. Preservationism was weakened by internal conflicts and by the apolitical or pro-Conservative stance of some of its leading component societies. Both local government and national government tended to look askance at the high cost in compensation which any really comprehensive national legislation on planning would, they assumed, entail. But despite the tenuous nature of the legislative achievements of planning and preservationism during the interwar period, these years did mark an important advance towards an effective rural planning regime. Not only was a flexible and, within its limitations, effective form of planning control developed in the form of Interim Development Control, but the passing of the 1932 Act represented an important acknowledgement of the National government's responsibility to institute a comprehensive and viable system of rural as well as urban planning. These were important foundations, on which the more far-reaching planning legislation of the post-1945 era was to be built.

In the next chapter we will look at the extent to which the ruralist bias of

English culture in the late nineteenth and early twentieth centuries had detrimental economic consequences, as alleged by Wiener, before moving on in subsequent chapters to look in more detail at three of the most dynamic manifestations of ruralism in the interwar period: the rise of rambling, the organic movement, and rural reconstruction. Subsequent chapters will gauge the legacy of interwar ruralism for the second half of the twentieth century through an assessment of the consequences of the 1947 Agriculture and Town and Country Planning Acts.

CHAPTER 9

. . . .

The Economic Consequences of Rural Nostalgia

§ THE decline of the British economy has been one of the staple elements of academic and political debate in Britain since at least the late nineteenth century, when anxiety that Britain was falling behind its chief political rival, Germany, in the output of key industrial products such as iron and steel first became apparent. In the post-Second World War years, the disquiet about British economic performance increased and became central to electoral competition between the Labour and Conservative parties. Elections were fought on the question of which party was better equipped to lead the nation out the economic malaise which was widely thought to be troubling it, culminating in 1979 with the election of Mrs Thatcher's Conservative government, which had campaigned against Labour under the slogan 'Labour isn't working'. Political commentators such as Anthony Sampson and Will Hutton drew attention to the anachronistic features of Britain's political system and alleged that these features had implications for Britain's economic performance. Historians such as Corelli Barnett and Martin Wiener also turned their attention to the question of British economic decline, and offered their own interpretations of its causes.[1]

In its most general form, the argument that Britain had suffered a severe economic setback since the late Victorian period tended to run along the following lines. For most of the second half of the nineteenth century, Britain was indisputably the world's leading economic and political power. Nor was this lead a slight one: on the contrary, no country before or since has ever enjoyed so large a territorial empire, nor (with the possible exception of the USA immediately after the Second World War) so great a margin of wealth over its nearest rivals. Britain was the 'workshop of the world', and British ships carried British industrial exports of textiles, railway vehicles, agricultural machinery and manufactured products of all kinds across the globe. From the 1870s onwards, however, this position of apparently unassailable dominance was progressively undermined. The extraordinarily rapid growth of the US economy in the last three decades of the century allowed it to overtake Britain on almost all measures of industrial production by the end of the century, while by the First World War Britain's great rival Germany had outstripped it in steel production, a source of particular concern because of its importance as a war *matériel*. While Britain's economic travails in the 1930s were less severe than those of most of its industrial competitors, including both Germany and the USA, after the Second World War Britain found itself not only hopelessly outproduced by the USA, but successively overtaken in terms of GNP by Germany, Japan, France, Italy and, by the end of the twentieth century, even some of what had previously been considered the 'undeveloped' countries of South-east Asia such as South Korea. The industries in which Britain had once led the world were especially badly affected. Cotton and shipbuilding were already in steep decline in the interwar period, and the decimation of manufacturing industry in the recession of 1979–81 effectively eliminated Britain's last remaining large-scale shipbuilding enterprises, as well as severely reducing the size of the steel industry. By the end of the 1980s even coal mining had virtually disappeared as a significant component of the British economy and, along with the other traditional heavy industries, was negligible as a proportion of world output.

Nor could this portrait of decline in the economic sectors of traditional strength be set off against more impressive performances in newer industries. On the contrary, an important element of the standard critique of British economic performance was that Britain had remained wedded to the staple nineteenth-century heavy industries for too long. There was a failure to invest adequately in the new industries where opportunities for growth, productivity gains and profits were higher. This failure, it is alleged, was apparent from the late nineteenth century onwards, when Britain did not develop a chemical or electrical industry to the same extent as Germany. In the twentieth century the same pattern was repeated, with the slow development and shortcomings of the British motor vehicle industry and subsequently of the electronics and communications industries. Conforming to this pattern, Britain was slow to innovate or adopt the latest technology even in the heavy industrial sectors. British industrialists often preferred to use machinery until it wore out rather than replace it as soon as a superior version became available. This was perhaps particularly apparent in the textile industry, in which much of the plant in use in the post-1945 era was of nineteenth-century vintage. As a result, the efficiency of Britain in the traditional industry sector was poor, accounting for the uncompetitiveness and ultimate demise of these industries.

This alleged failure to identify the economic opportunities offered by new industries, and to innovate and modernize effectively in the traditional sector, has often been linked to shortcomings in the educational sector. It has been argued that Britain's education system was singularly poorly adapted to maximizing the possibilities of economic growth. The absence of practical, business-related subjects from the curriculum, especially in the private but also in the state school system, is most often highlighted as the villain of the piece. Britain, it is claimed, did not develop an effective system of industrial training and education such as was provided by the German technical high schools.

Perhaps the leading explanation which has been put forward for this sad picture of economic failure, industrial decline and missed opportunities is the so-called 'cultural explanation'. This argues that the shortcomings of British economic performance derived ultimately not from economic variables such as resource endowments, but from a cultural environment which was antipathetic to industrial output and which generated scepticism about the benefits of economic growth. A leading element of the cultural explanation has usually been the claim that British culture was pervaded by rural nostalgia, and that this was damaging to Britain's economy. Attitudes to the countryside have therefore been accorded a central role in the explanation of what has perhaps been the most important unifying theme of modern British history. It is to the question of whether these large consequences can actually be attributed to the part played by the countryside in national culture that the present chapter is directed.[2]

Various links have been suggested between rural nostalgia and economic decline. Probably the most important relates pro-rural, anti-industrial attitudes to Britain's social structure and the unusually long-lasting persistence of dominance by the traditional landed elite within this. The aristocracy and gentry remained the leading element in national politics (and in rural local politics) until at least the 1880s and perhaps until the First World War. However, this social hegemony was persistently threatened from the mid-eighteenth century onwards by the rising proportion of national wealth attributable to non-land-based economic activities, much of which came into the hands of the middle class. Landowners sought to preserve their status by differentiating between sources of income. 'Old' money deriving from land was regarded as desirable and acceptable, while 'new' money made from manufacturing or to a certain extent from trade was less so, at least in the first generation and in the male line. This attitude has been characteristic of many aristocracies. But what (it has been alleged) is more distinctive about the British status system is that the British industrial bourgeoisie did not to any significant extent establish its own independent status hierarchy in the nineteenth or, more doubtfully, even in the twentieth century. Because landowners remained politically and economically dominant for most if not all of the nineteenth century, during the period in which industrialism was maturing in Britain, successful businessmen tended to seek social acceptance within the framework of the landowner status system to a greater degree than was the case in countries with a less powerful landowner class, such as the USA, or where relations between land and industry were more conflictual, as arguably in France. In order to gain acceptance in this way, industrialists had, it is suggested, to distance themselves from the sources of their wealth: too obvious or close a relationship to industrial or urban origins would impair efforts to achieve upwards social mobility. Hence there was a turning away from industry and the towns towards the countryside and the way of life associated with the rural elite, including country house ownership and engagement in gentry activities such as paternalism and field sports. This turning away from industry towards the countryside, it is argued, resulted in a seepage of talent out of industry into essentially unproductive rural activities based around landed estates. Rather than devoting themselves wholeheartedly to maximizing their business incomes, industrialists, seduced by the social values of landed society, spent time and invested money on purchasing, managing and improving their estates.

This tendency, it is argued, was reinforced by the effects of the public school system, in which the sons of many businessmen were educated. The public schools had developed as training grounds for the sons of the landed aristocracy and gentry, and even though many of them opened their doors to the offspring of the upper middle class in the course of the nineteenth century, they remained bastions of conservative, landed values. Most of the great public schools had a rural location in the southern English heartlands of landed society. In these schools, advocates of the 'cultural explanation' often maintain, the sons of businessmen learnt to be ashamed of their origins and to despise their fathers' occupations. A contempt for making money was instilled into them: an income ought to be decorously inherited, rather than earned. In this way, it is claimed, future businessmen were led to have ambivalent feelings about what was to become their occupation, and their 'industrial spirit' and competitive determination to outperform other businessmen was undermined. They felt half-apologetic about making money and tried to show that this was not what 'really' mattered to them; rather, they were concerned with more elevated, less grubby matters such as a love of the countryside, of fine art or of literature.

Furthermore, the pro-ruralism and anti-industrialism fostered by the public schools, and more broadly disseminated within national culture by the literary and intellectual traditions we have assessed in previous chapters, affected not only those who went into business, but also those who went on to determine the climate in which the national economy functioned: politicians and civil servants. A misty-eyed ruralism and barely concealed hostility towards industry was, it has sometimes been maintained, characteristic of many of Britain's leading politicians and civil servants in the twentieth century. The consequence, in the view of right-wing critics such as Corelli Barnett, was a succession of ill-considered, sentimental policies which adversely affected economic performance through their adherence to outdated modes of paternalistic thinking; most damagingly, in Corelli Barnett's view, the institution of the welfare state by the 1945–51 Labour government. Similarly, government policy often exhibited what could be seen as pro-rural policies which were limiting and damaging towards industry, as in the case of planning legislation which restricted industrial development in the countryside. Left-wing critics focus more on the relationship between the financial sector and government. They argue that landowners were more ready to assimilate commercial and financial wealth, because of its less 'dirty' and more discreet origins and its long-standing traditional ties to landownership. Anti-industrial and pro-finance assumptions among politicians and civil servants translated across, it is argued, into policies which systematically favoured the City of London at the expense of Britain's manufacturing sector. Hence the defence of sterling was regarded by a succession of twentieth-century governments as of more importance than the low interest rates and cheap finance which would most have benefited industry.[3]

This account of British economic decline and of the role played by rural nostalgia within it has, however, been challenged at a number of levels. We have already, in the previous chapter, assessed the claim that rural nostalgia was not in fact a particularly prominent element of British national identity. The remainder of the present chapter will consider arguments which relate to the question of the validity of the alleged economic consequences, as opposed to the validity of the alleged cultural cause.

First let us consider some objections to specific subsidiary elements of the claim that rural nostalgia had a damaging effect on the British economy. One element of this argument, it will be remembered, was that a deficiency of business acumen and competitive determination led Britain's businessmen to underperform through failing to invest appropriately in new, labour-saving technology. Most economic historians accept that Britain was indeed slower to invest in labour-saving technology than the USA. But it has been persuasively argued that this may have been, at least in many instances, a rational economic response to the abundance of skilled labour in the British economy. Whereas the scarcity of skilled labour in the USA made it imperative, and cost-effective, for industrialists to introduce expensive labour-saving technology to reduce the wages bill or even allow production to take place at all, this was not the case in Britain, where similar investment would actually not have paid for itself. This case has been argued most persuasively by Lars Sandberg with respect to the cotton industry. It had been assumed that the 'failure' of British cotton masters to invest in ring-spinning technology, in contrast to the US cotton industry, had played an important role in contributing to the decline of the British cotton industry, but Sandberg was able to show that ring-spinning would not in fact have been justified with respect to the economic return yielded if introduced on a large scale in British conditions.[4]

Similarly, the claim that hostility to industrialism resulted in a failure to develop technical education has been disputed. Michael Sanderson has argued that, in the main, Britain's record on technical education was not significantly worse than that of Germany or the USA. Nor is there any direct evidence that a lack of industrial training led British industrialists to make poor decisions, and still less that a pro-rural bias and ambivalence about the worthiness and merits of profit-making as a goal in life did so.[5]

More radical than these criticisms, which have merely chipped away at some of the component blocks of the edifice of the cultural explanation, was the critique made by W. D. Rubinstein. Rubinstein disputed one of the central elements of the case against the British economy by arguing that the assumption that Britain was essentially a manufacturing economy, and that the success or otherwise of the British economy could therefore be gauged by assessing the performance of British industry, was fundamentally flawed. On the contrary, Rubinstein claimed, the British economy was to a much greater extent a service economy, based on finance and commerce, than it was or had ever been a manufacturing economy. Britain had been the 'clearing house of the world' long before, in the early nineteenth century, it became the 'workshop of the world', and it remained so long after it ceased to be the world's workshop. Rubinstein drew on taxation records to demonstrate that throughout the nineteenth century more than half of middle-class wealth was based in London and its immediate surrounds, while the proportion of middle-class wealth in Lancashire and Yorkshire, although increasing in the early and mid-nineteenth century, remained negligible in comparison to that centred round London. The significance of this was that there is no serious doubt that London's economy and wealth structure was overwhelmingly based on commerce and finance, whereas in Lancashire and Yorkshire middle-class incomes derived to a greater extent from industry. Rubinstein's evidence therefore supported his central contention that the wealth structure in Britain had never been affected to a more than marginal degree by industrial incomes. He argued that this was because, contrary to the assumptions of many previous writers, Britain's comparative advantage in fact lay in trade and in financial services, not in industrial production. Policies which fostered the growth of the City at the expense of industry were therefore economically rational, and did not need to be explained in terms of an illogical anti-industrial or pro-rural bias.

Furthermore, Rubinstein argued, it was part of the natural long-term development of an advanced economy that it should shift from industrial to service-based activities, just as in an earlier phase of economic growth a movement from agricultural to industrial activities tends to occur. Rubinstein argued that as industrial technology and therefore industrial labour productivity improved, advanced economies had no need to employ so many workers in industrial production and could shift them into potentially more skilled and remunerative service occupations, where their labour added more value. On this argument, the decline and even virtual demise of the British manufacturing economy was largely inevitable anyway, and to be attributed to inescapable economic processes and sound policies and business decisions, not to an irrational anti-industrialism derived from persistent rural nostalgia.[6]

The implication of Rubinstein's argument is to downplay the seriousness of the economic problems which affected Britain during the twentieth century. However, a more radical and generalized argument has recently been put forward by several economic historians, notably C. H. Feinstein. This argument undercuts the entire debate by denying that Britain has in any significant sense experienced economic decline. The basis of the argument is a distinction which is drawn between absolute economic decline, regarded as a matter of valid concern, and decline relative to other economies, regarded as being of more questionable significance. While it may be desirable from a political point of view to maintain economic parity with other countries, the more important yardstick is the historical one of the past performance of the national economy in question. In these terms, Britain has experienced no 'absolute' economic decline. On the contrary, with only very brief remissions, the British economy continued to grow throughout the late nineteenth and twentieth centuries. This is true whether economic growth is measured in terms of total output or of output per caput. More strikingly still, it was in the three decades after 1945, when anxieties about British economic decline were at their height, that Britain's economic growth was by historical standards at its most impressive. It seems likely that in the years 1945–73 the rate of growth of the British economy was faster than during any period of similar length in the nineteenth century. Measured in per caput terms, British economic performance in the third quarter of the twentieth century was of course even more remarkable. Even in the more troubled years after 1973 British economic growth has been very high by historical standards, and comparable to that achieved during the nineteenth century as a whole.

Absolute decline did not, therefore, occur. Decline relative to the economies of some other industrialized countries is acknowledged, but it is argued that this decline was inevitable. Britain was the first nation to industrialize, but the technology and methods of business organization which allowed industrial-ization to occur could not for long be confined to Britain alone. Other countries were certain to adopt these methods in the course of time, and to close the economic gap with Britain. Not only was Britain's immense early and mid-nineteenth-century lead over all other countries therefore inherently unsustainable, it was also inevitable that Britain would not merely be caught up, but overtaken. This was because of the limited resource base of the British economy. As a small country, Britain was intrinsically and unavoidably disadvantaged with respect to many other countries in terms of population, land availability and ultimately even raw materials. Not only was Britain vastly inferior to the USA in all three respects, but even Germany was nearly twice as favourably endowed as Britain with regard to land area and population. Once the USA and Germany had applied the industrial technology developed in Britain in the first half of the nineteenth century (with additions of their own) to their much larger resource bases, it could only be a matter of time before each dwarfed the British economy.

This argument, in terms of the size of respective national resource bases, applies particularly persuasively to the period after the Second World War. Many countries, notably Germany, Japan, France and Italy, grew exceptionally rapidly in this period. This can be explained in part by a pre-existing lack of development and in part by the damage done by the war. There was as a result a wide productivity gap between these countries and the mature industrial economies which had not been severely damaged by the war (principally the USA and Britain), reflecting the scope for a massive increase in the efficiency with which the existing resources of the underdeveloped and war-damaged industrial economies were deployed. These countries had three main specific advantages over the mature industrial economies. In the first place, they could switch out of agriculture, with its inherently low productivity, into industry, which offered far more scope for efficiency gains. This was a once-only gain of which both the continental economies and Japan took advantage. Second, these countries were able to benefit by learning from the leading industrial countries, especially the USA, and adopting the most up-to-date and successful technologies. For this reason the war-damaged economies were able to develop an impressively modern and efficient industrial infrastructure in the postwar years, in contrast, for example, to Britain, in which outmoded pre-Second World War transport networks, machinery and buildings were a much more significant and problematic feature. Third, the citizens of underdeveloped and war-damaged countries were inevitably aware of the disadvantages they laboured under in comparison to the USA and Britain. They seem therefore often to have been more willing to work for longer hours, at lower wages and with more commitment than was the British workforce, because of a shared national awareness of the magnitude of the challenges presented by economic renewal.

The suggestion that the poor performance of the post-1945 British economy relative to those of many other industrialized economies can be explained in terms of the maturity of the economies in question is reinforced by a comparison between Britain and the other leading 'mature' economy in the immediate post-1945 period, the USA. This demonstrates that Britain's rate of GNP and productivity growth since 1945 approximates quite closely to that of the USA, and that explanations of British economic performance since 1945 framed in terms of Britain's exceptionalism are therefore probably misplaced.[7]

The argument outlined in the last few paragraphs undercuts the claim that rural nostalgia damaged the British economy because it implies that there is simply not a problem in need of explanation: the British economy performed as well as it could have been expected to do, given the limitations of its pre-existing resource endowment. The emphasis therefore shifts to explaining why it is that so many people have devoted so much effort to explaining a non-problem. The usual account is that the British obsession with economic decline is rooted in two experiences which were unique to Britain. The first was the loss of the British empire. In the short span of six decades (1910–70) Britain underwent the experience of losing almost the entirety of the largest empire the world has ever seen. This extraordinary episode inevitably left its mark, and contributed (in this view) to a misplaced presumption that the decline of Britain's 'greatness' was a generalized phenomenon involving national economic failure as well as political retreat. Second, it is suggested that another experience unique to Britain, that of being the first industrial nation, also left a mark on national culture. While to an objective observer it is clear that Britain's initial economic lead was unsustainable, this was not apparent to Britain's citizens, who therefore succumbed to an exaggerated sense of the significance of the inevitable slide in Britain's relative economic standing which ensued in the twentieth century.

A difficulty with the argument that there is nothing to explain because the British economy did not fail is that it is not only in terms of total output (GNP) but of output per caput and of productivity that Britain has been overtaken by many of its European and Far East competitors. However, it can be argued that the favourable conditions these countries benefited from after the Second World War generated a momentum which allowed them to 'over-shoot' Britain. Some evidence to support this is that income per caput and productivity in Britain have since the 1970s converged with those of other leading industrial countries, indicating perhaps that Britain has adjusted to its new status as a relatively underdeveloped economy, and reaped similar if less dramatic advantages from this to those which the war-damaged industrial economies did after the Second World War.

In conclusion, it seems clear that the more pessimistic claims of British economic failure have been exaggerated. Manufacturing was not as central to the economy as a whole as it was at one time believed to have been, and economic performance across the board was not as disappointing, once Britain's limited resource endowment has been taken into account, as has sometimes been alleged. This does not, of course, disprove Wiener's claim that ruralism was damaging to British economic growth, but it does put it into a more modest perspective. Even if ruralism did retard the British economy – and it should be emphasized that this remains at best an unproven hypothesis – the scale of this retardation is unlikely to have been as large as Wiener and his followers appear to have believed.

CHAPTER 10

Rambling

§ IN its broadest sense of walking for pleasure, rather than as a means to some other end, rambling is probably as old as civilization. Certainly it would be misleading to suggest that it was an invention of the modern period. In the fifteenth century, Petrarch recorded how he surprised his friends by walking to the top of a hill for no purpose other than the walk itself, but though Petrarch thought himself an innovator he was no doubt less original than he supposed.[1] However, for centuries after this, walking for pleasure remained an unusual and occasional activity practised by a few exceptional individuals. It was only in the late eighteenth and nineteenth centuries, at least in England, that rambling became an important social phenomenon. Three interrelated experiences underpinned this development: literary Romanticism, a rising interest in natural science, and urbanization.[2]

Literary Romanticism, as we have seen, elevated the role of nature in poetry by transforming it from background colouring to a creative agent working within and through the poet's imagination. This new conception of the relationship between the poet and nature necessarily brought poets more into the open air than had previously been the case. Wordsworth in particular eagerly sought out new experiences of nature which could provide the raw material for his writing, as W. J. Keith has shown. The intense and active engagement with nature which Wordsworth sought could scarcely be attained through a distanced or genteel mode of interaction, as might be obtained from driving in a carriage, riding on horseback, or admiring the prospect from some favoured viewpoint. Only by immersing himself in nature in the most direct way, by walking by the lakes, through the woods and over the fells could Wordsworth obtain the immediacy of experience he sought. He and Coleridge covered thousands of miles in their walks over the Westmoreland mountains; indeed, it has been estimated that Wordsworth walked more than 175,000 miles in the Lake District during his lifetime. This set a precedent for 'literary walking' which other writers, would-be writers and literati were to follow in the nineteenth century. Charles Lamb, who expressed his incomprehension of the fashion for rural walking which Wordsworth had established, was one of the few dissenting voices. In time, the practice spread beyond writers to embrace a broad spectrum of those who aspired to or were influenced by literary culture – a largely but not exclusively middle-class group.[3]

A second important early stimulus to rambling was the rising level of activity in and enthusiasm for natural science. In the late eighteenth and early nineteenth centuries, scientific investigation had a markedly outdoor character. The collection and classification of specimens was a major principle of development within many of the leading sciences. Geology was at the forefront of scientific advance in the early nineteenth century, and was inherently dependent on fieldwork. At a time when the geophysical structure of Britain was still almost entirely unmapped, and when even the basic processes of geological change were still far from clear, progress could be achieved only by identifying and recording stratification sequences. Early nineteenth-century geologists therefore of necessity traversed large distances on foot, searching for revealing outcrops which would fill in missing sequences. Other fieldwork-based sciences, notably botany, ornithology and entomology, were also developing rapidly in the early nineteenth century. All these sciences were still comparatively young, and, as a result, were more open to amateurs than more highly specialized and theorized branches of knowledge such as physics. Geological and biological interests consequently led quite large numbers of upper-middle-class 'gentleman scientists' on often lengthy rambles through the countryside in the early nineteenth century (and sometimes brought them into conflict with landowners who sought to bar them from trespassing over their estates, as in the case of the dispute between the Edinburgh Society and Scottish landowners in the late nineteenth century). There was therefore a scientific as well as a literary component to the rise of rambling in the nineteenth century.[4]

A third element which contributed to the rise of rambling was industrialization and urbanization. The bleak environmental conditions of urban society in the early and mid-nineteenth century gave a stimulus to the impulse to escape from the towns into more salubrious and attractive surroundings. Furthermore, the early industrial towns, particularly in the north-west, facilitated the development of a highly literate and intellectual artisan culture. This was perhaps most fully evident among the handloom weavers. Handloom weavers could read as they worked, and other groups of workers who could also do so (such as shoemakers) were similarly prominent in the artisan intellectual culture of the towns. Some aspects of 'high' culture were inaccessible to this artisan milieu, because of the cost of books or scientific equipment; but because the natural sciences were at this time passing through a phase in which, as described above, the collection and classification of specimens was the primary arena of activity, it was open to intelligent artisans to contribute to the development of these subjects. The passionate dedication of many artisans to collecting and classifying took them out into the countryside on walking excursions which, in some cases, might last for several days.[5]

A large part of the pleasure which intellectually minded artisans derived from such excursions clearly derived from their enthusiasm for the subject itself, and a further part of it can be attributed to the escape from unappealing social and environmental conditions. Part of the enjoyment also derived from a positive pleasure in being in the countryside. This aspect is conveyed vividly by the first chapter of Elizabeth Gaskell's *Mary Barton*, which describes how the artisans and factory workers of Manchester went out to the adjacent countryside in their leisure hours. What, however, remains unclear is how far the experience Gaskell outlines was typical – did working-class rambling occur independently of artisan scientific culture in the first half of the nineteenth century, or only as an adjunct to it?[6]

In the second half of the nineteenth century, the professionalization of science opened up a widening gulf between the contribution amateur scientists (whether of the gentlemanly or artisan variety) could make, and the work which professional scientists were doing. Partly, perhaps, because it was becoming isolated from its 'high science' roots, amateur science became more literary in tone, and one strand of it ultimately merged into the literary tradition of rambling. Literary rambling was invigorated by three further influences during the nineteenth century. First, John Ruskin's impassioned advocacy of the close study of nature's details encouraged a generation of his acolytes to sketch, paint and record rock forms, plants and animals. Second, the Pre-Raphaelites (themselves influenced by Ruskin) emphasized painting *en plein air* rather than in the studio, in order to capture a more life-like effect, and in doing so brought artists out into the open air in the same way that the Lake poets had done with respect to writers. Third, in the last third of the century, a section of the cultural avant-garde developed an interest in active outdoor pursuits, one of which was walking (characteristic of which was Leslie Stephen's 'Sunday Tramps', one of the earliest rambling clubs).[7]

It is quite clear that the sort of landscape preferred by both middle-class and working-class ramblers was 'wild' landscape, above all hills and mountains. The Scottish Highlands, the Lake District, Snowdonia and the Peak District were the most popular walking areas among committed ramblers in the nineteenth century. This raises further questions over the degree to which southern images of landscape dominated English national consciousness in the late nineteenth century.

As we have seen, preservationism at least in its early days was highly committed to maintaining and enhancing access to the countryside. This was mainly with a view to walking, although, in the case of urban commons, games and other forms of exercise also formed part of the intention. It was because access rather than merely preservation in itself was so large a part of its remit that the Commons Preservation Society was initially so concerned with London commons (notably in its resistance to the enclosure of Epping Forest). The London commons were not necessarily more threatened than many commons elsewhere, but they were more valuable in terms of access simply because of the size of the population which could potentially make use of them.[8]

A further indication of the congruence between preservationism and rambling is provided by the fact that footpath preservation societies were among the most frequently formed kind of preservation society in the second half of the nineteenth century. (The earliest societies had actually been formed in the first half of the nineteenth century, but it was only from the 1870s onwards that footpath societies became frequent.) Little research has been carried out on these societies, so it is as yet unclear what their composition was. It would be particularly interesting to find out whether the scattering of early footpath preservation societies based in northern cities such as Manchester had predominantly middle-class memberships, or whether they included a working-class or artisanal dimension.

One of the ways in which the preservationist–rambling axis sought to promote access was through legislation. The Commons Preservation Society was active in attempting to repeal those clauses of the 1235 Statute of Merton which gave legal comfort to would-be enclosers of commons. More important for ramblers, however, were the efforts of leading preservationists to promote an 'access to mountains' bill in Parliament. The Liberal MP James Bryce was the prime mover of access to mountains bills in the late nineteenth century, beginning with his first bill in 1884, on which subsequent bills (both those promoted by Bryce and by others) were largely based. These bills were aimed at legislating for unfettered rights of access for ramblers to uncultivated land. Most of them were restricted to specific parts of Britain, mainly Scotland or Wales, but some applied to the country as a whole. However, although some of the bills achieved second readings, none made it on to the statute books. In the main, the reason for the failure of the access legislation was opposition from Conservative MPs and peers. Such opposition was particularly vehement from politicians who were also landowners in Scotland, since it was Scottish landowners whom most of the bills would most directly affect. However, landowners were able to call on broad political sympathies in their resistance to access legislation by presenting such bills as attacks on the rights of property. Owners of land, like owners of any other kind of property, ought to be wholly free to determine how their property should be used, and so should be entitled to exclude the public from their land if they wished to.[9]

In the early twentieth century, rambling and preservationism developed in ways which accentuated and intensified the hitherto muted conflicts within the movements, and between them and other social elements. Late nineteenth-century rambling had been largely a minority pursuit, both among the 'bohemian' middle class and among the intellectual artisans of the working class. But particularly after the First World War, the popularity of rambling grew very rapidly. This was in part because of increasing leisure hours available at all levels of society, with reductions in the length of the working week occurring partly as a result of trade union successes, partly because of bank holiday legislation and partly through the regularization of working hours, which resulted in the Saturday half-holiday being offered in place of the traditional 'St Monday' in many places. By the early 1930s rambling had become a mainstream element of both middle- and working-class leisure. This inevitably focused attention on the relationship between preservation of the countryside and access to it. The optimistic nineteenth-century assumption that preservation and access were, or could be made to be, two sides of the same coin, proved increasingly vulnerable. As more and more people went out into the countryside, not only was the solitude which many preserva-tionists valued more and more disrupted, but physical damage or defacement occurred (for example through erosion or littering).

As rambling became an ordinary and integral part of popular culture, so its literary aspect diminished, although a convention of responsible and alert walking survived for several decades and was later embodied in the Country Code and in 'I-Spy' books. Commercialism colonized the rambling culture, which in its earlier more rarefied manifestations had been a self-consciously anti-materialistic and even ascetic tradition. Commercialism was particularly evident in the south-east of England, perhaps because the higher living stan-dards of this area allowed walkers to spend more on their leisure. Tea rooms, for example, proliferated around the edges of Burnham Beeches. However, even northern working-class ramblers were targets for commercialism, which in this case came mainly in the form of the railway companies, which ad-vertised special Sunday-morning trains for walkers to take them out to the hills.[10]

In addition to the large rise in the number of walkers and to the more commercial and even vulgar character of post-First World War rambling, a further development raised tensions between rambling and preservationism. In the early and mid-nineteenth centuries, rambling seems to have been an activity undertaken alone, or at most with a few friends. In the late nineteenth and early twentieth centuries, however, a new kind of collectivist rambling grew up alongside the older, more individualist or small-group tradition.[11] This was most marked among the industrial working class, many of whom began to walk in organized clubs. Nor was the new collectivism limited to the walking itself: ramblers also began to organize collectively in the early twen-tieth century. Both the Manchester and the Sheffield Federations of Rambling Clubs were established at this time. These organizations were to become powerful forces working to advance ramblers' interests and, because they held no brief for preservation but only for access, tended to widen the breach between rambling and preservationism.

Walking was not the only outdoor leisure activity which developed a collective dimension in these years – cycling also was, again especially among the working class, a predominantly collective activity. Working-class culture in general in the early twentieth century showed strongly collectivist traits, manifested in trade union membership growth, in the popularity of music hall, and in the seaside holiday.

Collectivist rambling was also important among the young, of both the middle and working classes. This in part reflected the success of the new youth movements, especially after the First World War, and the enthusiasm of many of these movements for outdoor activities as a means of moulding the young into physically and morally healthy citizens. The popularity of collective rambling among the young was reflected in the formation of new organizations to cater for it, notably the YHA and the Holiday Fellowship.[12]

While working-class and youth rambling were becoming increasingly collective, middle-class rambling appears to have remained more individualist or small-group-based. This opened up a further rift within the culture of rambling, evident in the cool relations between the northern federations and the London Federation. The Manchester Federation did not join the national organization (which became the Ramblers Association) for several years after it was set up, largely because it was not confident of the commitment of the London Federation to improving access. Rambling was therefore a fractured culture in the interwar period. But the trends towards popularism and commercialism apparent in most elements of the movement, and towards collectivism evident in the working-class and youth components of rambling, ran directly counter to the move in the older preservationist organizations during the interwar years towards greater elitism and exclusivism, both socially and in terms of policy with respect to access. The tensions between preservationism and middle-class rambling could often be accommodated, although the blatant intrusion of commercialism into beauty spots sparked discord.[13] The polarization between preservationism and working-class rambling was sharper, reflecting a wider process of polarization within society. The old liberal bloc with which late nineteenth-century access-oriented preservationism had been associated crumbled in the years immediately after the First World War. Under the pressure of the rise of the Labour Party, working-class political and economic organizations, and the politics of property against social welfare, Liberals increasingly migrated either rightwards into the Conservative Party or leftwards into the Labour Party. The older preservationist organizations drifted rightwards along with their leading supporters, and became more closely identified with the defence of property than they had previously been.

Working-class rambling developed its own organizations, which had little concern for preservation and focused almost exclusively on access.

This process of polarization and conflict reached its climax in the late 1920s and early 1930s in the struggles over access to the High Peak, the area of hills and moorland in northern Derbyshire between Manchester and Sheffield. Ramblers from these two large northern cities had been engaged in a struggle to maintain and improve access to the grouse moors of the High Peak since the late nineteenth century. The culminating episode was the Kinder Scout mass trespass of 1932, when hundreds of ramblers clashed with gamekeepers and police. Kinder Scout was not only the highest hill in the Peak District but was also readily accessible by railway from both Manchester and Sheffield, but despite this no public path crossed the huge expanse of heather moorland. In the course of the mass trespass, a scuffle occurred in which a gamekeeper was hurt. The leaders of the trespass were arrested, and later sentenced to prison terms. The harshness of the sentences caused outrage among ramblers, and the Kinder Scout mass trespass became enshrined in the folk-history of the rambling movement.[14]

Two questions arise from a consideration of the tensions over rambling in the High Peak in the interwar period. The first is: why was rambling so much more confrontational in this area than anywhere else in England? Second, what were the long-term effects of the Kinder Scout mass trespass (if any)?

The confrontational nature of rambling in the High Peak appears to have resulted from the conjunction of several factors. In the first place, nowhere else in Britain were major industrial conurbations and wide expanses of uncultivated hill country so closely juxtaposed. Sheffield and Manchester between them held more than a million people, and the moors began on the edge of each city. However, access to this moorland was extremely restricted. Only a few legal rights of way crossed most parts of the moors. Even the limited existing access was under pressure as landowners sought to maintain their incomes in the face of agricultural depression by converting large areas of the moorland from rough grazing to grouse moors. The landowners argued that walkers and grouse shooting were incompatible, not so much because of danger from the actual shooting but because walkers allegedly frightened the grouse and put them off breeding and raising young. At the same time, working-class demand for access to the moorland was rising steeply, because of the general rise in the popularity of rambling. This was substantially intensified in the late 1920s and early 1930s by the industrial depression following the Wall Street crash. High levels of unemployment meant that many working-class families had lower levels of disposable income than previously, which in turn caused a rising level of interest in cheap forms of leisure such as rambling, as other more expensive forms of purchased leisure became unaffordable. Unemployed workers also, of course, had plenty of time in which to go off on long moorland rambles.

In summary, then, a crisis in landowner incomes led to a change of land use, which in turn militated against access. This coincided with a crisis in working-class employment, leading to a marked increase in demand for access to land. This intrinsic conflict was given an additional twist by the political dimension to the relationship between ramblers and landowners. Northern working-class rambling was a near relative of socialism and non-conformity, both ideologies which identified the 'idle' aristocracy as especially objectionable. It so happened that many of the major landowners in the Peak District were in fact prominent aristocrats (such as the Duke of Devonshire). However, although the political confrontation between radical, morally earnest ramblers and conservative, game-preserving aristocrats was a real one, it was not this political dimension but the more immediate question of access that was the main issue at stake. This is demonstrated by the fact that the ramblers came into conflict with the local water companies, who had bought large areas of moorland as 'gathering grounds' for their reservoirs, as much as they did with aristocratic landowners.

At one level it could be argued that the physical confrontation between ramblers and gamekeepers on Kinder Scout merely continued the tradition of high-profile direct action which had been used successfully by many preservationist societies in the late nineteenth century. Perhaps the most notable example was provided by the Commons Preservation Society, which hired a gang of navvies to remove the fencing around Berkhamstead Common in the dead of night. As we saw in Chapter 8, however, many of the older preservationist organizations became more conservative in the years after 1918, and the Commons Preservation Society was less willing to engage in such public confrontation with landowners by the 1930s than it had been in the 1860s and 1870s. This no doubt left working-class rambling seeming more isolated than it would have done if the preservationist societies had retained their nineteenth-century activism. But there is in fact an important difference between what the Commons Preservation Society did at Berkhamstead and elsewhere, and the mass trespasses of the early 1930s. The whole point of the Commons Preservation Society's actions was that they had been legal, but while the northern working-class ramblers used legal means too in their efforts to enhance access, the point about trespass was precisely that it was not legal. On the contrary, it was a confrontation with and a challenge to the law. The political aim of the northern ramblers was to change the law, by securing effective access legislation, not to work within it.

Although there is an important contrast between the militancy of northern working-class rambling and the quietism of its southern counterpart, the differences between the two can easily be exaggerated. Rambling cannot in fact be divided quite so simply into two separate and non-overlapping groupings. There were, for example, often acute tensions within northern rambling organizations. The Kinder Scout mass trespass, for example, was not actually the work of the official rambling organizations. Neither the Manchester nor the Sheffield federations had approved the action. It was a much smaller and more recently established group, the British Workers Sports Federation (BWSF), which called and organized the trespass. The BWSF had close links with the Communist Party, which was one of the reasons the Labourist Manchester and Sheffield federations were unwilling to associate themselves with it. The tensions between the BWSF activists and the official rambling organizations simmered on for decades and had not been fully dissipated even in the late twentieth century, when accounts of the mass trespass offered by the BWSF leader Benny Rothman and by the Manchester Federation leader Tom Stephenson differed sharply (Stephenson claiming that Rothman and his trespassers never actually succeeded in setting foot on Kinder Scout itself, but only on the lower slopes to which access was permitted anyway). Nor was there even complete unity within the official rambling organizations in the north – the Sheffield Federation, for example, was often more activist and radical than its Manchester counterpart, giving stronger support to the imprisoned Kinder Scout trespassers than did the latter.[15]

If the Kinder Scout mass trespass exposed political tensions within northern rambling, it also showed generational tensions. The leadership of the official northern organizations was aged, on average, at least forty, while the BWSF was pre-eminently young – very few of the mass trespassers were older than twenty-one.[16] Nor can the confrontationalism of northern working-class rambling organizations necessarily be imputed to working-class ramblers in other parts of the country. Indeed, nowhere else in the country did the particular combination of elements which made the situation in the High Peak so charged obtain, and, unsurprisingly, working-class rambling mounted a less direct and sustained challenge to landowners in other parts of England. At the same time, just as working-class rambling was not always confrontational, middle-class rambling was not always entirely individualistic and passive in character. One example of collective rambling in the south of England would be the crowd of 16,000 ramblers who followed S. P. B. Mais to see the sunrise at Chanctonbury Ring in 1932. Middle-class ramblers were also caught up to some degree in the struggle against trespass. This took place both as part of orchestrated campaigns, as with the large demonstration of mainly southern ramblers at Leith Hill held to protest against the Kinder Scout sentences, and, much more frequently, through private confrontations between walkers and gamekeepers. The archetypal 'trespassers will be prosecuted' notice was as characteristic of southern woodlands as of northern moorlands, and the long-running sore of game preservation embittered relations between landowners and middle-class as well as working-class ramblers.[17]

Just as the course of events on Kinder Scout is disputed, so are the effects of the mass trespass. Stephenson argues that the trespass achieved nothing, while Howard Hill, who was associated with Benny Rothman, claims that it gave a decisive forwards impulse to rambling's legislative aims. Stephenson's argument is based on the premise that no political progress was actually made by ramblers in the 1930s, nor, given the political circumstances, was any progress possible. It is certainly true that the only major rambling legislation of the 1930s, the 1939 Access to Mountains Act, was greeted with bitter disappointment by ramblers, and that by criminalizing trespass in certain circumstances it actually worsened the legal position of ramblers in an important respect. But the 1939 Act was quickly superseded. The Scott report and the Dower report both recommended legislation to ensure enhanced access to the countryside for ramblers, and part of the 1949 National Parks and Access to the Countryside Act was devoted to this aim. One of the more significant achievements of the 1949 Act was the requirement placed on councils to draw up legally definitive maps of public rights of way. This safeguarded footpaths against closure and militated towards their proper maintenance. The creation of national parks also contributed to improving access by enlarging the areas in which walkers were able to roam at will (even though British national parks, unlike those in other countries, remained in the hands of private landowners). A further welcome feature of the Act to ramblers was that it repealed the detested 1939 Act.[18]

Clearly, the most important factor leading to the 1949 Act was the general leftwards shift brought about by the war and the election of a Labour government in 1945, but there is no doubt that the markedly raised political profile of rambling caused by the mass trespass and its aftermath (including the 1939 Act) meant that the issue was higher up the government's list of legislative priorities than it would otherwise have been. Governments always have more legislation that they would like to pass than they have time to do. It is at least arguable that had it not been for the Kinder Scout trespass the Labour government might not have given access legislation a high enough priority for it to make it to the statute book.

The 1949 Act represented the end of an era for rambling. Definitive (if still imperfect in that the cherished 'right to roam' had not actually been conceded) legislation had now been passed to facilitate access to the countryside and to safeguard rambling rights. The postwar period was to see a new era of rambling, in which the decisive factor was to be mass car ownership and the development of a popular, family-based countryside leisure culture, which we will assess in a subsequent chapter.

. . . .

CHAPTER II

The Organic Movement Before and During the Second World War

§ THE term 'organic' (especially in the guise of 'organic farming') is often associated with the environmentalist movement which developed in the United States and Western Europe in the 1960s and 1970s. In fact, there was an 'organic movement' in the interwar period too. It reflected contemporary attitudes to the countryside in interesting ways, and these connections will be the principal subject of the present chapter. An important question to ask about the interwar organic movement, one which the prior assessment of its ideological basis and political links will enable us to answer at least provisionally, is to what extent it can be considered as the direct forebear of the environmentalist movement of the 1960s and 1970s. As we shall see, continuities both of ideas and personnel are evident; but there are also ruptures. The concluding task of this chapter will be to weigh up the relative balance of continuity and change between the two movements.

Fundamental to the ideology of the interwar organic movement was the conviction that the earth – in the sense of the soil rather than the planet – was the essential basis of life, and that it was vital to recognize this if not only agriculture but society as a whole was to remain in good condition. Organicists saw the soil as a living entity, and one which required to be treated with care if it was to bring forth benefits. Because the soil was living rather than merely an inanimate mineral substance, it depended on organic rather than purely chemical processes. In particular, as Sir Albert Howard, the most influential figure within the organic movement at the time, argued, plant nutrition was no simple matter of absorbing chemicals in solution directly from the soil through root systems, for plants drew much of their nutrition from the presence of mycorrhizal organisms, which broke down organic material. Only once this had taken place was it possible for a plant's roots to absorb the nutrients.[1]

This emphasis on the importance of organic matter rather than a reliance on chemical ('artificial') fertilizers was linked to the characteristic organicist insistence that waste, of all kinds, should be returned to the soil. For organicists it was not only animal manure but also human excrement, plant matter and all other waste organic substances that ought to be returned to the soil rather than in a literal sense wasted (the so-called 'rule of return'). Great stress was placed on the part played by decayed vegetable matter in providing adequate nutrition for growing plants, in contrast to the tendency of British farmers to rely heavily on animal manure (to the extent that they were using organic fertilizers rather than depending entirely on artificials). This high regard for vegetable waste led to the practice of composting being lauded by organicists as the essential basis for proper replenishment of soil fertility through the formation of humus.

The significance of good soil management practices was far from confined to the maintenance of soil fertility. On the contrary, one of the characteristic features of the organic outlook was to see all aspects of life as linked together. If soil was kept in good health, plants would also be more healthy and less prone to disease (demonstrated experimentally by Howard during his time at the plant research station in the Indian state of Indore). Healthy plants were, in turn, more nourishing for the animals which ate them. Healthier plants and animals meant better-quality food for human beings, and so contributed essentially to human nutrition and health. Organicists liked to speak of a 'wheel of life' which expressed these relationships.[2]

The links between healthy soil, healthy plants and good nutrition led organicists to emphasize the central role of good-quality food, as opposed to the processed and sometimes adulterated foods too often sold to unwitting urban consumers. Processed foods such as white bread or tinned salmon contained, so organicists argued, much less of the original 'goodness' of unprocessed or minimally processed foods. Hence whole foods, notably whole-meal bread, were an important facet of organicist values.[3]

To some extent, organicism defined itself in opposition to the mainstream agricultural science of its day. While the latter tended to see agriculture overwhelmingly in economic terms, organicists were at least as concerned with quality as with cost. But it is important not to see the organic movement as entirely at odds with establishment science, far from it – in fact most of the leading figures within the organic movement had close links with or could even be considered part of the agricultural science establishment. Howard, for example, was appointed Imperial Economic Botanist to the government of India in 1905, and in 1924 he became Director of the Institute of Plant Industry in the State of Indore. Another highly influential organicist was the nutritionist Robert McCarrison, who was again an imperial employee. Sir George Stapledon, the grassland expert, was one of the most respected plant scientists of his generation, but was also an important figure in the organicist Kinship in Husbandry group.

Organicism's mixed relationship with agricultural science orthodoxy was paralleled by its ambivalence towards machinery. Some organicists, such as Henry Williamson and Viscount Lymington, were enthusiasts for machinery. Lymington, indeed, was one of the pioneers of the use of large-scale machinery in British agriculture. From their point of view, machinery was a means by which agriculture could be revitalized, and an exciting herald of the future. But other organicists, less concerned with the revitalization of agriculture than with the preservation of rural traditions and resistance to 'urban civilization', lamented the damage wrought by machinery on rural crafts. The writer H. J. Massingham was perhaps the foremost exponent of this view.[4]

One of the reasons for organicist ambivalence towards machinery was the high place which the movement accorded to physical labour. Organicists often admired the work of writers such as Hardy and Sturt who celebrated this, and many organicists did indeed actually go 'back to the land' to work the soil themselves. These included Williamson, who farmed at Stiffkey in Norfolk, the novelist Adrian Bell and the pacifist and writer Ronald Duncan. Several other leading organicists were already farmers or estate owners, including Rolf Gardiner, Viscount Lymington and the Sussex farmer Jorian Jenks.[5]

The commitment of organicists to natural processes and to rural tradition raises the question of the relationship between organic thought and another leading aspect of interwar attitudes to the countryside – rural planning. As we have seen, rural planning was strongly committed to preserving the countryside from urban despoliation, and in this respect it might seem that organicism and planning would have been natural allies. But in his detailed and subtle study of planning and organicism, *Landscape and Englishness*, David Matless has argued that the two were in fact opposites in most respects. Planning and preservationism marched hand in hand, but the version of the countryside which they sought to protect was markedly different from that espoused by the organicists. Planning was associated with the political left, and was informed by a modernist aesthetic which valued smooth lines, order and tidiness. Organic aesthetic values were less regimented: an unstructured principle of accretion and growth through time informed them. As we shall see, organicism tended to be aligned with the right in politics. 'Planner-preservationists', as Matless terms the movement he conflates, were not intrinsically anti-urban, but sought to regulate and rationalize the urban environment. Organicists were more prone to outright hostility to the city. The modernizing ethos of planner-preservationism was reflected in its desire to shape good citizens, while organicism, according to Matless, was more concerned with 'rooted residents' than with urban visitors to the countryside and wanted to foster distinctive traditional regional identities rather than a modernized nation-state. Planner-preservationists tended to look optimistically to a future which they believed they could shape, while organicists lamented a lost past they found it hard to believe could be revived.[6]

The contrast between planner-preservationists and organicists drawn by Matless is a useful one and marks a large advance on previous conceptual-izations which have tended to lump the two movements together and, consequently, present a misplaced picture of preservationism as a simple backwards-looking movement. But it is important not to overstate the degree of polarization between planning and organicism. There were links both of ideas and individuals between the two. This is particularly apparent in the continuing influence of the tradition deriving from John Ruskin ('there is no wealth but life') and William Morris, one of the interwar derivatives of which was guild socialism. Ruskin, Morris and guild socialism all espoused what could easily be described as an organic perspective, criticizing industrialism for its regimentation and mutilation of the human personality, and seeking an alternative in the never failing restorative powers of nature. George Sturt, highly regarded by many organicists, saw himself as a socialist, and some of the leading organicists such as Philip Mairet, the editor of organicism's leading journal, the *New English Weekly*, had close links with guild socialism. Yet, as we have seen, the tradition descending from Ruskin and Morris also contributed significantly to preservationism. There were, therefore, links between preserva-tionism and organicism both at the level of ideas and of personnel.

Why was it that an organic movement developed in interwar Britain? We need first to recognize that organic ideas were not new in the 1920s. Even before the First World War a few writers had drawn attention to the dangers of soil exhaustion and erosion, although this was not always set in the context of the relationship with nutrition and health in the 'wheel of life' metaphor so favoured by interwar organicists. Perhaps the most influential pre-First World War organicist text was F. H. King's *Farmers of Forty Centuries*, which described and celebrated the peasant agriculture of China. Chinese peasant agriculture, so King noted, was characterized by an almost complete avoidance of waste: virtually all organic products, notably human excrement, were returned to the soil. But although King and other writers expressed some of the major organicist concerns before 1914, it was only in the interwar period that a coherent organicism emerged which linked soil, health and social well-being. It was also only after 1914 that organicism developed the institutions and networks of communication that allow it to be described as a movement. The greater coherence, higher profile, larger number of adherents and more sophisticated organization of interwar organicism therefore justify the question of what it was that served to give such a stimulus to organicism after 1918.[7]

Part of the explanation is that soil fertility, the central practical concern of organicists, was becoming a major problem in the 1920s and 1930s. Low agricultural prices had led to underinvestment and cost-cutting in agriculture, as farmers sought to stem the flow of losses by limiting outlay. Soil fertility inevitably suffered as the land was not maintained in proper condition. Some farmers attempted to save money by reducing the quantity of manure applied, while others cut costs by limiting their investment in the preparation of the soil, thus damaging soil structure. Much former arable land, no longer worth ploughing, was allowed to 'tumble down' into weed-choked waste, of little use even as rough grazing. Some tenant farmers reacted to the adverse prices by extracting as much benefit as they could from a farm, exhausting its fertility, and then moving on to another farm. Others adopted the 'low input, low output' system, seen at its most extensive on the land of the Wilson brothers of Ramsbury, Berkshire, which was operated for grazing on a 'ranch' basis.[8]

This loss of soil fertility raised serious questions about the capacity of agriculture to increase production as would be required in the event of a war – and between 1919 and 1939 the shadow of another world war was never very far away. The problem was particularly acute in the case of grassland, which showed the effects of inadequate replenishment of nutrients less clearly than arable land and was therefore liable to even greater neglect. George Stapledon's work at the Welsh Plant Breeding Station at Aberystwyth demonstrated conclusively that the effects of neglecting the fertility of grassland were very damaging. Stapledon's results were quickly disseminated throughout the organic movement because of his close links with other leading organicists.

If soil fertility was a serious concern in interwar Britain, it was infinitely more so in many other parts of the world.[9] US agriculture was devastated in the 1920s and 1930s by the 'dustbowl' which developed in the Mid-West through soil erosion resulting from excessively intensive and exhausting agricultural practices. Less noted, but sometimes at a local level equally damaging, was environmental degradation in parts of the British empire, notably India although also in some African colonies such as Kenya. Imperial administrators and officials faced with combating these problems of soil erosion came to understand the crucial importance of soil structure to maintaining a viable and healthy agriculture. The Indian Forestry Service played an especially important role in this process.

Agricultural depression, fear of incipient war and the experience of empire all heightened concerns about soil fertility. At a more elevated intellectual level, anxiety about the progressive urbanization of Britain and about the 'imbalance' between urban and rural which had resulted was also an important contributor to the rise of an organic sensibility in the 1920s and 1930s. It was for this reason that organicism was closely associated with rural reconstruction, which we will assess in Chapter 12. Another respect in which the influence of hostility to urban influences is apparent in the formation of organicism is in the prominence of owners of landed estates in the movement (both Rolf Gardiner and Viscount Lymington, for example, were large landowners). Large landowners often regretted the passing of their social prestige and political influence; organicism served to express their rejection of the urban and industrial world order which had overseen their dispossession.

If hostility to an ever more dominant urbanism was one strand which helps to account for the rise of interwar organicism, another element was the preoccupation with national health, nutrition and fitness in the interwar years. This tended to magnify the appeal of the organicist stress on wholesome food and its links to health. One of the reasons for the prominence of concerns about health in national culture in the interwar years was the scientific work of nutritionists such as John Boyd Orr, which demonstrated the crucial importance of an adequate diet for good health. But fear of war was, yet again, in the background, and was particularly obvious in the national fitness programmes of the later 1930s. The relationship between organicism, health and fitness is apparent in the prominence of doctors within the organic movement. Many of the leading organicists were doctors, including Robert McCarrison, Lionel J. Picton, Guy Theodore Wrench, George Scott Williamson and Innes Hope Pearse. The latter two were the instigators of the Pioneer Health Centre in Peckham, where organicist principles were combined with a gymnasium in an attempt to provide a complete organicist programme for healthy bodies.[10]

While many of the aspects of interwar organicism which have been mentioned hitherto probably seemed benign if in some instances slightly eccentric to most contemporaries, the same cannot be said of what is still today the most controversial aspect of organicism: its connections with fascism. Certain aspects of organic ideology bore a close resemblance to some features of fascism, particularly in its National Socialist incarnation. Organicists and Nazis professed a common hostility both to 'big business' and to communism or state socialism. Organicists tended to see small-scale farming as more in sympathy with organic methods and principles. The 'finance system' was criticized for allegedly exploiting the soil of countries in other parts of the world in order to provide cheap food for urban consumers, leading to soil exhaustion and erosion. This hostility to the 'finance system' was expressed by the involvement of many within the British organic movement in Major C. H. Douglas's Social Credit movement, which argued that credit should be made available by the state and hence consumers and small-scale producers liberated from the tyranny of big finance. But organic hostility to high finance could easily elide with Nazi anti-Semitic interpretations of British and American capitalism as dominated by a ruthlessly exploitative clique of Jews. Similarly, the hostility of many within the organic movement to communism or state socialism was echoed within Nazism. The Nazi proclamation of a commitment to 'blood and soil' struck a chord with many organicists, and there was much interest in the ideas of the German agriculture minister Darré. Leading organicists made visits to Germany, notably Lymington and Gardiner who travelled to Berlin together in 1938 and met, respectively, Hitler and Darré. At least two other important organicists were members of Mosley's British Union of Fascists (Henry Williamson and Jorian Jenks).[11]

However, although most of the leading interwar organicists were associated with the political right, ideologically organicism was multi-faceted and could support a variety of political positions, including, as we have seen, guild socialism. The core organicist emphasis on 'life' as opposed to artificiality was capable of being deployed in a wide range of arguments. This helps to explain both the breadth of organicism in the interwar years, and its diffuseness; which in turn is relevant to the explanation of why despite its breadth the movement had few practical achievements to its credit.

The effects of the Second World War on organicism were paradoxical. It would be expected that a movement so strongly tainted by association with fascism would experience great difficulties during the war, but in fact organicism was invigorated by it. Rolf Gardiner founded the Kinship in Husbandry group two years after the outbreak of the war, involving many of the most significant voices of the organic movement, including Stapledon, Lymington, Bell and Massingham. In 1943 Lady Eve Balfour published *The Living Soil*, probably the most influential of the many organicist books published in Britain during the war. In the last year of the war in Europe, 1945, the Soil Association was founded by Kinship in Husbandry associates. The war therefore witnessed remarkable dynamism on the part of the organicists and a plethora of publications, radio broadcasts and organizational initiatives.[12]

How was it that organicism was able to flourish under such apparently adverse conditions? Part of the explanation is that although some organicists continued to voice admiration for fascism and even for Nazi Germany to a surprisingly late date (Arthur Bryant was still doing so in 1940, for example), most executed a swift about-turn and began to write and speak about Germany as a classic and terrible example of the dangers of allowing an urban and mechanistic cast of mind to trample over rurality and tradition. This new presentation of Germany bore little relationship to the pro-rural, organicist Germany which Gardiner, Lymington, Williamson, Jenks and other organicist fascists had extolled before the outbreak of the war. When organicists acknowledged this earlier version of Germany at all, it was to denounce wartime Germany for having betrayed the 'soil' element of Nazi 'blood and soil' ideology. Most organicists succeeded in this way in paying no price at all for their prewar allegiances, although a few, notably Jorian Jenks, were incarcerated.

Successful as the organicists' attempt to cover their political tracks on the whole was, it cannot in itself go very far in explaining why the organic movement made such advances during the war. More significant than the political repackaging was that the circumstances of the war shifted the exigencies of agricultural policy in favour of goals to which organic ideas were relevant. Before the war, government agricultural policy had been dominated by the economic, cost-based concerns so reprobated by organicists. The prime measure of efficiency was output per man in an economy which attempted to maintain its relatively high living standards by high labour productivity permitting industrial exports to the rest of the world in exchange for agricultural imports. But the submarine menace during the war meant not only that the cost of importing food rose sharply, but that questions arose about whether a sufficient food supply could be maintained at all unless domestic food output was sharply increased. The emphasis therefore shifted away from output per man to increasing output per acre. This was much more amenable to the organicist emphasis on improving soil fertility.

After the war, organicism declined quite sharply. This is again on the face of it surprising, since agriculture was buoyant and consumers prosperous in the 1950s, which might have made possible a further development of organicist ideas about higher-quality food and better nutrition, albeit at a higher cost per unit of output. In fact, the same factor which had promoted organicist ideas during the war now served to undermine them. The basis of the prosperity of agriculture after the war was the 1947 Agriculture Act, under the aegis of which farmers were offered guaranteed prices, but only in return for year-on-year efficiency gains, which were mainly to be achievable through mechanization and the application of ever-greater quantities of chemical fertilizers. This left little scope for organicist emphasis on labour-intensive mixed farming and composting, however high the yields gained in return.

Having assessed the development of organicism between the wars and during the Second World War, we are now in a position to consider the relationship between the organic movement of these years and the environmentalism of the post-1960 period. To what extent is the relationship between the two movements one of continuity, or are the differences between them so great that it is more useful to consider them as separate phenomena rather than as parts of a whole?

It is probably in political terms that the contrasts between the organicism of the first half of the twentieth century and the environmentalism of the second half are most evident. As we have seen, organicism was clearly a movement of the political right, even if with the potential to embrace some left-wing affiliates. Environmentalism since the 1960s has been equally strongly associated with the left, and sometimes even with the most radical, anarchist elements of the left. There are also differences between organicism and environmentalism with respect to attitudes to nature. While organicists looked to nature as a model, they did not always see a need for a rigid separation of the natural from the artificial. Organicists were more concerned with demonstrating and insisting upon the positive importance of humus than they were with demanding the complete exclusion of artificial fertilizers. It may be fair to suggest that late twentieth-century environmentalism and organicism were more exercised by a negative demand to exclude or avoid chemical treatments, whereas interwar organicism was more strongly concerned with advocating the positive benefits of 'the rule of return'.

An important aspect of late twentieth-century environmentalism is its ambivalence or even outright hostility to economic growth. Organicists, by contrast, were not anti-productionist. On the contrary, they argued that the use of organic methods would result in *higher* output per acre than conventional methods. Achieving improved yields was an important concern of many of the most influential agricultural scientists within the organic movement, notably Howard and Stapledon. Connected with this pro-production stance, organicists regarded themselves as being unequivocally in favour of agriculture. Here again the contrast with the attitude of late twentieth-century environmentalism is clear: environmentalists have been among the sharpest critics of farmers since the 1980s. Interwar organicists, however, saw themselves as taking a stand *for* farmers and agriculture against the neglect, contempt and misunderstanding of a nation-state which was damagingly dominated by urban influences.

What organicists rejected was not productionism but a certain version of it – a version which in their eyes was a delusion. This was the notion that output per man could be indefinitely improved by applying ever larger quantities of artificial fertilizer and introducing ever more mechanization. Once again, the influence of the experience of empire is readily apparent. In India, high population densities set a premium on land rather than labour productivity. Because organicists wanted to see high land rather than high labour productivity, and because of their admiration for the small farmers of India and China, they tended to favour the concept of peasant farming. This links organicism to rural reconstruction and to 'back-to-the-land' ideas, which also aimed to preserve a large agricultural population on the land, and points to another important difference between organicism and later environmentalism. The former was in many ways a rural and agricultural movement. Almost all its leading figures either were or became farmers or landowners. Environmentalism was very much an urban movement, and even when it spilled over into the countryside in the 1980s and thereafter this was as a result of commuting and retirement migration which brought people who worked or had worked in urban-based jobs into the countryside, but not into agriculture or into pre-existent rural cultures.

Yet if the differences between organicism and environmentalism are clear, so too are the continuities. The core emphasis of organicism on natural processes and on the need to respect these if human life was to be sustainable survived intact at the ideological centre of late twentieth-century environmentalism. Nor were the continuities only at the level of ideas. While many of the leading organicists died shortly after the war, figures such as Gardiner and Jenks provide a link with later environmentalism, as of course does the Soil Association itself. Organicism therefore pointed the way to the more powerful and influential environmentalism of the late twentieth century. In its own time, it had much less effect than the later movement, but what it lacked in results it made up in breadth of influence, partly because of the protean character of its central metaphor of 'life'. In the next chapter we will look at an aspect of attitudes to the countryside in the interwar years which related at many points to organicism and yet also pointed in quite different directions: rural reconstruction.

. . . .

CHAPTER 12

Rural Reconstruction Between the Wars

§ FEW of the characteristic aspects of attitudes to the countryside held during the interwar years had their origins after the First World War, yet many of them developed much more fully and impressively after 1918. This is particularly true of 'rural reconstruction', by which is meant efforts and plans to stimulate and improve rural society in the late nineteenth and first half of the twentieth century, particularly those which were principally concerned with the quality of rural social and cultural life as opposed to being narrowly focused on agriculture.

Rural reconstruction initially emerged in response to the agricultural depression of the late nineteenth century. This damaged the profitability of farming in many parts of the country and created an ongoing discussion of how farming could be made to pay. As the depression continued, fears began to extend beyond the issue of farming profitability to broader aspects of rural society. One of the phenomena associated with, and partly caused by, the agricultural depression was rural depopulation. Many villages began to lose population in the 1870s and often continued to do so until the second half of the twentieth century. This raised anxieties about the sustainability of rural social life. Villages with declining populations could no longer support the range of commercial services or leisure activities that they had once done. Furthermore, as population drained away from the villages to the towns and cities, it became apparent that the political and cultural balance between town and country, already skewed towards the former, was becoming radically and seemingly irreversibly biased in that direction. This seemed to imply a re-making of the social fabric of the nation which, in the eyes of some, was dangerous and undesirable.

Many remedies for rural depopulation were suggested by late nineteenth-century writers such as P. A. Graham, author of *The Rural Exodus* (1892). One of the most favoured solutions was to promote smallholdings. It was argued that among the main reasons agricultural labourers were migrating to the towns or to the New World in such large numbers was that they had no prospect of upwards social mobility in the English countryside. Farm size had increased to the point where the hope of renting a farm was an unrealistic one for a labourer. What was needed, according to this view, was a 'rural ladder' reaching from allotments through smallholdings of graded sizes up to full-scale farms.[1]

Probably the second most popular remedy proposed for rural depopulation was agricultural education. Many (especially farmers) alleged that young labourers were leaving the countryside in large numbers because of an urban bias in the education they had received, which taught them skills and values which were appreciated in towns, such as good handwriting and mathematics, but left them ignorant or even contemptuous of rural skills such as hedge-laying, thatching or any one of dozens of traditional rural crafts and agricultural activities.

At a more narrowly agricultural level, the main proposals before 1914 were for a switch to more profitable if less familiar branches of agriculture such as fruit and vegetable growing, for the adoption of new methods and techniques and for political assistance to agriculture. The main suggestion as regards the latter was tariff reform, which Rider Haggard in his influential 1902 survey *Rural England* saw as the only solution of sufficient depth to meet the real needs of British agriculture while remaining convinced that it was politically unobtainable. However, in the years immediately following the publication of *Rural England*, tariff reform began to seem less of a pipe dream because of the advocacy of an influential section of the Conservative Party, headed by Joseph Chamberlain. The crushing political failure of tariff reform delivered by the landslide victory of the Liberals in the 1906 general election destroyed this hope until the outbreak of the First World War, which led to government intervention to increase agricultural production. In order to ensure this, the government offered farmers guaranteed prices under the 1917 Corn Production Act and its successors. It appeared that the 1920 Agriculture Act had established a guaranteed-price regime for peace time, but escalating costs led to the repeal of the Act the next year, with the connivance of farmers' leaders who were hostile to the minimum wages which were a concomitant of guaranteed prices. After the repeal of the Agriculture Act, it became clear the protectionism was again a politically unacceptable option for the foreseeable future.[2]

In the twenty years from 1919 to 1939 the discourse of rural reconstruction established before the war continued, but with significant changes in content and tone. Smallholdings, perhaps the most popular panacea of pre-1914 rural reconstructionism, no longer attracted much support in the 1920s and 1930s. This was for a number of reasons. In the first place, effective legislation to promote smallholdings had been placed on the statute book in the years immediately before and after the war. Second, the rise in living standards after the war made it improbable that agricultural labourers would be attracted by smallholdings, because the gap between the living standard of a smallholder and of a factory worker, or even of most agricultural labourers, had grown too wide. Third, many soldiers had found it difficult to settle back into civilian life after demobilization, and some had taken smallholdings as a means whereby they could live independently and in relative seclusion, but these men had generally struggled to make a living, and many had given up.[3] This experience was discouraging to those who argued that a national policy of smallholdings provision was desirable. Finally, the economic circumstances of the 1920s and 1930s were unfavourable to smallholdings. The depression of the late nineteenth century had raised the price of fruit, vegetables and milk relative to arable products, and because the former were at that time more profitably cultivated on a small scale, smallholders stood to gain at the expense of larger farmers. In the interwar period, competition in the sectors where small farmers had a cost advantage was more intense, and it was larger farmers able to spread their costs who were less disadvantaged by the difficult economic circumstances.

Proposals for improved agricultural techniques and methods also continued to be made in the interwar period, with an emphasis on mechanization. Associated with this was a small influx of businessmen, such as John Spedan Lewis and Ernest Debenham, to agriculture. These businessmen attempted to apply the methods which had succeeded in urban conditions to farming, including the adoption of labour-saving machinery and careful accounting and cost monitoring. However, ideas about improved agricultural efficiency, especially as implemented by businessmen-turned-farmers, were to a greater extent than before the war developed in isolation from more broadly based plans for rural reconstruction which aimed to achieve a better quality of rural life rather than merely more adequate profits for farmers and landowners.[4]

Rural reconstruction in its fuller sense was given a powerful stimulus and a new direction by the events and effects of the war. The most important influence was the changes caused by the war in the outlook and expectations of rural workers themselves. Many male rural workers had been in the army, while rural women had often worked in munitions factories. Both experiences often led to a revaluation of previous assumptions. In the trenches, the deference characteristic of prewar rural life was threatened by the camaraderie of soldiers in imminent danger of death. To a certain extent the fact that most officers came from the elite, with a substantial overrepresentation of the landed gentry, and that these officers led their men with conspicuous courage, counteracted the hierarchy-dissolving effects of trench comradeship. But other wartime influences were also inimical to deference. Rural recruits inevitably came into contact with men drawn from urban areas, and in doing so encountered their typically less submissive relationship to authority. The leisure culture which emerged in the army during the war was also characterized by informality and egalitarian comradeship. Women munitions workers were exposed to the less deferential urban outlook even more directly through their work in factories. The result, widely reported at the time, was that the mood of the young men and women returning to their villages in 1918 and 1919 was one of discontent. The less constrained leisure opportunities which many had enjoyed during the war contrasted unfavourably with the often limited and excessively supervised leisure that had been offered in most villages before 1914. There was a general expectation of, and demand for, something better.

Several new organizations were formed in the late stages of the war or in the immediate post-1918 years in response to this demand. Notable among them were the Women's Institutes, formed with government support in 1917 and an almost immediate runaway success. Several other important organizations emerged in the years that followed, including the rural section of the National Council of Social Service, the Rural Community Councils, and the Young Farmers' Clubs. At the same time, organizations which had been established before the war but which had made only limited progress in the countryside began to make greater headway. In this category were the Boy Scouts and Girl Guides, the WEA and the YMCA.[5]

These organizations were important for several reasons. Their growing influence in rural areas tended to diminish the local predominance of organized religion. They represented a shift away from parish-based leisure organizations to nationally constituted organizations. Still more importantly, the new social organizations catered for social groups which had previously been neglected in the countryside, and in some cases even gave these groups some experience of self-management. Most obviously this occurred in terms of gender, with the WI, but it was also apparent with respect to youth, through organizations such as the Scouts, Guides and Young Farmers' Clubs, and to a certain extent as regards class, since agricultural labourers seem to have been represented on the management committees of at least some of the new social organizations (such as village halls).[6]

Rural reconstruction was the major rural aim of most of the new social organizations with a specifically rural remit. All of these organizations sought to make living in the countryside more interesting and fulfilling, and to give back to the countryside some of the life which it was agreed it had lost since the mid-nineteenth century. To some degree the organizations co-operated with each other in this aim. An important influence here was Barnett House in Oxford, which emerged as a centre for the co-ordination of rural leisure and social work in the years after the war under the leadership of Grace

Hadow, a vice-president of the National Federation of Women's Institutes. Hadow worked together with W. S. Adams, the Chairman of the National Council of Social Service and later Warden of All Souls, to facilitate the co-ordination of the new rural social organizations. It was as a result of a series of conferences convened in Oxford by Hadow and Adams that the National Council of Social Service established a rural department, and, in its wake, Rural Community Councils began to be formed. Rural Community Councils were composed of county representatives from voluntary organizations work-ing in the countryside, such as the WEA, the YMCA, the WI, the Girls' Friendly Society, the Scouts and Guides, the Village Clubs Association and others. In the main the Rural Community Councils were intended to perform on a country-wide basis the function that Barnett House had been fulfilling in Oxfordshire.[7]

The social organizations at work in the countryside after 1918 did not always agree with each other. There were, for example, quite severe tensions between the WI and the Village Clubs Association over the question of mixed village clubs, which the latter believed were essential but the former regarded as a threat to its independence. But although organizational rivalry and turf wars were common and could not always be avoided even when a local Rural Community Council had been formed, the occasional disputes between the new rural social organizations should not be allowed to overshadow the basic unity of outlook and purpose which guided them. A central value which was common to virtually all the new social organizations was citizenship. This emerged particularly forcefully in the WI, which took very seriously its func-tion of shaping the first generation of women voters into responsible electors, providing them with lectures on improving, if largely uncontroversial, topics of public interest such as the League of Nations. The more recently formed youth organizations, particularly the Scouts and Guides, also showed a strong concern with developing a sense of civic responsibility in their members. The National Council of Social Service shared the same perspective, and it was in part for this reason that it attempted to promote 'village social councils', which would consist of representatives of village leisure organizations and which would act as 'schools of democracy' at the village level (an ambition which bore a family resemblance to the WI intention of functioning as 'village parliaments'). An important aspect of the citizenship which the new rural social organizations attempted to foster was that, although citizenship clearly referred to a sense of national belonging, it was to be achieved through unity at a village level. Almost all the new social organizations had the village as their lowest unit of administration. Fostering citizenship was linked to, and dependent on, develop-ing a stronger sense of community identity and cohesion.[8]

Rural reconstruction was therefore centrally concerned not only with the countryside but also with the community. At one level, this was a matter of reviving a sense of collective identity and local spirit which had been battered by years of low agricultural product prices and by depopulation. This was what rural reconstruction meant before the First World War. But this older sense of reconstruction was increasingly overlaid in the post-1918 years by a new meaning. The 'reconstruction' required for rural communities after 1918 was not merely the repair of economic ravages, but of the damage wrought by the war. The holes torn in the fabric of village social life by the war were visible on the war memorials erected in virtually every village in England after the end of the 'Great War'. How it was appropriate to commemorate the dead was a fiercely contested and divisive issue, but rural reconstruction placed most emphasis on making a better future for the living.[9] Village halls built as war memorials with war memorial collection funds were an example of this approach; but in relation to the war, rural reconstruction became reconstruction not just for the people of the countryside but for the nation as a whole. What those committed to rural reconstruction were ultimately seeking to reconstruct was not any actual village, but a mythical image of a tranquil village England from before the shattering effect of the war; the 'village in the mind'. So rural reconstruction represented a psychological retreat into the countryside – a retreat which served the wounded minds of the often elite or urban-based organizers who led the new social organizations as much as the villagers towards whom reconstruction was ostensibly directed. Furthermore, as the war receded this became a retreat not only from an unbearable past, but from a troubled present dominated by economic difficulties, unemployment and the rising threat of another war.

Rural reconstruction had an interesting relationship with the organic movement. Some organicists were actively involved in it, perhaps the best example being Montague Fordham, who was one of the leading writers on rural reconstruction and the founder of the Rural Reconstruction Association (1926). The commitment of many organizations (such as the National Council of Social Service and the WI) involved in rural reconstruction to reviving rural craftsmanship and preserving rural traditions won sympathy from organicists. At the same time, many organicists were suspicious of rural reconstruction because it tended to emphasize leisure and social life rather than the earth, labour and production.[10]

Rural reconstruction was almost wholly a voluntary, non-governmental domain. This voluntaryism suited the Conservative governments which predominated during the interwar period very well. Voluntary provision of social and leisure services saved the government money, since rural communities were to a large extent in effect paying for their own needs, supplemented by assistance from some of the wealthy philanthropic trusts such as the Carnegie Trust and the Pilgrim Trust. Voluntaryism also had other advantages. It allowed for more flexibility than provision by national or even local government could easily have done. It was possible to tailor local effort to local circumstances, whereas it would have been difficult if not prohibitively costly for national government or county councils to vary the administrative struc-ture of social and leisure provision on a village-by-village basis. Voluntaryism also offered a large measure of local autonomy: decisions were taken in the village rather than in the council chamber or at Westminster. But despite these evident advantages, there is another side to the voluntaryism which rural reconstruction established so extensively in the interwar countryside. Flexibility and local autonomy also meant patchy and limited provision; where local leadership and initiative were lacking, no mechanism existed to ensure that provision was nevertheless offered. This was unfortunate in that places deficient in social resources were often those where local initiative was at its weakest, so those villages where need was greatest were less likely to be recipients of assistance from voluntary organizations than other villages. Voluntaryism also tended to mean that small villages, which again were more likely to be disadvantaged with respect to social provision, lost out in com-parison to larger communities; a situation reinforced after the Second World War by planning policies which concentrated public services on larger 'key' villages (see Chapter 13).

An even sharper question which needs to be posed is whether the local autonomy secured by voluntaryism did not really in practice mean 'continuing elite dominance'. It is difficult to answer this question with confidence in the current state of research, but it seems probable that the answer to it is 'yes'. In the main, interwar rural voluntaryism appears to have served the function of reconstituting authority structures which had been damaged and shaken by the war. Paradoxically, this was done through a formal broadening of authority. Most of the new rural social organizations had democratic con-stitutions, but the position of the rural elite was strong enough, and surviving deference sufficiently persistent, that despite this it still tended to be members of the elite who emerged as leaders of village social organizations. Because the elite were now leaders *by the choice* of their communities, their tarnished authority was reaffirmed and relegitimated.[11]

Rural voluntaryism was in fact an alternative to the creation of an effective tier of local government at the parish level. Rising demand for social and leisure provision would almost certainly have forced a greater development of parish-level government had it not been for the new social organizations. So rural reconstruction helped to confirm the demotion of village local gov-ernment. Parish Councils had been created in 1894, but Lord Salisbury's government had hobbled their capacity to effect significant change from the start by limiting their tax-raising powers to a rate of 4d in the pound. In many respects village local government has never recovered, and its continuing weakness is the counterpart of the strength of voluntary organizations in the countryside. 'Rural reconstruction' bears a share of the responsibility for bringing this situation about.

At its best, then, rural reconstruction brought new life to the countryside by improving the quality and quantity of rural leisure, including many previously marginalized groups in social activities, and by introducing a greater element of democratic process into village social life. But the broadening of authority this entailed served in the end to entrench rather than displace existing status hierarchies.

Rural reconstruction had undoubted successes, foremost among which were the Women's Institutes and the provision of village halls. Both of these spread through hundreds and eventually thousands of villages and resulted in a much increased number and variety of rural leisure activities and a strengthened sense of rural community. Despite these successes, rural reconstruction was limited in other ways. Partly this limitation was self-imposed: by choosing to concentrate on leisure, rural reconstruction set itself a manageable task, but at the same time one which could not reverse the economic realities of the decline in the need for labour in agriculture. While mechanization continued to reduce the size of the farm labour force required by farmers on the one hand, and urban wages continued to be sufficiently higher than rural wages to tempt rural workers to migrate to the towns on the other, there would always be a limit to how much any reconstruction programme could achieve. Furthermore, not only could rural reconstruction do relatively little to check depopulation, but this limitation soon rebounded on it. While the new social organizations had great success between 1918 and the mid-1920s, the continuing decline of village populations tended to sap them of membership. This was exacerbated by the effects of the particularly severe slump in agricultural prices between 1929 and 1932. By the mid-1930s there were reports of village halls struggling to make ends meet, and even the WIs were no longer always quite so well attended as they had been in their early years.

Less obvious, but in the long run even more damaging to the project of rural reconstruction, was the worm in the bud: that the reconstruction attempted was only at a superficial level intended for the ordinary villagers who were the apparent target. The belief in a 'rural community' which could be rebuilt and then safeguarded was to no small degree a reflection of the desire to see the countryside as a haven from the ugliness and unsatisfactoriness of urban industrial life in the 1920s and 1930s. But most rural inhabitants had little interest in reconstituting an imaginary village of the past. Partly for this reason, the success of rural reconstruction in shoring up rural traditions was distinctly limited. It was possible, for example, for the National Council of Social Service to insist that villages applying for funding from its Village Halls Loan Fund should use local building materials and techniques in applying the funds. But the NCSS could do nothing about the use that villagers subsequently made of their halls. In fact many villagers chose to use village halls for archetypally urban forms of leisure activity such as film shows, keep-fit classes or fashionable dances. To a certain extent other rural social organizations also facilitated the diffusion of urban culture into rural areas. Ironically, therefore, rural reconstruction may have hastened the intrusion of urbanism into rural life.[12]

Perhaps the most lasting legacy of rural reconstruction was in enshrining the concept of 'the rural community' in the national mind. Before 1914 the phrase 'rural community' was not in common use, but the concern of the new social organizations with citizenship and social cohesion, and the impulse to retreat to an imagined countryside which underlay rural reconstruction, brought the term into common usage. Since then, the two concepts of rurality and community, which have no necessary or even empirical connection, have become axiomatically linked. Once again, this is a legacy which has had ambiguous effects. On the one hand, it has contributed to the preservation of the outward form of villages because, as the embodiment of community, villages acquired an iconic status enshrined in post-1945 planning legislation. On the other hand, the powerful association between rurality and community has contributed more than anything else to the mass migration of urban dwellers to the countryside since the Second World War. This, in a self-defeating action, has in turn done more than anything else to undermine the distinctiveness of rural life, as we shall see in more detail in Chapter 16.

CHAPTER 13

Rural Change and the Legislative Framework, 1939 to 2000

§ AN appropriate way of beginning this chapter is by referring back to the poem by Thomas Hardy quoted in full in Chapter 6 (see page 73). Two themes emerge powerfully from the poem: those of continuity and change, and of image and reality. Hardy evokes the timelessness of rural work practices against the transient horrors of the 1915 present, yet, as we saw in Chapter 6, this evocation is predicated on an intense awareness of change and of the threatened status of the rural traditions in which Hardy finds solace. Similarly, Hardy's presentation of a rural idyll, understated but all the more persuasive and powerful for that, raises the question of what the social realities which have been transmuted into poetic symbols actually were.

Although Hardy wrote this poem during the First World War, the poem's themes are peculiarly apposite to the experience of the countryside in the years during and after the Second World War. In this chapter we will initially assess the balance between continuity and change in agriculture and the countryside in England since 1939, and then provide some explanations of this balance through considering the relationship between the image of the countryside and the realities of rural social and economic change.

Perhaps the first thought to strike a modern reader of Hardy's poem is likely to be that his predictions about the durability of rural work practices have been dramatically falsified since he wrote. Seen from the perspective of the early years of the twenty-first century, it seems inescapably obvious that there have been colossal changes in the countryside in general, and perhaps above all in the nature of agricultural work, since the second decade of the twentieth century.

Perhaps the most obvious of these changes has been mechanization in agriculture. Before the Second World War, machinery played an incomparably less important role in farming than it has done since 1939. There was, in the first place, far less machinery in use in the prewar period. Furthermore, what machinery existed was very much less powerful. It was far less specialized and sophisticated, and was correspondingly less expensive than it has since become. As regards powered machinery, the main items of equipment in use on farms in 1939 were tractors, barn machinery such as threshers and chaff-cutters, and, to a lesser extent, milking machines. Tractors were still far from universal, and continued to be outnumbered by farm horses throughout the interwar years, while most barn machinery was driven by oil or petrol engines with very low output by comparison with postwar installations. Milking machines were plagued by technical problems in their early years, and on many farms, including some of the most progressive such as those of John Spedan Lewis on the Leckford estate, they were abandoned in favour of a return to hand-milking during the interwar period. As a result, over 90 per cent of dairy herds in England and Wales were still hand-milked in 1939.[1]

Since the Second World War, there has been a very large increase in the power available per worker in British agriculture, with corresponding implications for labour productivity. Furthermore, there has been an extraordinary development of specialized equipment, as a result of which many tasks which were previously done by hand became routine operations for machinery. Tasks which fall into this category include the mucking out of stables and cowsheds, hedging and ditching, and the harvesting of root and vegetable crops.

One of the most important effects of agricultural mechanization has been the almost complete elimination of what in the nineteenth century was one of the most important rural social classes: the rural craftsmen and crafts-women. In the nineteenth century, and until well into the twentieth, most villages had a blacksmith, wheelwright and carpenter, and many had one or more thatchers and even perhaps a saddler as well. These had been largely employed by the farmers and landowners. But mechanization then resulted in a shift from wood-based to iron- or steel-based implements, which removed what had been the primary source of work for both wheelwrights and rural carpenters. Mechanization also led to the replacement of horses by tractors, which eliminated the agricultural need for saddlers. Blacksmiths were also adversely affected; they had played an important role in the repair, or even manufacture, of the simpler kinds of farm machinery in use in the nineteenth century, but all but a few blacksmiths lacked either the expertise or the equipment to repair the complex and expensive machinery which began to be introduced from the late nineteenth century onwards, and which was adopted *en masse* from the late 1930s. Thatchers had also been integral to the agri-cultural economy in the nineteenth and early twentieth centuries. Their services had been required not only, indeed in many parts of the country not even primarily, for roofing residential buildings, but for thatching hay and corn ricks and stacks to protect them against rain and weather. Once combine harvesters reduced or even superseded the need for ricks to stand in the fields drying before being transported to the farmyard for threshing, the thatcher was no longer needed in the corn field. A residual demand for the services of thatchers continued to exist for the maintenance of cottage roofs, although in the interwar years thatch was increasingly replaced by cheaper materials such as corrugated iron or more durable ones such as tiles or slate.

Some indication of the scale of the decline in the numbers of rural craft-workers can be derived from evidence taken from trade directories. A study of Hampshire craftworkers based on this source showed, for example, that the number of blacksmiths recorded in the county had declined from approximately two hundred and fifty in 1939 to only about eighty-five in 1996, while the number of wheelwrights had fallen even more precipitously, from forty-two in 1939 to a single individual in 1996. Some other crafts, however, such as thatching and saddlery, although declining over the twentieth century as a whole, had in fact shown a slight revival since 1939, presumably because of the non-agricultural demand generated, respectively, by rural in-migration and by the rising popularity of horse-riding as a leisure activity. Nevertheless, taken as a whole it was clear that mechanization in agriculture had gravely affected rural crafts and had brought some, notably wheelwrighting, to the point of extinction.[2]

The effects of agricultural mechanization on farmworkers, while not quite as catastrophic as on rural craftworkers, have nevertheless been dramatic. In raising labour productivity, mechanization sharply reduced the size of the labour force required in agriculture. This in turn has resulted in a steep decline in the number of farmworkers, apparent from the late nineteenth century onwards, but especially striking in the post-Second World War period. Some indication of the shrinkage of the agricultural workforce can be given by statistics. In 1931, for example, the proportion of the British workforce employed in agriculture was 8 per cent, but by 1996 this had fallen to a mere 2 per cent.[3]

The decline in the total number of farmworkers in Britain was reflected in the decline of the average number of farmworkers employed per farm; indeed, the national figures essentially reflect the reduction in the number of farm-workers employed per farm, as a direct result of individual farmers' decisions to replace labour with machinery. In the nineteenth century and, to some extent, still in the first half of the twentieth century, a high proportion of farms employed several farmworkers. Large farms, such as those typical of the Berkshire Downs or of Lincolnshire, often employed as many as thirty or even forty workers for much of the year, and more at harvest-time, but by the 1970s, most farmworkers were the only full-time employee on the farm on which they worked.

The decline in the number of farmworkers per farm had important implications both for the relationship between one farmworker and another, and between farmworkers and farmers. When there had been many farmworkers employed on a farm, the workers naturally met each other frequently in a work context as they went about their tasks. Often they worked alongside each other. Horse ploughing teams, for example, needed a man to hold the plough and a boy to lead the horses, and it was common practice to use two teams alongside each other in one field. Threshing, even after threshing machines had been introduced, needed several farmworkers; in the case of a threshing machine, perhaps two or more men were needed to pitchfork the unthreshed sheaves to the top of the machine, another to feed the corn into the machine, and others to replace the filled bags of threshed grain and carry them to a cart for removal.

This experience of shared work could create strong ties of solidarity between farmworkers, manifested, for example, in the culture of farmworkers, which incorporated collective features such as part-singing of hymns and other songs at work. This solidarity provided the social basis for agricultural trade unionism, which was an important feature of English agriculture in the late nineteenth and for much of the first half of the twentieth century. However, the decline in the number of farmworkers per farm which was so characteristic a feature of postwar farming made the typical agricultural worker much more isolated than he had previously been. What had once been a collective experience became, with the pervasive mechanization of the post-1939 period, an increasingly solitary occupation.

At the same time, and in contrast, the relationship between the individual farmworker and his (or in rare instances her) employer became much closer. This was partly because the farmer was now often the only other person the farmworker met in the course of his daily work. But there were other reasons too. The decline in the number of farmworkers per farm also meant that the farmer, who in the nineteenth century had typically been a manager who did not engage in manual work but exercised an essentially supervisory role, now more often took a full share of manual work alongside his employee. The work roles of farmer and farmworker therefore became closer and less distinct.[4] Furthermore, farms which had previously employed many people now often relied wholly on family labour, so the employee alongside whom the farmer was working was quite likely to be his own son.

Factors other than mechanization also served to bring farmers and farmworkers closer together after 1939. An important shift, which we will consider in more detail subsequently in this chapter, occurred in the social composition of many villages. Incomers, often urban and middle-class by background, moved into villages, eventually displacing agriculture from predominance in village life in many parts of the country. This contributed to making farmers and farmworkers more conscious of what united than of what divided them. The two-fold process whereby the bonds between farmworkers loosened while those between farmworkers and farmers tightened was one of the main reasons for the great weakness of agricultural trade unionism in England in the postwar period, in contrast to industrial trade unionism which reached the apogee of its strength in the 1970s.[5]

If, as we have seen, mechanization had important effects in reducing the number of farmworkers employed per farm, its effects on the nature of farmwork were no less significant. One of the most interesting, but least noticed, effects of mechanization in agriculture was, for example, to make the relationship between farmworkers and animals less close than it had been. In the nineteenth and early twentieth centuries, farmworkers often were directly and deeply involved in the care of animals. Horsemen, for example, seem frequently to have taken great pride in the appearance of their charges, spending additional hours grooming them, and resorting to a remarkable variety of sometimes questionable methods to improve their horses' looks (such as applying arsenic to make the mane more shiny). Shepherds were no less deeply involved with their sheep, although this closeness was based on care and responsibility rather than on pride in appearance. Shepherds often lived in mobile huts out in the fields with their flocks at lambing time (as described, for example, in the opening chapters of Hardy's *Far from the Madding Crowd*). Even closer to the typical shepherd than his flock, however, was his dog. Shepherds and sheepdogs were often almost inseparable, and few nineteenth-century photographs of shepherds do not also show the shepherd's dog. The remarkable bond between shepherds and their dogs is vividly described in W. H. Hudson's *A Shepherd's Life*, based on his conversations with a Salisbury Plain shepherd. The proximity of agricultural workers to animals was experienced physically in the era before general mechanization to a much greater extent than it was after the Second World War. A good example of this is hand-milking. A milkmaid rested her head against the flank of the cow she was milking while she did so, and squeezed the teat directly with her hand – a delicate and skilled task which required sensitivity to the nature of the cow's udder. Similarly physical was the relationship between an agricultural worker's household and the pig which a high proportion of labourers kept in the late nineteenth and early twentieth centuries. Pigs were a vital supplement to the diet and income of many labouring families, and were often treated with great affection; they were tickled, slapped and scratched by all members of the family.[6]

The contrast afforded by the relationship between agricultural workers and animals since the Second World War could scarcely be greater. Farmworkers, and for that matter farmers too, became increasingly separated from their animals by labour-saving machinery, such as milking machines, while draught animals were replaced by tractors. These labour-saving machines led to a sharp increase in the animal-to-human ratio in agriculture, which has

1. **The Countryside March.** Hundreds of thousands marched through London on 1 March 1998 to defend the countryside. The strength of support for the march was impressive, but as was indicated by the wide range of interests and causes represented 'defending the countryside' meant very different things to different people.

2. ABOVE. **Grasmere in the Lake District.** Literary attitudes to the countryside were decisively reshaped by the English romantic poets, for many of whom the landscape of the lakes was a formative influence.

3. BELOW. **Dove Cottage,** where Wordsworth lived from 1799 to 1808.

4. ABOVE. **Richmond Park.**
Eighteenth and nineteenth-century urbanisation fostered a popular appetite for access to urban green space, before which the crown's persistent efforts to maintain the exclusivity of the London royal parks were ultimately forced to yield.

5. RIGHT. **Sir Robert Hunter,** a key figure within the late nineteenth-century preservationist movement and together with Octavia Hill and Hardwicke Rawnsley one of the founders of the National Trust.

6. LEFT. **Epping Forest.** The struggle to maintain rights of access to Epping Forest and other London commons was the major preoccupation of the Commons Preservation Society in its early days.

7. LEFT. **Ramblers at Styhead Pass in the Lake District, 1922.** Rambling became immensely popular among the urban working class in the interwar period.

8. ABOVE. **Advertising hoardings on the North Downs, near Esher, Surrey.** The rise of motoring after the First World War brought in its wake what the CPRE referred to as a 'mushroom growth' of roadside advertising, petrol stations and tea rooms to serve or exploit the motorist, until these were tardily controlled by planning legislation.

9. BELOW. **Taynton village hall, Oxfordshire,** built in 1938 with a National Council of Social Service grant, on condition that traditional building materials rather than asbestos be used for the roof. Along with other organisations involved in 'rural reconstruction', the N.C.S.S. hoped to sustain rural traditions through reviving the village community.

10. LEFT. **Wheelwrights, 1907.** Organised efforts to sustain 'traditional' rural crafts in the face of changing agricultural technology met with little success for much of the twentieth century, but paradoxically counter-urbanisation in the late twentieth century allowed crafts such as blacksmithing, saddlery and thatching to exploit a new, non-agricultural market.

11. RIGHT. **Hand-milking, Amery Farm, Alton, Hampshire, 1910.** Notice the close physical contact between cows and milkmen. One of the major consequences of agricultural mechanization has been to increase the physical and emotional distance between farm workers and animals.

12. LEFT. **Claas combine harvester, October 1968.** Mechanization vastly increased the productivity of farm labour, reducing the size of the agricultural workforce and creating a housing surplus which facilitated middle-class immigration into the countryside.

13. RIGHT. **Pylons,** photographed for the CPRE. The CPRE's hostility to modern intrusions into the countryside was more discriminating than has sometimes been acknowledged: in its early days, for example, the organisation admired the clean lines of modernist architecture and design, including steel pylons.

14. BELOW. **Prairie farming, Bedfordshire.** To maximize the economies of scale obtainable from mechanization, arable farmers removed thousands of kilometres of hedgerows in the second half of the twentieth century, provoking considerable environmentalist criticism.

15. ABOVE. **The Evenlode at Combe, Oxfordshire.** Some historians, notably Martin Wiener and Alun Howkins, have argued that perceptions of rural England have been dominated by the lush, gentle landscapes of the 'south country', reinforcing notions of social stability and traditional authority.

16. BELOW. **Halvergate Marshes, Norfolk,** scene of fierce conflict between environmentalists and farmers in the 1980s.

contributed to a growing tendency within agriculture to regard animals less as individual creatures than as one of a mass – a process which has been taken to its extreme in the case of battery poultry.[7]

To a lesser but still important extent, the same process of distancing which has affected the relationship between farmworkers and animals as a result of mechanization has also been apparent in the relationship between farmworkers and the land. In the nineteenth century, farmworkers spent much of their time in direct contact with the soil. Hoeing and harvesting were still largely carried out by hand, and even ploughing involved actually treading the soil. But in the twentieth century, especially in the post-1939 era, farmworkers spent an increasing proportion of their time cocooned in the cabs of their tractors, touching plastic, glass and metal rather than earth and vegetation, and hearing the sound of tractor engines and radios rather than of horses' hooves, the wind in the trees and the cries of birds.

Agricultural production has, in short, become more technologized, industrialized and 'cold' than it was before the Second World War. It has also sometimes been suggested that mechanization led to a deskilling of the farm workforce. Here, however, the situation is a little more complex. On the one hand, it is undoubtedly true that machines and new technology have taken over or made unnecessary many complex and skilled tasks performed by agricultural workers in the nineteenth and early twentieth centuries, such as hand-milking, scything, hedging or thatching hay ricks. Furthermore, in some cases operating the machinery appears to be a much less complex task than the task the machinery replaces. For example, it takes no more than a few afternoons to learn the rudiments of driving a tractor off the public roads, but it takes years to learn how to control heavy agricultural horses effectively. To set against this, however, it can hardly be denied that mechanization and new technology have placed many new demands on the agricultural workforce. Even the simplest repairs to steel machinery, for example, are likely to require welding skills. Applying fertilizers and herbicides at the right time, in the right quantity, and on the right soils and crops, requires considerable expertise. At the same time, the reduction in the size of the farm labour force has meant that farmers and farmworkers now often have to carry out a wider range of tasks than their nineteenth-century predecessors. Where, as so often, a mixed farm now employs no or very little hired labour, the farmer must of necessity combine the formerly separate roles of ploughman, stockman, shepherd, hedger and general labourer. Perhaps the most exacting of the new requirements, however, is the need for farmers to learn to discriminate effectively between the torrent of competing products which manufacturers have made ever more strenuous attempts to persuade them to buy in the postwar period.

While, then, there is some truth in the suggestion that mechanization has led to deskilling, a more accurate statement would be that although mechanization has tended to reduce the significance of manual skills, it made it increasingly important for farmers and farmworkers to have adequate intellectual and knowledge-based skills. For this reason, mechanization was closely associated with a major expansion of agricultural education. Once again, before the Second World War agricultural education had been rudimentary. There were many complaints from farmers and landowners, especially during the agricultural depression of the late nineteenth century, of the lack of agricultural content in the school curriculum, and very little training was available for farmworkers after they had left school (which they characteristically did early). The advent of pervasive mechanization changed this, although there was a time lag. It was only from the 1970s onwards that the educational qualifications of most farmworkers were radically transformed by the establishment of a wider range of specialist agricultural colleges and by the increased provision of specialized agricultural training, mainly in the form of short evening and day-release courses, by further and adult education institutions. While the farm labour force (not excluding farmers) had been one of the most poorly educated elements of society in the mid-twentieth century, this was much less true by the end of the twentieth century. Institutional changes had lagged behind the economic and technological changes which drove them forwards, but they had come nevertheless.

Change has therefore been a dramatic and startling feature of the countryside since the Second World War, but the respects in which the countryside has *not* changed are also very significant. Continuity is perhaps most evident with respect to the physical appearance of the countryside. It is true that there have been some important changes in the rural landscape since 1939. Both urban encroachment and, once again, agricultural mechanization have had effects. Urban encroachment has resulted in new housing being built in many villages, and in the spread of suburbs into what was once open country around cities and larger towns. Agricultural mechanization, as has often been pointed out, led to the rearrangement of fields and farmyards to suit the specifications of the new machinery. But although many fields were amalgamated after 1939, and some were turned into houses, roads, industrial estates or put to other non-agricultural uses, an observer returning to the British countryside after a sixty-year absence would find few features which he or she did not recognize. The basic pattern of fields, hedgerows and outlying farms which dominated the English countryside in the first years of the twenty-first century dates back to the period of parliamentary enclosure in the late eighteenth and early nineteenth centuries, or in those parts of the country where enclosure took place earlier, such as Kent, to even before this. While some crops, such as oilseed rape and linseed, have become more important than they were in the early twentieth century as a result of changing relative prices and EEC/EU policies, the colours of the English countryside remain essentially as they were: a patchwork of green, yellow and brown in the lowlands, and mottled green, brown and purple in the grass and heather uplands. Furthermore, the major landscape features of the English country-side, such as small woods, streams and gentle hills have been modified only modestly since 1939, other than in a few exceptional areas of the countryside where extensive afforestation has taken place, such as Kielder Forest in Northumberland, or where large reservoirs have been built, as at Rutland Water (occupying almost a third of the surface area of England's smallest county). It is true that there has been some change in the balance of different elements constituting the English countryside. The total acreage of hedgerow, woodland, marshland and downland pasture has fallen, while that of arable has risen. The loss of habitats associated with these changes has had serious effects on wildlife which, as we shall see in the next chapter, has prompted environmentalist concern. But the ingredients of the mix from which the English countryside is constituted have hardly changed at all, and even if their relative quantities have altered, this has generally had much more significant consequences with respect to habitat than it has for landscape. The topography and even vegetative cover of the countryside remains to a remarkable degree as it was a hundred or even two hundred years ago.

Even the appearance of the built environment in the countryside, inevitably subject to more intensive pressures and processes of change over a shorter time-scale than the land itself, has altered surprisingly little. Most villages in the year 2000 looked very similar to how they did in 1940. Most have a core of pre-twentieth-century buildings, including a few which stand out visually because of their size or quality, such as a church, manor house, rectory or large farmhouse. These older buildings have almost invariably been carefully conserved. Nor has modern building, in most cases, been allowed to over-whelm older structures. There has, indeed, been significant house building in many villages since 1945, but this has often been relatively discreet. In a high proportion of cases, sensitivity to local architecture has been shown by the use of local building materials and styles. Furthermore, the location of new housing developments in villages has usually been carefully considered. Typic-ally, new housing is based on infill rather than built on fields; new houses are often tucked away behind older houses in positions which intrude little on the visual character of villages. Partly as a result, the basic pattern of streets almost invariably closely resembles, and is indeed in many cases identical with, that of sixty years ago. Since existing villages have been modified with a sometimes almost obsessive eye to their 'historic character', and since the number of entirely new villages built since 1945 has been negligible, most villages are still in the early twenty-first century dominated by the same visual features as they were in the early twentieth century.

In visual and landscape terms, then, the English countryside has in many ways changed remarkably little since the Second World War. The physical continuity of the countryside therefore belies the socio-economic transformation which, as we have seen, has been wrought on it in the same period. To explain the paradox of a countryside which was radically transformed in socio-economic terms, but remained surprisingly unchanged in landscape and land use, we need to invoke the second theme of Hardy's 'In Time of "The Breaking of Nations"': the relationship between image and reality. In particular, we need to understand the pivotal role that urban attitudes to and expectations of the countryside have played in shaping its development in the modern period.

In broad terms we can say that, since the industrial revolution, urban Britain has valued the countryside for two quite different products: food on the one hand, and beauty on the other. It is the relationship between these two requirements that explains much about the history of the modern countryside, especially since the Second World War. With respect to food, urban Britain sought a modern, efficient, highly productive agriculture which would ensure that the nation was adequately fed at low cost. This requirement can be traced back at least as far as the repeal of the corn laws in 1846, when landowners and farmers were forced to sacrifice agricultural protection for the sake of cheap food. Working-class living standards rose only slowly in the first half of the nineteenth century, and an impoverished, hungry and rapidly increasing urban working-class population saw the corn laws as an aristocratic conspiracy to redistribute income away from the urban poor towards the rural wealthy. Middle-class manufacturers often regarded the corn laws as raising the cost of industrial production, since high food prices necessitated higher wages. The repeal of the corn laws established free trade as a powerful cultural symbol of British politics, closely identified with other key concepts such as 'progress' and, in the twentieth century, 'democracy'. Efforts to re-introduce protection, as by the Conservative tariff reformers in the first decade of the twentieth century, were liable to be thwarted by the almost iconic status which free trade had achieved as a distinguishing characteristic of British national identity. This strong bias in favour of low food prices was in some ways reinforced by the depression of the 1930s, when many working-class families in the areas of the country where unemployment was widespread went short of food, and also by the privations of the Second World War and of the period of austerity which followed it.

Yet if urban Britain wanted cheap food, at the same time it also wanted an unchanging, old-fashioned, 'quaint' countryside which would provide city dwellers with a refuge, both in physical reality and in the imagination, from the pressures, limitations and ugliness of the urban industrial world. This cultural tendency was at least as old and every bit as deep-rooted as the concern with cheap food. We have examined some of its sources and components in earlier chapters, noting, for example, the fury with which many writers (especially in the late nineteenth and early twentieth centuries) attacked the intrusion of industry into the countryside. Wordsworth lambasted proposals to build a railway from Kendal to Windermere; Dickens in *Hard Times* pilloried the polluting effects of factories. John Ruskin assaulted the dreariness of London's spreading suburbs in *The Crown of Wild Olive*, while E. M. Forster adopted a more ironic, but equally biting tone in denouncing the northwards creep of the 'red rust' of London into Hertfordshire in *Howards End*. Most uncompromising of all was D. H. Lawrence's fierce critique of the urban landscape as spiritually deadening, a charge repeated in many of his books, but perhaps most graphically in *The Rainbow*.[8]

By the early twentieth century, the beauty and purity of the countryside was, as we have seen, firmly established in contrast to the supposed ugliness and corruption of urban Britain, as one of the dominant motifs of high culture in Britain. The most significant development in the interwar period with respect to attitudes towards the countryside was that this idealization, which had been most obvious and marked among writers, intellectuals and artists in the nineteenth century, more and more filtered down to less culturally elevated levels of society. By 1945 powerful idealizing assumptions about the countryside were probably as important a feature of popular culture as they had already become of high culture. The travails of urban working-class experience in the interwar years, marked by deteriorating slum housing, industrial pollution (including deadly smog in London) and unemployment, contributed to this.

This process of filtering down was apparent in the formation and growth of the organizations aiming at rural preservation and at enhancing access to the countryside which were assessed in the preceding chapters on preservationism and rambling. The Council for the Preservation of Rural England (1926), the Ramblers Association (1935) and the Youth Hostels Association were all established in the interwar period, and all not only reflected the filtering down of idealizing attitudes towards the countryside, but also had the effect of fostering them. At the same time there was also a marked expansion of existing organizations dedicated to the same purposes, as is apparent in the rise in membership of the National Trust and the Commons Preservation Society.

The effects of the two world wars strongly reinforced the diffusion of the idealization of the countryside among the urban population: although 80 per cent of British people lived in towns by 1914, wartime governments in both wars sought to foster patriotism by encouraging citizens to identify with images of rural England. Such images avoided confronting the awkward realities of poverty, class conflict and dissatisfaction with living conditions which would have been evoked by images of the urban scenes in which most people's lives were actually played out. Partly for this reason, almost all wartime posters using the theme of 'Your Britain – Fight for It' were of idyllic rural beauty.[9]

The dual requirement of urban Britain from the countryside for, on the one hand, cheap food, and on the other, untarnished beauty, were reflected in the legislation by which the Labour government, elected in 1945, attempted to define the role of the countryside in the new postwar era. The most important components of this legislation were two Acts of Parliament, both passed in the same year: the Agriculture Act, and the Town and Country Planning Act, both of 1947. While the significance of the former for rural Britain has been widely acknowledged, the latter is less well known. But, especially in conjunction with the Agriculture Act, it was one of the most important pieces of postwar legislation in terms of its effect on the countryside.

Both the 1947 Acts need to be considered in a little more detail. The Agriculture Act was born very much out of the circumstances of the war and of the immediate prewar years. During the war, Britain had come perilously close to starvation through the U-boat threat. The conclusion which many strategists drew was that it had been extremely dangerous to allow British agriculture to decline to the point where it met barely one-third of domestic food consumption, as it did in 1939. For strategic reasons it was essential that a higher proportion of domestic food requirements should be produced at home in the postwar period. This meant that farmers had to be given an assurance that it was in their financial interests to raise output levels.

In addition to the perception of a need for higher incomes to farmers to encourage them to produce more food, there was also a widespread feeling that farmers deserved higher incomes. Prior to the war, farmers' incomes had often been very low – according to some estimates scarcely higher than those of farmworkers in the late 1930s. Yet farmers had made an impressive contribution to the war effort through their participation in the 'plough campaign' whereby the arable acreage and grain harvest had been sharply increased. It was felt that farmers should be rewarded for this by a higher standard of living once the war was over, and that there should be no repetition of the events of the years immediately following the First World War, when government promises to farmers had rapidly evaporated with the collapse of world food prices in 1920 and 1921.

The solution to low farm incomes adopted by the 1947 Agriculture Act was to guarantee farm product prices by means of deficiency payments. Under this arrangement, a price for each farm product would be agreed between representatives of the farmers and of government at an annual price negotiation. If, for a given product, the market price fell below this level, government would compensate producers by paying them the difference between the actual market price and the deficiency price. This payment would go directly to the farmer, so the consumer would pay no more than the world market price.[10]

The deficiency price system shielded farmers from the worst effects of price fluctuations and low prices, but government did not intend to provide farmers with a free hand to produce inefficiently, secure in the knowledge that they would be protected by guaranteed prices. On the contrary, the other side of the coin of deficiency payments was that government expected farmers to make effectively year-on-year productivity improvements. Hence, the government hoped to achieve both higher farm incomes, greater national food self-sufficiency and cheap food, all under the aegis of the same Act.

The second of the twin acts of 1947 was the Town and Country Planning Act. As its name implies, this piece of legislation was, unlike the Agriculture Act, not solely concerned with the countryside. It needs to be seen in the context of the rise in prestige of planning which occurred during the war. The war effort had been highly planned, and had, at least as it seemed at the time, clearly been a resounding success. Furthermore, not only had the outcome of the war vindicated the superior efficiency of planning as a means of co-ordinating economic production and social policy, but this contrasted with the disrepute into which *laissez-faire* economics had fallen as a result of the world depression of the 1930s and of the economic theories associated with J. M. Keynes, which demonstrated that government action could alleviate economic difficulties in certain circumstances. The Town and Country Planning Act was therefore part of a broader vision of a new postwar society in which planning, under the eye of the state and of its adviser-experts, would be the decisive agent of social reconstruction.

Nevertheless, if the name of the Town and Country Planning Act indicates that it was not solely concerned with the countryside, it also shows that the whole problem of planning was conceptualized in terms of the town–country dichotomy.[11] In this, the Act showed the influence of the Scott Committee report of 1942. This highly influential wartime parliamentary committee had argued that the countryside had, in the interwar years, been sacrificed to urban interests in ways which were profoundly damaging to the nation as a whole; the way forward was alleged to be government assistance for agriculture and tighter controls on industrial and urban development to ensure that town and country were kept properly separate in future.[12]

The thrust of the Town and Country Planning Act was very similar to the objectives outlined by the Scott report, with the emphasis falling on the careful preservation of the countryside against the urban threat. The Act therefore formed an 'aesthetic' counterpart to the productionism of the Agriculture Act, with which the former's assumptions resonated. Just as part of the rationale for the Agriculture Act had been the perception that agriculture had been unwisely neglected in the interwar years, so the Town and Country

Planning Act incorporated the assumption that the neglect of agriculture had had damaging consequences for the rural environment. In the 1930s, as the Scott report had emphasized, low farm incomes had led to collapsing farm buildings, fields allowed to run to waste, unkempt hedges, choked-up ditches and other symptoms of the decay of the fabric of rural England. Furthermore, the economic weakness of agriculture and the correspondingly low price of agricultural land were believed to have been in part responsible for the very rapid rate at which rural land had been converted to urban and industrial uses in the interwar years. This loss of rural land, and decay of the infrastructure of the countryside, was seen as damaging not only to agriculture, but at a more fundamental level to national identity itself. By putting agriculture back on its feet through the Agriculture Act, one source of the problem had, it was believed, been remedied. What the Town and Country Planning Act attempted to do was to avert, or at least control, the other danger: urban or industrial take-over. Hence the Town and Country Planning Act specified that agricultural land was to be considered as primarily earmarked for agricultural uses; it was to be built over only in exceptional circumstances. Tight controls were imposed on urban development and expansion, but in contrast to these tight controls on urban activities, agriculture was not subject to planning controls. The framers of the Town and Country Planning Act, in common with the majority of the Scott Committee, identified rural Britain with agricultural Britain.

Agriculture was thus given very favourable treatment by the first postwar Labour government. One of the paradoxes of twentieth-century British rural history is that it was in general the Labour Party, both in theory and in practice, which courted farmers most assiduously, yet since at least the 1920s in most parts of the country farmers have persistently voted Conservative, despite the increasing hostility of the Thatcher government to public subsidies in the 1980s.[13]

The two 1947 Acts set a framework for rural Britain which in some respects endures to the time of writing. It is true that the entry of Britain into the European Economic Community (as it was in 1973 when Britain joined) significantly altered the way in which farm incomes were supported. The EEC relied upon tariff barriers and price support (i.e. the purchase of large quantities of a given farm product once it had fallen below its 'intervention price', in order to drive the price back up to the intervention level) to maintain farm incomes, a system which placed the burden of farm support on to consumers rather than tax-payers (in the main). But the basic principle that the community as a whole should ensure farmers a decent living standard, independent of fluctuations in market prices, was maintained. Similarly, although the Town and Country Planning Act has been amended many times, its basic principle of protecting agricultural land in particular, and the countryside in general, from urban and industrial intrusion, has survived.

It is as a result of the regime established by the two 1947 Acts that the paradox of socio-economic transformation and yet visual stasis derives. The price squeeze by which, under the Agriculture Act and its successor the Common Agricultural Policy, government authorities have sought to reduce the cost of food and of the intervention bill led directly to the imperative to raise productivity and hence to agricultural mechanization and capital intensification, with all the consequences already described. The Town and Country Planning Act was equally effective in achieving its different aims. The tight control on non-agricultural building and industrial development in the countryside introduced by the Act was the main factor responsible for the 'freezing' of the appearance of the countryside, and the predominance of agriculture in rural land use characteristic of the postwar countryside. In other countries, where the planning regime has been less strict or less antipathetic to urban intrusions into the countryside, the results have been very different (for example in many parts of the USA and in Australia).

Although the legislation of 1947 established a powerful and long-lasting framework for British agriculture and the countryside, it was a framework ultimately based on an illusion: that the countryside could be radically modernized and yet remain an unchanging refuge from modernity at the same time. For this illusion to be sustained, it was necessary for urban and rural to remain separate, so that people with urban backgrounds who subscribed to the myth of a traditional, idyllic countryside would not be brought into direct contact with the radical forces of modernization at work beneath the relatively unchanging visual appearance of the countryside. This condition was progressively undermined almost from the outset by the migration from the towns to the countryside which was, in part, a consequence of this very illusion.

Migration to the countryside began to affect the home counties from the late nineteenth century, with the development of an extended suburban railway network which reached out into the Kent, Surrey, Berkshire, Buckinghamshire and Hertfordshire countryside. This remained on a small scale until the 1930s. Outside the home counties, migration to the countryside became a significant trend only after 1945. Population totals give some indication of the scale of the outflow from the cities since then, however. In 1951 there were 10.4 million people in the administratively rural districts of England, Wales and Northern Ireland, and the county districts of Scotland. This represented only 20 per cent of the national total. But by 1971 the corresponding figures were 12.8 million and 23 per cent. By 2001 over 14 million people were living in the English countryside, representing 28 per cent of the national total. These figures can only to a very limited extent be attributed to natural increase, which, although briefly high in the late 1940s and again in the 1960s, has slowed to a trickle since then. Overwhelmingly the most important cause of rural population growth in the second half of the twentieth century was in-migration. This consisted of two main components: urban decentralization, and retirement migration. Of these, the first was more important.

Urban decentralization has been a phenomenon affecting all British cities since about 1960, but it affected the largest centres from before that date. The population of Greater London, for example, peaked at 8.6 million in 1939. Urban decentralization can be understood in terms of the development of Metropolitan Economic Labour Areas (MELAs). A MELA consists of a densely populated urban core, an inner commuting ring in which a high proportion of the employed population commutes to work in the urban core, and an outer commuting ring in which only a small proportion of the employed population commutes to work in the urban core. Each large city or town can be thought of as possessing a MELA. Geographical mobility improved in the second half of the twentieth century, mainly through the provision of better roads such as the linking up of the motorway network in the 1960s and through the wider distribution of car ownership. As mobility has improved, so the physical size of the inner and outer rings of each MELA has expanded. As a result, by the 1980s virtually the whole of lowland England was within the urban system as defined by MELAs. However, urban decentralization has advanced in a wave-like motion. It affected the most populous centres first, in a period in which the smaller centres were still centralizing. Later it affected the medium-sized and finally the smaller centres, by which time decentralization from the largest centres was already slowing down.[14]

The second main component of rural in-migration other than commuting has been retirement migration, which in many ways is a simpler phenomenon. While the distribution of commuter migration is highly complex and is related to factors such as centres of employment and the characteristics of local transport networks, retirement migration is to a greater extent a 'one-way' process, rather than an interactive one. Elderly people seem to have a preference for retiring to areas which are rural, coastal and warm. The south-west (especially Devon and Cornwall), the south coast, Wales and East Anglia have, unsurprisingly in view of this structure of preferences, been the most favoured regions.

The rural population has, as we have seen, grown in total since the Second World War. This pattern of overall growth conceals marked variations from region to region and village to village. In the most remote areas of Britain, depopulation continued for several decades after 1945, essentially for the same reasons that depopulation had occurred in the interwar years: the lack of employment opportunities in agriculture, the low wages and incomes, and the lack of services and facilities in comparison with those offered by even modest-sized towns. However, some of the factors contributing to the outflow of population from Britain's remote rural regions in the early postwar years were actually intensified by developments in these years as compared to the interwar situation. The dominance of urban culture, especially as manifested through television, became almost total in the 1950s and 1960s, while the collapse of the agricultural community through rural depopulation meant that living in the remoter rural areas, such as northern Northumberland or the central Pennines, no longer meant accepting merely a more limited rural culture in place of a more varied urban one, but accepting exclusion from national culture as a whole. To a disproportionate extent, it was young people who continued to leave the remote rural regions, and to a lesser degree even many of the more accessible regions. The outflow of young people to the cities had important implications for the age structure of rural communities, especially in view of the steep decline in the average number of children per family. The countryside developed an increasingly unbalanced age structure, dominated by older people. This created difficulties in the provision of some services, particularly education, where the small numbers of children in many villages made it inefficient to continue to provide schooling at the village level and led to the closure of many local primary schools in rural Britain.[15]

The main growth in the rural population occurred initially in the more accessible regions, especially the south-east of England. It gradually spread outwards as the accessibility of the more distant regions increased. The growth of the south-west became particularly striking in the 1970s, while East Anglia, a region which until the last two decades of the twentieth century had a surprisingly poor transport infrastructure in view of its unchallenging topography and proximity to London, grew especially rapidly in the 1980s and 1990s (partly due to motorway development and to the electrification of the London to Norwich railway line).

By the end of the twentieth century, however, the process of rural repopulation had extended so far that virtually all rural areas, even some of the most remote, are gaining population again. While for much of rural Britain, and especially rural England, this is in large part due to the expansion of MELAs attendant on an improved transport system, the most remote rural areas still lie outside the range of normal commuting. In these areas it is the influence of retirement migration, and to a lesser extent the purchase of second homes by the affluent, which has been the primary force contributing to the reversal of depopulation. Very few of the new inhabitants of Ross and Cromarty or Cornwall, for example, travel to work in a major urban centre, but many retired people find these areas attractive precisely because of their remoteness and presumed rural tranquillity.

If different rural regions have experienced differing patterns of in-migration, there have also been significant differences between one village and another. These differences too are in part related to relative accessibility. In general, villages with good transport links (such as direct road routes or a bus service) to nearby towns grew more rapidly than neighbouring villages with poorer links in the post-1945 period. The situation was complicated by three further factors: the aesthetic character of the village, the size of the village, and local and national planning policy. One of the most influential studies of urban–rural migration in postwar Britain was conducted by Ray Pahl. Pahl's study of mid-Hertfordshire drew particular attention to the difference which the aesthetic character of a village made to its capacity to attract in-migrants. Villages with thatched cottages and a medieval church were more likely than those with few picturesque buildings to attract commuters or retirement migrants. Size was also important: larger villages were more attractive because they tended to support a greater number and variety of services. Planning policy reinforced this effect by encouraging the growth of villages which already had a substantial population (the so-called 'key village' concept). This was largely for economic reasons. It was less expensive for councils to provide services to a small number of large villages than to a large number of small villages; and economies of scale would allow a better quality of services to be provided in large villages too.[16]

Part of the reason for the flow of migrants from urban to rural areas in the second half of the twentieth century was, as has been indicated, that a much improved transport network and enhanced levels of personal mobility as a result of the diffusion of car ownership made commuting feasible on a large scale in a way it had not been in the interwar years. This was especially significant in view of the growth of employment opportunities in medium-sized provincial towns such as Newbury, Huntingdon and Chelmsford and in the New Towns such as Harlow and Telford. Because of the limited size of these towns, their travel-to-work areas included an extensive rural hinterland. Another important development was the major improvement in the extent and quality of rural services after the Second World War. Prior to the war many villages lacked electricity and even mains water and sewerage, but by the 1970s very few villages lacked these amenities. However, improved transport, the relocation of employment and improved services were in the main enabling rather than motivating factors: they represented a reduction in the relative disadvantage of the countryside, rather than a positive attraction in their own terms. What made people actually want to live in the countryside rather than in a town? In the early postwar years, the cost of housing was one significant factor. But especially from the 1970s onwards, the price differential between rural and urban property narrowed rapidly and in many parts of the country even swung in favour of the latter. Increasingly, the positive attraction which drew so many urban residents to move to rural areas was the idealized view of the countryside as beautiful, unspoiled, peaceful and a refuge from modernity which had previously informed the 1947 Town and Country Planning Act.

This idealized view was clearly far from being an accurate perception of rural life even in 1947. Yet, perversely, the more commuters and retirees that arrived in the countryside seeking the rural idyll, the further from reality the idyll became. Rural in-migration resulted in major conflict between idealized expectations and the often dissonant and incompatible realities which increasingly obtruded on them. Because the rural newcomers were above all concerned with the countryside as a landscape, rather than (in the main) as a place where people lived and worked, the conflict between long-standing inhabitants, who usually had connections to and sympathies with agriculture, and the newcomers, who were usually economically detached from agriculture, became increasingly focused on environmental issues. As we shall see when we examine this conflict in more detail in the following chapter, developments in farming technology and practices in the post-Second World War period had intensified the inherent but hitherto largely unacknowledged conflict between agriculture and the environment to the point where the interests of the one seemed to stand in stark opposition to those of the other.

. . . .

CHAPTER 14

Agriculture and the Environment

§ THE assumption that the interests of agriculture and of the countryside were one and the same, embodied in the Scott report and the legislation of 1947, was increasingly challenged from the 1960s onwards on environmental grounds. By the end of the century the environmentalist critique had not only largely displaced the pro-agriculture consensus of the early postwar years in the public mind, but seemed to have attained an ascendancy over producer interests even within policy-making circles. Nevertheless, it was becoming increasingly apparent that the hegemonic claims of the environmentalist version of 'the countryside' were no less contentious and socially inflected than the productionist values they sought to supersede.

The awakening of public concern about the effects of modern agriculture on the environment is often attributed to Rachel Carson's *Silent Spring*, published in 1962. But this is a simplification of a more complex and in certain respects uncomfortable history. As we saw in Chapter 11, organicist and environmentalist thought flourished in the interwar period, even though it remained on the margins of British intellectual life. But the close links between some of the organicists and fascism served to diminish their influence. Furthermore, much of the emotional force of organicism came from the economic context of the 1920s and 1930s. An agriculture visibly brought to its knees by international trade and a depressed world market could plausibly be described as the victim of an international financial and industrial system. But the organic movement's attempts to claim the mantle of champion of agriculture were disputed by the planner-preservationists, and the circumstances of the postwar years allowed the latter to attain an unchallengeable ascendancy in the late 1940s and 1950s. The significance of *Silent Spring* is that it marks a new phase of rural environmentalism, in which many of the old arguments were redeployed, but shorn of their embarrassing far-right associations, and with the aim of reaching a wider populist constituency.[1]

Even in this context, the effects of *Silent Spring* should not be exaggerated. Carson's book was almost exclusively concerned with the effects of agricultural pesticides, in particular DDT. She demonstrated vividly how these entered the food chain and posed a danger not only to the survival of top carnivores such as birds of prey, but potentially also to human health. The public response to Carson focused sharply on this pesticides issue and did not initially develop into a generalized concern over the relationship between modern agriculture and the environment *tout court*. On the contrary, in Britain at least, farmers continued to be held in high esteem. This was partly because of the continuing sense that they had been unfairly and unwisely neglected in the period before the war, and because of public gratitude for the heroic efforts made by agriculture to expand domestic food output during the war. A more pragmatic and immediate reason for continuing to value farmers and admire their success in raising production was the ongoing contribution agriculture made to easing postwar Britain's chronic balance of payments problems. The oil crisis of the early 1970s and the prospect of world commodity shortages contributed to prolonging the currency of this perspective. It was only in the 1980s that concern about the total impact of modern farming practices on the country-side became widespread, and if a single book is to be picked out as marking the onset of environmentalism as a force affecting the character of the English countryside, Marion Shoard's *The Theft of the Countryside* (1980) is a more persuasive candidate than *Silent Spring*. Certainly, since the early 1980s farming in Britain has been under ever more intense scrutiny from an expanding and increasingly active environmentalist movement.[2]

The core of the environmentalist critique of postwar British agriculture is that since the Second World War British farmers, aided and abetted by the Ministry of Agriculture, have pursued the goal of increasing production irrespective of all other considerations, and in particular of the environmental cost of so doing. Lured by the promise of the guaranteed prices and production grants offered by MAFF and, after 1973, by the protectionism of the Common Agricultural Policy, farmers have progressively sought production gains at both the extensive and intensive margins. At the extensive margin, farmers have brought new land into use, or upgraded the use of existing agricultural land, by draining marshland, ploughing up moorland, grubbing up woods, and, in some instances, reclaiming land from the sea. This has incurred much criticism from environmentalists for its effects on wildlife and landscape. Many of the habitats threatened by land improvement were, or were becoming, nationally rare and harboured some of Britain's rarest plant and animal life. The Halvergate Marshes in Norfolk, for example, were the subject of a major confrontation between environmentalists and farmers in the 1980s. The farmers wanted to drain the marshes, but they sheltered endangered indigenous species such as bitterns, swallowtail butterflies and marsh sowthistle. More common habitats such as woodland were of course less rich in rare species than marshes like Halvergate, but were important for the diversity of wildlife species they contained, which far exceeded that of the farmland into which farmers sometimes sought to convert them. Nor was wildlife the only environmental asset threatened by agricultural land reclamation schemes. Even more contentious than the Halvergate Marshes dispute was the battle to save Exmoor the plough. The scenic qualities of moorland proved to be as highly cherished as the wildlife importance of marshes. But although the direct threat to the landscape of the moors or the wildlife of the marshes came from the farmers who initiated attempts to reclaim them, environmentalists reserved their most bitter criticism for the Ministry of Agriculture, whose grants encouraged and paid for much of the alleged destruction.[3]

If reclamation at the extensive margin prompted environmentalist concern, so to an at least equal degree did agriculture's efforts to raise output at the intensive margin by increasing capital inputs. Improvements in technology and scientific understanding reduced the real cost of capital inputs after the war, while government subsidies on building and equipment had a similar effect. One of the major consequences of the increased application of capital to agriculture was a much accelerated tendency towards specialization. Farmers who had invested in expensive items of equipment such as combine harvesters were anxious to obtain the best value from them by using them over as large an area of their farms as possible. In this way economies of scale could be achieved. Specialization maximized the productivity gains which mechanization made possible. The large arable farms of East Anglia were only one example. Specialization made equal inroads into other types of agriculture such as dairy farming and egg or broiler chicken production. It was, however, in lowland farms that these processes occurred most fully; capital investment in upland farms has been more limited and specialization has proceeded more slowly.[4]

One of the consequences of specialization has been a steep decline in the old system of mixed farming. Mixed farming was, at least according to many environmentalist critics, in harmony with the environment, because it depended on the recycling of nutrients. Fodder crops were grown to feed animals over the winter; these animals were then folded or depastured on the land which grew the crops; and the manure dropped on the land restored fertility to it. In this idealized version of the mixed farming system, only endogenous resources were used, and all waste products were recycled within the system. Specialized farming, by contrast, relies on importing exogenous resources into the system, and typically produces unused waste products. Arable farming, for example, imports off-farm chemical fertilizers and produces unused straw; specialized dairy farming imports processed feedstuffs and produces large quantities of sewage.

A highly contentious aspect of this process of agricultural specialization and of the attendant shift from endogenous to exogenous resource-use has been that, for the first time in history, farming has allegedly become a net user of energy rather than a producer. This allegation caused particular concern in the context of growing awareness that the world's energy supplies were being depleted at a potentially unsustainable rate, particularly in view of the fact that agriculture is overwhelmingly the greatest renewable source of energy available to mankind, through the photosynthetic conversion of sunlight into plantstuffs. This feature of postwar farming has been criticized not only on the grounds that it is intrinsically at odds with good environmental management, but because the greater use of exogenous resources has been implicated in rising levels of agricultural pollution. The damaging effects of some pesticides and herbicides on the food chain were already well-known by the 1980s, but a newer concern was with nitrates from chemical fertilizers leaching from soil into watercourses. This, it was argued, led to eutrophication, whereby high levels of algal growth in rivers, streams, lakes and ponds choked off oxygen availability and killed fish and invertebrates. Sewage and silage effluent from dairy farming had, it was alleged, similar effects.

It has also been claimed that the increased use of manufactured off-farm inputs has had a damaging effect on food safety. Concerns were raised about pesticide sprays used on fruit in the 1980s, and about hormone injections to stimulate cattle growth. More recently these anxieties have been put into the shade by the BSE (Bovine Spongiform Encephalitis) epidemic. This devastated the British herd, resulting in the slaughter of millions of affected cattle and in the loss of billions of pounds to agriculture, because of the reported link between BSE and the fatal and incurable human disease Creutzfeld-Jacob Disease (CJD).

Not only does specialization result in a less environmentally balanced form of production, but it also often has two other environmentally undesirable side-effects. First, it tends to result in monoculture, as a direct consequence of the shift away from the complex, multiple land uses of mixed farming to the simpler pattern required by specialized agriculture. Monoculture is detrimental to wildlife, as most species require a range of habitat in order to flourish. It also produces a 'prairie-like' landscape which is often regarded as aesthetically inferior. Arable monoculture was subjected to the fiercest criticism, because it supports a particularly limited range of wildlife and creates a quasi-uniform landscape.[5] Environmentalists have pointed out that postwar guaranteed prices, and the greater scope for cost-reducing economies of scale within arable, have maintained the arable sector at a level far higher than in the prewar period. Second, specialization tends to be associated with an increase in physical size in order to maximize the economies of scale it offers. Examples are the larger fields, grain silos and straw bales of specialized arable and the larger broiler houses of specialized poultry production. This increase in scale can sometimes be damaging to wildlife and is often visually intrusive.

Specialization and its associated economies of scale have resulted in remarkable gains in efficiency for farmers since the 1940s, especially in arable and milk production. Government has sought to promote this through a 'price squeeze', whereby real unit prices have been progressively lowered over time. One of the further effects of the price squeeze was that it put pressure on livestock farmers to cut costs by maximizing animal stocking rates (i.e. the number of animals kept per acre) and throughput (i.e. the length of time between purchase and disposal of each individual animal). Stocking rates have been raised by increasing purchased inputs such as oilcakes for feeding cattle, and by shifting to 'battery'-type production, which proved especially adaptable to poultry, pigs and calves. Throughput was improved mainly by slaughtering animals at an earlier age, notably in the case of veal calves and poultry. But the attempt to intensify livestock production by raising stocking rates and throughput generated increasing animal welfare concerns in the 1980s. Subsequently these concerns have extended to cover previously unquestioned aspects of farming such as live animal exports.[6]

The main thrust of environmentalist criticism of modern agriculture, however, at least in Europe, has been directed not so much at farmers themselves as at the government agencies which have steered farmers towards environmentally destructive practices. In Britain, it has been the Ministry of Agriculture's guaranteed prices and production grants under the 1947 Agriculture Act, and after 1973 the effects of CAP membership, which have been chiefly criticized, on the grounds that by these means the state has created the conditions which have led to the noxious developments outlined above.

A further criticism which relates more exclusively to the role of the state and less to farming practice has also been made. This is that the efforts of the state to promote conservation have been half-hearted and relatively ineffective; and that agricultural policy and conservation policy have worked against each other. Because the agricultural lobby has until recently been vastly more influential both inside and outside government, for most of the period since the Second World War agricultural policy dominated and to a certain extent negated conservation policy.

To understand this criticism we need to consider the evolution of conservation policy in Britain. As with agricultural policy, legislation passed in the immediate postwar years established the foundations of policies which endured with only relatively minor changes until the 1990s. The crucial act was the National Parks Act of 1949, which established National Parks and the National Parks Commission. The genesis of the National Parks Act and its recreational (as opposed to environmental) consequences are assessed in more detail in the next chapter. This act was intended to complement the 1947 Agriculture Act and the Town and Country Planning Act of the same year in establishing a framework for the future of the English countryside. But the

1949 Act was always very much the poor relation of the other two. Local authorities, endowed with control over planning under the Town and Country Planning Act, lobbied successfully to retain their full planning powers even over areas designated for inclusion in National Parks. As a result, the National Parks Commission was deprived of control over planning in the National Parks from its inception. In the event, the National Parks Commission was in fact left essentially as a purely advisory body, with no executive powers of its own at all. The National Parks themselves were widely regarded as successful within their own terms, and some environmentalists have seen them as a useful model on which further conservation legislation could be based. But it has often been pointed out that they are highly skewed both in terms of their geographical position and of the landscape types they exemplify. With the exception of the recently created Norfolk Broads National Park, all are located in the north or west of England and Wales, and all consist predominantly of upland terrain. Partly because of this skewed distribution, almost all the land within the National Parks is of low agricultural value and so is less exposed to the effects of agricultural intensification. Where there has been a major clash between agricultural and preservationist interests, National Park status has often proved of limited effectiveness in preventing a change of land use, partly because agricultural interests have had a dominant position on many local authority land management committees. The most notorious case was probably Exmoor, where National Park status did little to check the destruction of up to a third of the area of moorland within the National Park boundaries between the end of the war and the 1980s. But Exmoor was unusual in being a western upland area which nevertheless had significant potential for agricultural improvement. The more serious criticism of the value of the National Parks in protecting natural habitat and landscape is that they do nothing to protect the areas of the country which are in fact far more vulnerable to modern farming: the southern and eastern lowlands.[7]

In addition to creating National Parks, the 1949 Act also set up the Nature Conservancy (now English Nature), which was empowered to establish a core of National Nature Reserves. Again, these have been quite successful in their own terms, but have been criticized for representing a misconceived approach to nature conservation. Many bird and animal species are dependent on large feeding areas, and it has been argued that if these disappear, nature reserves, even of generous proportions, can do little to maintain the viability of natural populations.

The least successful innovation of the 1949 Act, at least from the point of view of habitat conservation, was probably the creation of Areas of Outstanding Natural Beauty (AONBs). These were intended to provide a grade of protection one step lower than that offered by National Parks. But AONBs have been largely ineffective in preventing habitat loss, partly because of their low public profile and the limited powers and restrictions associated with them. A good example of the failure of AONBs to protect valued habitats is the Berkshire Downs AONB. The 'traditional' character of the high downland was defined by sheep pasture with low fertility and high plant biodiversity, but much of the remaining unimproved grassland was either ploughed up or enriched with artificial fertilizers after 1947.[8]

Conservation legislation between 1947 and the 1980s is often regarded as having done little to improve the situation. The 1968 Countryside Act (which created the Countryside Commission) was more concerned with increasing access to the countryside than protecting it; while the 1981 Wildlife and Countryside Act was widely regarded as a great missed opportunity, institutionalizing a voluntary system of landscape and habitat protection that had already been shown to be ineffective.

These, then, have been the leading features of the environmentalist critique of modern agriculture and of its relationship to conservation policy. This critique has been increasingly influential. At the same time it has become apparent that the environmentalist case is by no means as coherent or unproblematic as some of its adherents might like to believe. Rural environmentalism needs to be carefully assessed, by setting it in an appropriate historical perspective, by testing its coherence in terms of policy recommendations, and by considering its social provenance and political implications.

The historical perspective that many environmentalist critics of agriculture adopt is predicated on a comparison of the present-day countryside with that of the period immediately before the Second World War. This, however, is an arbitrary and even misleading comparison. The late 1930s were the end of a period of seventy years of almost continuous agricultural depression, in which there had been a marked reduction in the intensity of exploitation and in which the margin of cultivation had retreated. By the late 1930s wildlife was probably more plentiful and the landscape more 'natural' than it had been since the first half of the nineteenth century or before. The contrast with the impoverished flora and fauna of the countryside of the early twenty-first century is considerable. But if the early 1870s rather than the late 1930s were taken as the benchmark, the contrasts between the present situation and the era before modern agricultural technology would be less marked. The 1870s were the last years of the 'high farming' era which had seen massive investment in agricultural infrastructure and a high level of expenditure on variable capital (such as fertilizers). Wildlife was less abundant and the landscape more tamed in the early 1870s than in the 1930s. This suggests that the bleak monodirectional schema adopted by most environmentalist critiques of agriculture may be unrealistic. It could be argued that it is more appropriate to see an alternation between periods in which agriculture has exerted strong pressure on the environment and periods in which it has exerted less pressure, corresponding to periods of high and low prices. Periods of high prices and pressure since the late eighteenth century included the Napoleonic wars, the 'golden age' of the third quarter of the nineteenth century, and the years between the Second World War and the 1990s; while periods of low prices and pressure occurred in the second quarter of the nineteenth century and during the long agricultural depression from the 1870s to the 1930s, interrupted only by the higher prices during the First World War and its aftermath.[9]

It is, of course, only a broad rule of thumb that high prices produce high pressure. One of the effects of the high prices of the Napoleonic wars, for example, was to stimulate enclosure, which led to the proliferation of hedgerows and was at least in that respect beneficial for wildlife. But in general the relationship between farm product prices and pressure on the environment is likely to hold good. When prices are high, farmers will want to utilize land as intensively as possible and to drive out natural plant and animal species which compete with the farmed plants or animals. To some extent, therefore, the unidirectional catastrophism of rural environmentalism is based on a historically short-sighted view. It could even be argued that, seen in a longer historical perspective, what has happened since the Second World War is simply one of the periodic upswings in the intensiveness of cultivation to which agriculture is subject.

A closer examination of the policy recommendations which can arise from an environmentalist perspective also suggests that some of the more totalizing claims of rural environmentalism require critical interrogation. Broadly speaking, rural environmentalism can be considered as being concerned with three different (although overlapping) types of conservation: landscape conservation, wildlife conservation and resource conservation. The difficulty is that these three types of conservation frequently conflict. For example: rubbish dumps, sewage farms, concrete reservoirs and motorways are all generally considered to be blots on the landscape, but the first three provide feeding or resting sites for some of Britain's rarest birds, while the verges of motorways are exceptionally rich in wildflowers. Similarly, the intermittently proposed Severn Barrage would be a catastrophe for wildlife in the area, but at the same time would massively reduce fossil fuel consumption. Wildlife conservation can therefore conflict with both landscape and resource conservation. Conflicts between the latter are not infrequent either, one of the most controversial examples in recent years being windfarms. These generate energy in a way that conserves resources, but they have also been bitterly attacked in the name of environmentalism as a form of 'visual pollution'.

Further complexities are introduced when we attempt to define the meaning of each kind of conservation. The question of what constitutes a desirable landscape is, for example, highly subjective. To a fell walker, a hill covered by purple heather in bloom might epitomize landscape beauty, but to many farmers the same hill might appear more beautiful if carrying a fine crop of wheat. Nature conservation might at first glance appear less subjective, but immediately questions arise about the relationship between nature and humanity. Since at least in Britain all habitats have evolved in the context of greater or lesser degrees of human intervention over several thousand years, most ecosystems are products of human intervention and management. On what grounds should one be preferred to another? Subjective considerations soon re-enter the debate.

More complex is the question of resource conservation, since the concept of sustainable agriculture, which lies at the heart of the idea of resource conservation in rural areas, has become a major topic of debate. One of the difficulties with sustainability as a concept for evaluating agricultural systems is that its meaning is unclear. A narrow definition would be that a sustainable system must a closed one, in the sense of functioning essentially without exogenous inputs. A broader definition would be a system which is indefinitely sustainable given a continued supply of exogenous inputs. The difficulty with the narrow definition is that the last time English agriculture was sustainable in this sense was probably in the 1840s. The quantum leap in agricultural productivity since that time has been almost entirely a consequence of exogenous inputs, and few if any policy-makers are prepared to contemplate a reversion to the levels of agricultural productivity characteristic of the first half of the nineteenth century. More plausible is the broad definition of agricultural sustainability, but it is unclear that there has ever been a time when English agriculture has been unsustainable in this second sense. It is true that there are valid concerns about the effects of some modern agricultural practices on soil fertility, as for example the damage to soil structure caused by heavy equipment, or the shrinking of drained fenland through the drying out of peat. But these concerns are peripheral and localized, and hardly present a major long-term threat to the productivity of English agriculture. Truly unsustainable agricultural practices, like those which caused the 'dustbowl' in the American Mid-West in the 1920s and 1930s, were not an important feature of English agriculture in the nineteenth and twentieth centuries.

In attempting to understand the rise of rural environmentalism, and to assess the validity of its critique of modern agriculture, we need to consider not only the arguments themselves, but also their social genesis. From this point of view, the most important dimension is the close relationship between rural environmentalism and the great internal migration of middle-class commuters and retirees into the countryside since the Second World War ('counterurbanization'). Counterurbanization occurred at least in part because those who moved to the countryside had a vision of the countryside as embodying distinctive rural characteristics which were absent in urban Britain. Once settled in the countryside, these ex-urban migrants have, quite naturally, been determined to keep the countryside as close to their vision as possible, not only because that was why they moved there in the first place, but also because as home owners they now have a vested interest in maintaining the attractiveness of the countryside to potential purchasers of the same ilk as themselves.

These newcomers have rarely been a merely passive presence in the countryside to which they have moved. Characteristically, migrants to the countryside since the Second World War have been wealthier, better educated, more articulate and more used to wielding influence than the existing rural inhabitants. By the 1990s ex-urban immigrants were also often in a numerical majority in the villages they had moved to. They were able to use their increasing political muscle to impose their view of the countryside on other residents, notably those employed in agriculture. This has often been to the detriment of the interests of farmers, who may have been prevented from removing unwanted hedgerows, operating noisy agricultural machinery at night, and so forth, and still more so of agricultural workers, who have suffered from the prevention of industrial and housing development in the countryside.[10]

The environmentalist critique of modern agriculture therefore, inevitably, incorporates a selective view of what the countryside should be like. It is a view which militates in favour of the interests of one particular group in rural society but, to a greater or lesser degree, conflicts with those of other groups. As such, it has acted as a source of division in rural communities.

It is, therefore, essential to put the environmentalist critique of postwar agriculture into its historical, policy and social contexts. This may lead us to regard environmentalism as one voice among many rural voices deserving to be heard. It should not, however, lead us to deny the importance of the environmentalist viewpoint. While it is true that there is a price-related alternation in the intensity with which agricultural land is cultivated, environmentalists make a legitimate point in arguing that the current phase of intensification has gone well beyond the furthest point ever reached before. So it behoves us to assess the environmental implications of future efforts to increase food output with more care than was sometimes taken in the past. Ironically, it is possible that the end of the current phase of agricultural intensification may already be in sight, if the emergent trend within the Common Agricultural Policy towards lower-intensity farming develops and persists.

. . . .

CHAPTER 15

Recreation in the Countryside Since the Second World War

§ IN this chapter we are in general concerned not with any and every recreational activity that took place in the countryside, but with those forms of recreation of which the countryside was an essential component. Many forms of recreation take place in the countryside purely because the people who engage in them live in rural areas. There is little, for example, which is specifically rural in watching television in a country cottage, or even about playing football on a village football pitch. Such activities have little significance in terms of understanding the evolution of attitudes to the countryside in the second half of the twentieth century. The forms of recreation with which we are concerned are those which are distinctive to the countryside. These activities are, of course, to a very large extent engaged in by people who live in towns.

The pattern of rural recreation since the end of the Second World War falls into two main periods. Between 1945 and the early 1970s there was a vigorous expansion of demand for rural recreation. More and more people wanted to visit the countryside for car-touring, picnics, walking, visiting country houses and a host of other activities. This rise in demand, and in the number of people making use of the countryside, was in large part a consequence of the very great improvement in mobility resulting from the diffusion of car owner-ship in the 1950s and 1960s. Other factors were, however, also at work. Population levels rose quite significantly between 1945 and 1970. At the same time, average income increased as a result of the sustained economic prosperity of the third quarter of the twentieth century. Higher incomes were associated with shorter working hours, so most people had both more money and more time to spend on leisure by the 1960s than they had before the war. Particularly important was the shift from a five-and-a-half-day week to a five-day week, making possible the emergence of the 'weekend' as a leisure phenomenon.

By the early 1970s planners and leisure specialists were becoming aware of the scale of the transformation of rural recreation which had occurred, and of many of the characteristic forms it was taking. This led (by extrapolation from contemporary trends) to predictions of a huge expansion in the demand for rural leisure by the end of the twentieth century, but while rural recreation continued to enjoy wide popularity in the years after the early 1970s, the predictions of a manifold rise in demand have not been realized. This seems to have been largely because the economic factors which facilitated the upsurge of rural leisure in the 1950s and 1960s have not been sustained in the subsequent period. Economic growth faltered after 1973, and, perhaps partly in consequence, population growth did too. Inequality increased, with the poorest fifth of British society registering very limited gains in real incomes between 1973 and 2000, with consequences for the continuing broadening of the demand for rural recreation. For many, the length of the working week increased, resulting in less available leisure time, while many others experienced unemployment, which was correlated with a reduced participation in most leisure activities.[1]

One of the most striking features of rural leisure after the Second World War was the remarkable extent to which it was car-based. This was perhaps especially true of the first half of the period. In these years most people who sought rural recreation not only arrived at their destination by car, but appear to have regarded the journey itself as an integral part of their leisure enjoyment. Often circuitous routes were followed, allowing for a longer journeys, with different scenery on the two legs of the journey. Once people arrived at their destination, they often chose to stay in their cars rather than get out and walk somewhere else. This was particularly true of older people. The car appears to have been regarded as an extension of the home, which could be driven out into attractive countryside and parked for the admiration of the view and the setting. Where people did get out of the car, it was often only to use the immediately surrounding area for a picnic, sunbathing or some similar use (it has been suggested that if the car can be regarded as an extension of the home in such circumstances, the area around the parked car was analogous to the garden). The emphasis on relatively modest forms of recreation, notably picnics, which could be enjoyed in or in the immediate vicinity of a parked car, was characteristic of rural recreation in the 1950s and 1960s. To some extent rural recreation has become more ambitious, varied and less closely tied to the car in the last quarter of the twentieth century, although the car has retained its pre-eminence as overwhelmingly the most important means of access to the countryside. But for car owners of the 1970s, 1980s and 1990s a number of factors came together to reduce the significance of the car as an object of leisure, rather than merely a means of reaching another leisure goal. Probably the most important of these was the increased level of traffic on rural roads, itself ironically in part a result of the popularity of motoring as a form of rural recreation. As traffic levels increased, driving became a more demanding and less enjoyable activity, often entailing the frustration and discomfort of long queues in hot weather (particularly in the case of car tours through rural beauty spots in summer, which had been among the most popular forms of rural recreation in the 1950s and 1960s). To some degree, it was probably also the case that the enthusiasm for the car as an object of leisure consumption decreased as car ownership itself became less novel. Many car owners in the 1950s and even the 1960s were not only first-time owners, but belonged to social strata which before the war had never expected or in some instances even aspired to own a car.

This mobility-based flood of day-trippers into the countryside directly occasioned one of the chief features of post-Second World War rural recreation planning: the fear that an explosion of demand for rural recreation was underway or was imminent. Planners were anxious that a huge and putatively ongoing rise in the number of visitors to rural Britain would swamp the countryside, destroying the characteristics of solitude, landscape distinctiveness and beauty, and rich flora and fauna for which it was valued. One of the consequences of this fear has been that rural recreation planning has been persistently cautious and restrictive with regard to access, tending to favour the interests of landowners (and latterly of conservationists) against those of people in search of recreation.[2] This was apparent in perhaps the most important statute relating to rural recreation since the late 1940s: the 1968 Countryside Act. This made provision for country parks, which were intended to act as 'honeypots' which would draw in car-based urban visitors. Facilities such as refreshments, toilets, picnic tables and extensive parking space would be provided, and as a result urban visitors in search of rural recreation would be concentrated in a few segregated areas, removing visitors from the rest of the countryside.

A failing of the legislative framework governing rural recreation since 1945 is that it has tended to be behind the times. Since the war, the basic framework of rural recreation has been set by the 1949 Access to the Countryside Act. This in the main reflected the priorities of the 1930s: it sought to facilitate pedestrian access to a few selected areas of high scenic value, which were designated National Parks. These were characteristically upland areas popular with committed ramblers, such as the Peak District and the Lake District. The 1949 Act also promoted the interests and wishes of dedicated ramblers through promoting and protecting the public footpath network. But the chief characteristic of rural recreation in the postwar years was the very rapid rise in car-based access and the corresponding demand for better roads, parking places, picnic sites, toilets, catering outlets and so forth. The 1968 Act caught up with this, but the priorities of the 1950s and 1960s which it reflected were not to be those of the 1970s, 1980s and 1990s. In these years, a great widening of the geographical scope of rural recreation took place. Increasingly, it was the entire country, not just a few specifically designated areas, which was regarded (and used) as a recreation resource.[3]

Part of the reason for the failure of rural planning legislation to reflect changes in the pattern of leisure usage adequately was that planners and academics working in the area of rural recreation adopted a narrow perspective on land use, based on the concept of separating out different uses by zoning them. The decision to promote country parks was characteristic of this approach. Country parks would occupy a very small proportion of the total land area of the countryside, but they would be entirely given over to recreation. It was intended that this would keep visitors away from other areas of the countryside, in which other similarly zoned uses (primarily agriculture and forestry) could be carried on undisturbed. However, it was not in fact practicable to establish a strict version of zoning, simply because the public was not willing to restrict its leisure consumption of the countryside to designated approved sites designed with recreation in mind. Partly in recognition of the fact that actual patterns of use did not conform to the single-use model, academics and planners began to move towards the more sophisticated concept of multiple use of land. It was realized that many alternative uses of the countryside were in fact compatible. Forestry, for example, was for large parts of the life-cycle of trees not in conflict with walking or picnicking; reservoirs or lakes need not only be used for water supply but could also be used for fishing, sailing, bird-watching and other water-related leisure activities.[4]

By the 1980s rural recreation had become one of the dominant uses of leisure time in rural England. In 1996, for example, an astonishing 1.3 billion day visits were made to the English countryside.[5] Despite its quite exceptional position in the pattern of recreation, however, the British countryside of course remains almost entirely in private ownership, and access to it is patchy. Calls for a 'right to roam' were not a new feature of this period – indeed, as we saw in a previous chapter, they date back at least to Bryce's Access to Mountains Bill of 1884. But the enormous increase in the leisure use of the countryside, and the failure of the 1949 Act to provide for a right of free access to open countryside, gave a new impetus to the call for a right to roam, especially from the 1970s onwards. The Ramblers Association was, once again, at the forefront of this demand.[6] During the years of Conservative government between 1979 and 1997, little progress towards meeting a demand that implied such a curtailment of private property rights was likely. But after a long delay brought about by opposition from landowning and agricultural interests, the Labour government elected in 1997 finally enacted the right to roam with the passing of the Countryside and Rights of Way Act in November 2000. At the time of writing, however, it remained to be seen how much land would actually be designated as accessible open country under the mapping process on which the Act's provisions depended.

However, the question of the role of government in providing and promoting access to the countryside is complicated by a consideration of the class-specific pattern of rural recreation. Many studies have shown that the higher social classes enjoy more than their fair share of rural recreation, while the lowest social classes had less of all types of rural recreation. Surprisingly, there is some evidence to suggest that the lower social classes were less under-represented in the more commercialized forms of rural recreation, such as country fayres and car boot sales, than with respect to less commercialized forms such as rambling and cycling. This has led to speculation about whether rural recreation should be approached in terms of social need, as has at least to some extent traditionally been the case. It has been argued that the main reasons for underparticipation by the lower social classes in rural recreation appear to relate to very broad socio-economic phenomena about which recreation planners could do little, such as long working hours, unemployment, poor education and poverty among the least affluent. In so far as the trend of government policy has been to promote free access with minimal commercial facilities, it has even been argued that what is apparently socially inclusive has in fact been the opposite: greater freedom for commercial development of rural recreation might have increased, rather than decreased, uptake by the least affluent. Since the 1949 Act applied national resources (through national and local taxation) to facilitate forms of leisure which are primarily enjoyed by those who are already privileged, it has been suggested that this may have been socially regressive – transferring resources from the poor to the rich.[7] These claims are debatable; it can and has also been argued that underparticipation by the least affluent should direct attention to measures to increase equality and improve educational standards. Whatever conclusion is drawn from patterns of access, the claim that government policy on rural recreation has centred on facilitating free access, in particular for walking, can scarcely be disputed.

Probably the central plank of post-Second World War government policy on access to the countryside was the provision of National Parks. The history of National Parks in Britain falls into three main periods. In the 1930s, the idea of National Parks was promoted and developed. In the 1940s, changed political circumstances allowed these ideas to be adapted to and incorporated in legislation. From the 1950s onwards, the legislative machinery created in the 1940s was in operation and was subject to a few, surprisingly minor, alterations. National Parks were created in Britain later than in some other countries, notably the USA. British National Parks also differed from the US originals in two other important respects. First, the US parks were much larger, reducing the potential conflict between preservation and access. Second, the US parks were in public ownership, eliminating the difficulties which have been experienced in Britain in the relationship between national parks and the planning system.[8]

The origins of National Parks legislation in Britain can be traced back to a memorandum sent by the Council for the Preservation for Rural England, with support from the Council for the Preservation for Rural Wales and the Association for the Preservation of Rural Scotland, to Prime Minister Ramsay MacDonald in 1929. While others, including the Society for the Promotion of Nature Reserves and Lord Bledisloe, had made calls for the establishment of one or more National Parks in Britain, the significance of the CPRE's 1929 memorandum was that it began a chain of events which can be traced through to the actual creation of the National Parks. MacDonald's response was to set up a committee, chaired by Christopher Addison. Addison's report was published in 1931, and recommended the establishment of National Parks. The timing, though, was extremely unfortunate. MacDonald's Labour administration was replaced in 1931 by the National government dominated by the Conservative Party, and partly because of the change of government and partly because of the financial crisis of 1932, the new Minister of Health (who had responsibility for planning at this time) refused to request funding for the Addison recommendations from the Treasury. By the time the national finances were re-established on a stable basis, the political opportunity had passed. The Town and Country Planning Act of 1932 had obliged county councils to develop county plans, and by the mid-1930s most county councils had commenced this task. To implement the Addison proposals at this stage would have meant depriving several of the councils of a large part of their newly acquired planning powers, which the government was not prepared to do.

The idea of National Parks was, however, kept alive during the 1930s by the Standing Committee on National Parks formed by the CPRE and the CPRW. Partly under the influence of the Standing Committee, Lord Reith, Minister of Works in the wartime administration, commissioned John Dower, a noted advocate of National Parks, to produce a report on the subject. Dower's report recommended the establishment of a series of twelve National Parks, mostly located in upland areas of northern and western Britain but also including the South Downs and the Norfolk Broads. There was some concern about Dower's report within government, particularly from the Ministry of Agriculture which was uneasy about the impact of National Park designation on farming. In order to allay these concerns and produce an acceptable basis for legislation, the government asked Sir Arthur Hobhouse to chair a committee to investigate the proper legislative framework for National Parks. John Dower sat on this committee, which perhaps unsurprisingly largely endorsed Dower's original report. The Hobhouse report formed the groundwork for the 1949 National Parks and Access to the Countryside Act, but the delay between Dower's and Hobhouse's reports had been costly to the cause of

National Parks. In the meantime, plans for legislation on town and country planning had matured and, by the time the Hobhouse report appeared, what was to become the 1947 Town and Country Planning Act was already at an advanced stage. This allocated responsibility for planning controls to local authorities. In a repeat of the situation with respect to the Addison report of 1931, the result was that it became politically difficult to grant full planning powers to National Park authorities. The momentum behind National Parks was greater in the late 1940s than it had been in the early 1930s (partly because of the effects of the war, partly because of the election of a Labour government, and partly because of the endorsement of National Parks by the Scott, Dower and Hobhouse reports), and as a result National Parks legislation was not shelved as it had been in the 1930s. But the powers of the new National Parks committees constituted under the 1949 Act were very much less than they might have been had it not been for the 1947 Town and Country Planning Act. In the event, the only National Park authorities with independence in respect of planning from their local county councils were the Peak District and the Lake District National Parks.[9]

One of the unfortunate by-products of the failure of the 1949 Act to wrest control over planning from county councils was that, because the new National Park authorities were, with the exception of the Peak District and Lake District boards, essentially committees of the relevant county councils, central government was not willing to provide them with a regular annual grant income. A second unfortunate result was that the effectiveness and level of activity of the National Park authorities varied greatly. Where county councils were committed to making them work, they flourished, but in areas where county councils had other urgent priorities (such as Northumberland, faced with the precipitous decline of the Northumberland coalfield in the 1950s to 1970s), less was achieved. Reorganization of the structure of National Park authorities under local government legislation in 1972 and 1974 improved the situation somewhat, but the National Parks still remained administratively weak, especially in the crucial arena of planning. Ironically, the main threat to the landscape integrity of National Parks came not from the small-scale, piecemeal commercial, industrial and residential development which had been anticipated (but which planning legislation proved sufficiently robust to hold in check), but from national government itself (often acting in conjunction with big business). Perhaps the most glaring intrusions into National Parks after 1949 were the construction of Fylingdales ballistic missile early warning station in the North Yorkshire Moors National Park, the building of Trawsfynydd nuclear power station in the Snowdonia National Park, and the creation of oil refineries at Milford Haven in the Pembrokeshire Coast National Park. The first two of these projects were initiated by national government, and the third endorsed and imposed by it.[10]

National Parks were not the only means by which the 1949 Act attempted to preserve rural amenity and promote access. A lower grade of landscape protection was established through the category of Areas of Outstanding Natural Beauty (AONBs). The record of AONBs compares poorly, however, with that of the National Parks. Whatever the deficiencies of their administration and powers, the National Parks have achieved a high public profile and have had much success in reconciling access with conservation (if less in protecting landscape against other threats). AONBs have never had the same level of public profile, largely because they lack specific responsible bodies. Nor, as we saw in the last chapter, have they had as much success in preserving the landscapes they were intended to protect against modifications of their character, although, as in the well-known cases of the South Downs and the Berkshire Downs, this has resulted more from changes in agricultural practices than from industrial or residential development.

What do patterns of rural leisure since the Second World War tell us about attitudes to the countryside in this period? Perhaps the first question we need to ask is to what extent rural recreation should be seen in terms of attitudes to the countryside. We need to distinguish between two different types of rural recreation if we are to answer this question. The first type is where the countryside is simply the setting in which the recreation activity takes place. Examples include angling, rock-climbing and sailing. The second type is where the countryside is itself the object of recreation, for example walking. In practice, most examples of the first type in fact involve a large component of the second type. Rock-climbing, for example, may only require a sheer and jagged rock surface, such as exists in places like urban quarries, but it tends to take place in wild and beautiful parts of the countryside, because for most rock-climbers the countryside is an important part of their leisure experience rather than merely where it takes place.

Most rural recreation is, therefore, at least in part a consequence of attitudes to the countryside. Paradoxically, the upsurge of rural recreation has taken place in the context of (and has in part indeed caused) a marked reduction in the distinctiveness of the countryside (at least in social and cultural terms). The countryside had become an object of leisure consumption to a greater degree than ever before by the last quarter of the twentieth century, but at the same time the real differences on which this consumption was putatively based were becoming ever less significant (a change which will be examined in more detail in the next chapter).

This has led some theorists, particularly cultural geographers such as Paul Cloke, to argue that the 'image' of the countryside has now become almost completely detached from its reality. Cloke draws on the work of the French sociologist Baudrillard to argue that many aspects of rural recreation in the late twentieth century had become characterized by a radical commodification in which images bore almost no coherent connection to any underlying reality. Cloke cites the example of medieval castles that attract visitors by staging events such as vintage car rallies and craft fairs, both of which are consumed as part of an inclusive package of symbols by visitors, but neither of which actually has a significant relationship with the real history of such a castle.[11]

What can we conclude about rural leisure and attitudes to the countryside since the Second World War? In broad terms, rural leisure has been transformed in these years by the mobility revolution caused by the diffusion of car ownership, and to a lesser extent by mass affluence and increased available leisure time. But the conflict between recreation and other uses of rural land, anticipated to become severe by the end of the twentieth century by planners in the 1970s, has not fully materialized. In the main it has proved possible to reconcile access and conservation more easily than was anticipated.

Policy has been slow to adjust to changes in leisure patterns and demands, adopting an overcautious approach to access and for too long persisting with a clumsy single-use zoning-based approach. Nevertheless, the 1949 National Parks and Access to the Countryside Act, the chief legislative milestone of the period, did succeed in creating a valuable resource in the National Parks, which have facilitated access and preserved landscapes (even if the AONBs have in general been less successful).

The rise in demand for rural recreation reflects the continuing (or even increasing) power of the rural myth in Britain. Yet paradoxically, the flood tide of rural recreation began to flow at the same time that rural Britain was becoming socially and culturally almost indistinguishable from urban Britain. As we have seen, this has led cultural theorists to argue that the explanation for rural recreation must in part lie in the commodification of the countryside, in which the image has become widely separated from the reality of rural life, and it is the image which is largely consumed. It would be possible to interpret this as indicating the essential irrelevance of attitudes to the countryside to an understanding of rural society, but a less shallow approach would be to see it as underlining how powerful the needs and concerns which prompt people to accept images so widely variant from reality actually are.

In the next chapter, we will look at how these powerful needs have shaped conflicting attitudes to the countryside in a more specific social setting: the village itself, one of the most central and enduring symbols of rural England.

. . . .

CHAPTER 16

Intra-village Social Change and Attitudinal Conflict in the Twentieth Century

§ IN this chapter we will look at social change in English villages in the twentieth century and how this has been shaped by and in turn affected attitudes towards the countryside. The focus will be on developments since 1945, but as the most vivid contrast is between the late twentieth-century village and the nineteenth-century village (with the first half of the twentieth century as in many respects a period of transition), in several cases evidence will be offered from the nineteenth century to bring out the striking and radical nature of change in English villages since that time. The chapter will initially assess village social change and the attitudes underpinning this in five different respects. Villages can be seen, first, as places of work; second, as places of residence; third, as places where consumption takes place; fourth, as sites for recreation; and fifth, as arenas in which political power is exercised. We will assess how social change and attitudes have interacted in these spheres of life, and then look in more detail at two contrasting case-study villages for which in-depth studies by researchers allow a fuller picture to be provided, Ringmer in Sussex and Elmdon in Essex. In conclusion, an assessment will be made of how twentieth-century social change has affected the character of English villages as communities.

As a place of work, the most striking feature of the typical English village in the twentieth century has been the decline in the number of its inhabitants working in agriculture. This decline has been both relative to the total village population, and absolute. As we saw in Chapter 14, its main cause was the revolutionary technological changes which affected agriculture, especially since the Second World War. There has also been a decline of those working in agricultural servicing trades, most of which have either disappeared (as in the case of wheelwrights), or become mechanized and as a result have shifted to urban locations where economies of scale and better facilities and labour are available (as in the case of agricultural machinery repairing). Many villages have also experienced a decline in general services, such as shops, post offices and schools. In the first part of the twentieth century, this was largely due to falling local populations, although school closures also owed something to official education policy which sought to rationalize provision and raise standards by eliminating the smaller village schools. As a result of the decline of rural crafts, trades and industries and of the general service sector, despite the contraction of agricultural employment most villages were probably more purely agricultural in terms of employment in the interwar years than they had been for several hundred years. Since the mid-twentieth century, the pattern of change in the village as a place of work has varied primarily according to population. Partly as a natural result of the better services they are able to offer, and partly as a result of the 'key settlement' policies promoted by many planning authorities, large villages have tended to retain a wider range of non-agricultural employment than smaller villages. Indeed, some of the larger villages in which population has increased significantly since 1945 have seen a revival in the numbers employed in some rural service sector occupations, such as shopkeeping. Other (especially smaller) villages have, however, continued to lose employment and may retain no non-agricultural employment.[1]

In the nineteenth and early twentieth centuries there was an almost complete overlap between the village as a place of work and as a place of residence, but the invention and diffusion of the internal combustion engine was to bring radical change. Initially, the impact was muted, because in the first several decades of the twentieth century it was only the wealthy who could afford to own a private car. While motor bus services did significantly improve the accessibility of many villages, this was of limited significance in terms of the impact of mass car ownership after the Second World War. In the wealthiest and most accessible areas, closest to the greatest centres of population, however, commuting from the countryside was already becoming a significant phenomenon in the 1930s. This applies particularly to the more accessible areas of the home counties such as the Thames valley and parts of Surrey and Hertfordshire. More of southern and midland England came within the scope of commuting in the 1950s and by the 1980s there were few parts of the country which had not been touched to some degree by commuting (although this was predominantly short-hop commuting to a local town, rather than long-distance commuting to a more distant major city). By the year 2000 a majority of the employed population resident in English villages worked outside those villages. This was not only because incoming migrants bought houses while continuing to work elsewhere. Increased personal mobility also affected those born and brought up in villages, as we shall see when we consider the case-study village of Elmdon. However, a common pattern was for 'traditional' village residents to commute a shorter distance to work.

Nor is it only in terms of where their inhabitants work that English villages have changed as places of residence. There have also been important changes in age structure, which has shifted sharply towards the older end of the spectrum, and household size, which has fallen rapidly. Both these are national trends, applying to urban England as well as rural England, but they apply with more force to the latter, partly because of the restriction on housing supply in the English countryside caused, mainly, by the planning system. The shortage of housing has meant that house prices in the last three decades of the twentieth century rose more quickly than in urban England. As a result, young villagers leaving their parental homes have been unable to afford to buy houses in their own villages, and have been forced to move out. The lack of non-agricultural employment available in villages has worked in the same direction. The cost of housing has made it very difficult for most first-time buyers to afford village property, and the typical buyer has been middle-aged and prosperous. Usually these buyers no longer have young children, giving a further skew to the age distribution. The popularity of many parts of the countryside as places to which to retire to has added to this tendency. The low average household size of many villages is largely a direct consequence of the skewed age distribution: older people have fewer children living at home, and are more likely to form single-person households.

With respect to its role as a place where consumption occurs, the English village has had a more complex history in the modern era. In the early nineteenth century, most villagers were too poor to be able to afford anything beyond a minimal level of consumption. Basic services such as shoemaking, retailing and public house ownership were common, but little existed in the way of consumer services beyond this. Real incomes rose late in the century, but in most villages population declined and often the decline in the population outweighed the rise in living standards, resulting in a decline in services in many villages in the last part of the nineteenth century. To some extent, however, the decline of commercial services was counterbalanced by quite extensive investment by the state, by landowners, by religious institutions and by villagers themselves in social provision, notably schools, churches and chapels, reading rooms, village halls and sports facilities. While some of this, notably the provision of village halls and of sports facilities, continued in the interwar years, in other cases the continuing contraction of the village population and the decline of the estate system led to a decline also in public services and facilities.[2]

It might have been anticipated that the reversal of rural depopulation after the Second World War would also have reversed the slow decline in village services, especially in view of the affluence of many of the new inhabitants. In some villages, especially the larger ones, this has indeed occurred; but taking English villages overall, there has been a steady decline in the number of village shops, post offices, pubs, doctors' surgeries and schools since 1945.[3] The explanation seems to be that villages have in many cases been the victims of their own rising levels of prosperity and mobility. Both public planners and private retailers have realized that since most villagers are now highly mobile (over 80 per cent of the rural population had access to a car by the late 1990s), services can be concentrated on the larger settlements where economies of scale can be achieved and the quality of provision raised. In the public sector this process has been a planned one, operating through the key settlements concept, while in the private sector it has operated through market forces eliminating less cost-efficient small shops in favour of larger shops and supermarkets.[4] One consequence of these developments has of course been that those who are already most disadvantaged have become even more disadvantaged; it is in general the poor and elderly whose access to transport is least satisfactory and who have suffered most from the decline of the village as a place of consumption.

The history of English villages as places in which leisure and recreation take place has also been complex in the modern era. While in the eighteenth and early nineteenth centuries many villages appear to have possessed a vibrant but rough popular leisure culture, based on physical activity, animal sports and alcohol consumption, in the mid- and late nineteenth century these rough forms of recreation were stamped out or sanitized by elite and middle-class reformers, who sought to impose their own more respectable version of recreation. One of the consequences was that much of the life went out of rural popular culture, and by the late nineteenth and early twentieth centuries young farmworkers tended to look to the towns, accessible now by bicycle on a Sunday, for fulfilment of their leisure aspirations, rather than their own villages. This was exacerbated by the gender gap in villages of this period among young people: many young women were out 'in service' in towns. In the interwar years, declining population in many ways further sapped village leisure life, although there were some improvements notably with respect to leisure building provision and the range of voluntary organizations with a remit for leisure operating in the countryside. Subsequently, improved levels of mobility had some tendency to make village life less unattractive, in so far as leisure could more easily and frequently be enjoyed in nearby towns even while residence continued to be in the village. But at least until the 1980s such mobility was markedly less available to the less wealthy inhabitants, above all farmworkers. Furthermore, women of all social classes (but again disproportionately of the lower social classes) enjoyed less good access to transport than men, while also often experiencing less social contact in the course of the working day. It was rural women, therefore, who suffered most from the deficiencies of villages as places in which recreation took place (or did not take place) in the post-1945 period. The arrival of middle-class newcomers after the Second World War had ambiguous effects. On the one hand it sometimes led to a revival of village leisure activities, with newcomers taking an active role in fostering clubs and societies, as was apparent in Ruth Crichton's study of the large commuter village of Mortimer in Berkshire, but in other instances the active involvement of newcomers in village leisure had less desirable consequences, sometimes leading residents of longer standing to feel excluded from activities which had previously been 'theirs'.[5]

As arenas of political power, English villages have also been subject to major changes since the late nineteenth and early twentieth centuries. At this time, most villages were hierarchical communities, reflecting the fact that virtually all employment was in one industry (agriculture), and that there was an almost complete identification between the village as a place of work and as a place of residence. Landowners and clergymen were at the apex of this hierarchy, and the two groups reinforced each other since clergymen were also typically major landowners, while landowners regarded the Church of England as an ideological bulwark against threats to the status quo, and gave it overwhelming support. In day-to-day terms, however, it was very often the farmers who ran the village, since landowners were often willing to delegate control over the minutiae of local administration. It was farmers who dominated the parish vestry in most rural parishes in nineteenth-century England, and so made the vital decisions about poor relief until 1834; after 1834 farmers continued to exercise considerable influence over relief policies through their involvement as poor law guardians. It was also, of course, farmers who took most decisions about employment in villages. Other social classes in most nineteenth- and early twentieth-century English villages were essentially subordinate, with agricultural labourers forming the base of the pyramid of power. Craftsmen were often self-employed and so enjoyed a slightly greater measure of independence, but since farmers were by far their most important customers they too had powerful reasons for maintaining good relations with them.

The first great blow to this system came with the decline of the non-economic advantages of land ownership and the simultaneous, if more temporary, decline of its economic advantages. This became apparent in the years of the agricultural depression in the late nineteenth century between the 1870s and 1890s. Many landowners held on to much of their land until the First World War, but a combination of death duties, loss of heirs due to war deaths and the revival of land prices in the immediate aftermath of the war encouraged a very large number of landowners to sell much of their land, mainly to their tenant farmers. A few of the traditional landed elite lingered on as large landowners, but by the 1960s land ownership in most English villages was overwhelmingly in the hands of farmers, and the old tripartite social structure of the English countryside had permanently disappeared. These developments might have been expected to enhance the political power of farmers within villages, and this indeed was what occurred in most villages – but only for a relatively brief period of time. The influx of newcomers into villages in the second half of the twentieth century introduced a new and not easily assimilated element into the situation. Most of the newcomers were well-educated middle-class people, who were both affluent and politically astute. Furthermore, and crucially, they were not economically dependent on farmers in any way. This created a new line of division in villages to supplement the old class divide: that between old inhabitant and new in-migrant. This division closely mirrored the division between those employed in agriculture and those employed in non-agriculture-related occupations. Quite often the social division was so sharp that it gave rise to visible mani-festations. In many village pubs, for example, the incomers moved into the lounge bar while the old inhabitants ensconced themselves in the public bar. Similar divisions were often apparent at village fetes and shows, where the newcomers were more likely to engage in flower-arranging or wine-making competitions than they were in more traditional activities such as the fruit and vegetable show.[6]

The main area of conflict between newcomers and long-established village residents has been over land use in the countryside. The newcomers have, by and large, come to the countryside to enjoy its amenity value, and wish to preserve this.[7] Frequently this concern conflicts with modern farming methods, as we saw in Chapter 14. The one major aspect of social life in English villages which has changed little since the nineteenth century is the political subordination of farmworkers. Indeed, it could even be argued that this has actually increased. The fall in the number of farmworkers per farm has meant that the likelihood of farmworkers developing a sense of solidarity with other farmworkers is much reduced, while also tending to increase the farmworker's economic dependence on and personal bond with his employer. Furthermore, the arrival of middle-class incomers, with their often alien urban values, has reinforced the strength of the personal bond between farmer and farmworker. As a result, the agricultural trade unionism of the late nineteenth and early twentieth centuries declined steeply from the 1920s onwards, with the last major strike occurring in 1923. But although the farmworker and the farmer may have drawn closer together in personal terms, in reaction to the middle-class incomers, in political terms the situation has worked rather differently. Newcomers and farmers now together form a large numerical majority in most English villages, and have used their control of the levers of local state power to combine against the interests of farmworkers, who have largely lost what little political influence they ever had due to the decline in their numbers. The classic case is the provision of council housing in villages. Both farmers and newcomers have in general wanted to prevent the development of council housing, the farmers because they want to keep rates low, and the newcomers for this reason and also because of their concern to preserve the 'rural character' of the village they have expensively moved into. A similar *de facto* alliance has operated with respect to planning restrictions on industrial development: farmers have not necessarily welcomed the competition for labour this might bring, while newcomers have again objected to the 'spoiling' of the rural environment. Politically, therefore, it has been the farmworker who has been the loser, unable to find alternative work within the village, or to provide housing for his children in the village once they leave home.[8]

Before moving on to consider what the effects of these trends on villages as communities have been, let us now look at examples of two contrasting English villages to illustrate these changes in more detail.

Ringmer is situated three miles north-east of Lewes, in East Sussex. During the twentieth century Ringmer changed dramatically as a place of work, especially in regard to the sharp fall in the proportion of the population employed in agriculture: 83 per cent of Ringmer heads of households were in manual work in 1871, the vast majority of them involved in agriculture; by 1971, only 34 per cent of heads of households were in manual work, and of 150 households only one had a head of household who was an agricultural worker.[9]

Changes in Ringmer's characteristics as a place of residence have also been marked. Population increased dramatically between the late nineteenth and the late twentieth centuries. In 1861 the population was only just over 1,500, while by 1971 it was about 3,700. At the same time, the age structure of the population had changed markedly. The proportion of residents aged under ten years fell from 30 per cent in 1871 to half that figure in 1971, while those aged sixty-five or over increased from 6 per cent in 1871 to 11 per cent in 1971. Both these last two changes, however, occurred mainly in the late nineteenth and early twentieth centuries. At the same time, average household size fell, from 4.6 people in 1871 to 3.0 people in 1971, the mode household size falling from five in 1871 to two in 1971. The population was also to a much greater extent than it had been non-local in its origins. By the early 1970s, 65 per cent of the population had moved from elsewhere in Sussex and a further 29 per cent from outside Sussex. Villagers were also more likely to marry partners from outside Ringmer. The proportion of church marriages in which both parties were from the parish fell from 58 per cent between 1857 and 1868 to 25 per cent between 1961 and 1971, with most of the reduction occurring in the mid-twentieth century.[10]

Ringmer was a much more comfortable place in the late twentieth century than it had been in the late nineteenth century: its houses had central heating and mains electricity, water and sewerage, rather than the oil stoves and lamps, wells, pumps, buckets and middens on which the village had relied a hundred years earlier.

There were also notable improvements in the quality of leisure in Ringmer over these years. The length of the average working week fell; most Ringmer employees worked about 100 hours per week in the 1870s, but by the 1970s most worked less than half that number of hours. The role of paternalistic provision of leisure decreased, but the number of leisure organizations in the village increased to more than thirty by 1971, with membership spread fairly evenly across the social spectrum. The most popular leisure activities, including going to a pub, taking a car trip, and watching or playing sport, did not reflect social status at all. Leisure activities had become age specific rather than class specific. Women were far more involved in formal village leisure activities than they had been, partly because of the effect of domestic appliances in reducing the burden of housework, and partly because of a shift which had occurred from an individual to a family-based pattern of leisure.[11]

As an arena of political power, Ringmer demonstrates the changes which were outlined earlier in this chapter. As late as the 1920s the village was still dominated by a gentry elite, but by 1971 the situation was very different. In a survey of villagers only 20 per cent of those questioned saw 'clear signs' of social differentiation in the village, and of those who did perceive status differences, most based their judgement on length of residence in the village rather than class-based status criteria.[12]

In the mid-nineteenth century the vicar of Ringmer lived in the largest house in the village and employed by far the largest domestic staff. Through his position on the vestry he exerted considerable political influence in the village, and his dominant position with respect to institutional and personal charity enhanced his influence. In the 1920s the vicar remained an important figure, sitting on local government committees and other decision-making bodies, while church-going remained a normal experience for villagers. But by the 1970s fewer than 20 per cent of village households included a regular church-goer, and the church no longer had any great political, social or even recreational significance in the village.[13]

House ownership was another indicator of the widening basis of power within the village. In 1867 only thirty of 280 householders were owner-occupiers, but by 1971 as many as 878 of 1,263 householders owned their own homes. The degree of concentration of land ownership, however, had scarcely diminished between the 1860s and the 1970s, while the political constituency of which Ringmer formed a part had been represented by the same family, with one short break, for the entire period between 1920 and 1970. The loss of political authority by the traditional elite had therefore been considerable, but landowners had nevertheless succeeded in hanging on to some of their former power, whereas the Church of England had lost virtually all its social influence.[14]

The north-west Essex village of Elmdon shows many of the same changes as Ringmer, but also some interesting differences. Elmdon is set in an arable area of Essex about seven miles west of Saffron Walden, and fourteen miles south of Cambridge. The most significant changes in Elmdon as a place of work between the late nineteenth and the late twentieth centuries was, once again, the decline of the agricultural labour force: the proportion of male employees who were farmworkers fell from 66 per cent to 33 per cent. At the same time, the number of professional families rose significantly, from one (the vicar) in 1861 to thirteen in 1964. By the 1960s there were no longer any live-in domestic servants in the village, but there had been a large rise in the number of villagers doing part-time work in private households (mainly cleaning and gardening). The nature of women's work had changed radically: in 1861 about three-quarters of women in full-time work were in manual labour, while in 1964 about four-fifths of women in full-time work were in professional jobs. There had, however, been a slight fall in the proportion of women who were in full-time work.[15]

As a place of residence, the most notable feature of Elmdon was that (unlike Ringmer) its population fell between the late nineteenth and the late twentieth centuries. In 1861 the population was 520, but in 1964 it had fallen to 321. The age structure changed in a comparable but perhaps even more dramatic way to that of Ringmer. The percentage of children aged under fifteen fell from 41 per cent of the village population in 1861 to 19 per cent in 1964, while that of older people (aged over sixty) rose from 10 per cent in 1861 to 25 per cent in 1964. Household structure also changed; indeed, the average size of household fell so greatly that despite the large fall in the population of the village there had been virtually no change in the number of households (which had fallen from 115 to 114).[16]

The percentage of households with only one or two members in Elmdon rose from 29 per cent in 1861 to 54 per cent in 1964, while the proportion of inhabitants born outside the parish increased dramatically, from 27 per cent to 59 per cent. However, this was mainly the result of the tendency to marry someone from outside the parish. The proportion of marriages in which both partners had been born in the parish fell from 38 per cent in 1861 to only 5 per cent in 1964. A high proportion of Elmdon marriages (47 per cent) in 1964, however, still included at least one partner born in the parish.[17]

The tendency for the village as a place of residence to separate from the village as a place of work is particularly apparent in Elmdon. In 1861, virtually all the villagers worked within the parish. But by 1964 only 46 per cent of the male workforce continued to do so. Interestingly, this tendency affected those born and raised in Elmdon almost as much as it did incomers: 52 per cent of the former worked outside the parish in 1964, as opposed to 55 per cent of the latter. Many of the incomers were in fact not middle-class but farm-workers. Elmdon men were increasingly moving out of farm labour into jobs such as working in the paper factories in the nearby towns, or for the local bus company.

As a place of consumption, Elmdon exhibited a picture of decline between 1861 and 1964, in accordance with the fall in the population. There was still a grocer, two butchers and two pubs in Elmdon in the latter year, but both the drapery and the baker's had closed. To some extent, however, declining services were compensated for by mobile shops, fish-and-chip vans and other mobile services.[18]

As an arena of political power, Elmdon's most startling change in the twentieth century was when the 'squire', Jack Wilkes, sold his land in 1927. It was the farmers who initially inherited local political power, through the parish council, employment and their control of 15 per cent of the village's housing stock. By 1964, however, this dominance had been much reduced, partly because of a shortage of farmworkers, partly because of the building of twenty-five new council houses, and partly because newcomers had taken up positions on the parish council.[19]

Elmdon and Ringmer therefore together exhibit most of the main trends affecting villages in the period between the late nineteenth and the late twentieth centuries. Both showed a fall in the proportion of the population engaged in agriculture, the development of a split between occupation and residence, declining household sizes, an increasingly elderly population, and the erosion of the social and political dominance of the traditional landed elite. However, comparing the two villages also indicates that in some respects these tendencies affected different villages very differently. This is especially notable as regards the significance of agriculture in the two villages. In Ringmer the collapse of the significance of agriculture was almost complete, due to very rapid population growth. In Elmdon, much more remote than Ringmer, population actually declined between 1861 and 1964, and, partly as a result, agriculture retained a much more important share of the total workforce.

Having examined social change in English villages with respect to work, residence, consumption, recreation and political power, let us conclude this chapter by assessing how social change has affected the village seen as a community. It will be clear from what has been indicated above that whether we think villages have 'declined' as communities will depend very much on, in the first place, what periods we are comparing, and, in the second place, from whose perspective we are judging. If we were, for example, to take the 1820s as our benchmark, it would be hard to argue that there had been a decline in the village as a community. Most villages at least in southern England in the 1820s were marked by bitter social conflict and discontent, including the destruction of farm equipment and crops by angry farmworkers, animal maiming, and even threats to the life of farmers. The late twentieth-century village was almost entirely free from violent conflict and social tension of this kind. But if we were to compare the 1930s with the late twentieth century, it could be argued that the level of social conflict had increased. Whereas in the 1930s the supremacy of agriculture and of farmers was unchallenged within most villages, this was no longer so by the 1980s.

If periodization is crucial to our perception of whether there has been a decline in the extent to which English villages form communities, so is the social perspective we adopt. From the point of view of farmers, it might well seem that community has declined. The village which they largely ruled in the interwar period is now invaded by urban incomers. Some limited compensation, however, has arisen through closer ties with farmworkers. For farmworkers, the brief flowering of solidarity and independent social organization of the late nineteenth and early twentieth centuries was nipped in the bud from the late 1920s onwards, and farmworkers have increasingly become strangers within their own villages as their numbers have declined and new cultural values come to predominate. Yet it must be questioned how rich the old village community really was for farmworkers. There can be no doubt that increasing real incomes and mobility allow them opportunities for leisure in nearby urban centres much greater than anything they knew in the nineteenth century. The newcomers are often the people who most loudly bewail the decline of the village community; yet as we have seen it is questionable to what extent this community ever really existed. The community whose demise newcomers often bemoan is, all too often, the imaginary one of their disappointed dreams. Social change in English villages since 1945 have, therefore, been inextricably bound up with assumptions about what the countryside is or ought to be. Attitudes have shaped responses just as much as they have been modified by independent socio-economic forces. In the last chapter of this book, we will see how the powerful cultural meanings with which the countryside has been invested, and the social changes which these meanings have in part reflected, in part constituted, but also in part radically contradicted, generated a crisis in the relationship between countryside and town in the last decade of the twentieth century.

CHAPTER 17

Town, Country and Politics at the End of the Twentieth Century

§ THE last decade of the twentieth century witnessed a remarkable upsurge in the political profile of the countryside in national politics. In a striking break with the apparent pattern of two centuries – that is, rural issues and influences becoming less and less important in relation to their urban equivalents – the countryside emerged as a major focus of discontent and of political instability in the 1990s. At the forefront of this development was an organization calling itself the Countryside Alliance. This body claimed to speak for the interests of rural England as a whole, and attempted to present itself as the authentic, but hitherto unexpressed, voice of the countryside. One of the most impressive aspects of the Countryside Alliance was its scale. It acted mainly as a public pressure group, in the classic manner of 'outsider' pressure groups such as the Campaign for Nuclear Disarmament in the 1980s, and accordingly chose as its chief means of expression the mass demonstration. Two very large demonstrations were arranged to take place in London in 1997 and 1998, the second of which brought as many as a quarter of a million protesters into the capital – the largest demonstration seen in London for a decade. Prior to the 1998 demonstration, more than 5,000 beacons had been lit across the country by supporters of the Countryside Alliance to indicate their strength in numbers, and, by allusion with the wartime invasion-scare symbolism of lighting beacons, to make clear their belief that the countryside was under threat. The number of protesters at the two demonstrations was such that the demonstrations could not simply be written off as a narrowly based defence of hunting, as the League Against Cruel Sports attempted to do. Particularly significant was the massive media coverage the Countryside Alliance succeeded in generating, particularly in connection with the London marches. Virtually without exception the national dailies (both the broadsheets and the tabloids) led with the 1 March 1998 demonstration, and coverage was overwhelmingly sympathetic. Nor was the media coverage transient: on the contrary, the issues raised by the Countryside Alliance continued to make frequent headlines right up to the time of writing.[1]

What made the Countryside Alliance, and the marches it organized, particularly impressive and effective was not just the number of people who were successfully mobilized – giving the lie to those who believed that the 'countryside lobby' consisted of no more than an exiguous number of large landowners and wealthy farmers – but the strength of feeling it manifested. This was apparent from the fact that most of the people on the marches did not in any way belong to a 'culture of protest'; almost certainly the majority had never been on a demonstration before in their lives (or in the case of those with university educations, not since their student days). Most of the Countryside Alliance's supporters almost certainly regarded themselves as in sympathy with the establishment, or at least as grudging supporters of it; to adopt the oppositional tactics and traditions of radical protest groups therefore represented a striking breach with customary modes of feeling, behaviour and self-identity.

The Countryside Alliance had a long list of grievances. Near the top of this list was the crisis in farm incomes which had developed from the mid-1980s, largely as a result of the fall in real prices for farm products within the European Union. This had been much exacerbated by the outbreak of Bovine Spongiform Encephalitis, a fatal disease of cattle, which had broken out in Britain in the late 1980s and devastated the British dairy herd. Other complaints included the decline in rural service provision, including public transport, health, education, post offices and commercial services (notably shops and pubs). The degradation of the rural environment and the failure of government to take more effective steps to protect the countryside from despoliation was another grievance. Some of the protesters at the London marches wanted better access to land, through better maintained and signposted footpaths or even a 'right to roam' across uncultivated land. Another important focus was the question of hunting: the Countryside Alliance gave strong support to hunting and shooting as embodying and sustaining a characteristic, distinctive and threatened 'rural way of life'. Government plans to build more new houses on 'green field' sites in the countryside were also an object of disquiet to many of the alliance's supporters. More broadly, the movement alleged that there was a general urban incomprehension of rural life and values, and that urban domination of British politics, government, the economy and national culture was leading to a systematic bias against and marginalization of the countryside, evident, for example, in policy on transport, which through raising petrol prices unfairly discriminated against rural residents, who typically had limited access to public transport.[2]

Many of these complaints were rooted in real social processes which had been occurring in some cases over many years, in others over a shorter time-span, but often with an acceleration or higher degree of visibility in the late 1980s and the 1990s. Farm incomes, for example, were suffering from a long-term fall. In the broadest terms, the fall in farm incomes was deeply rooted in demographic and economic changes affecting all advanced economies. Engel's Law predicted that as per caput income rose, the proportion of income spent on food would fall. This would necessarily lead to a diminution of the relative significance of agriculture in the national economy, a trend which has indeed occurred without exception in advanced economies in the twentieth century. Furthermore, the radical improvements in total factor productivity obtained within agriculture in Britain (and elsewhere) in the twentieth century, particularly since 1945, were achieved in large part by the massive uptake of labour-displacing machinery. Agriculture therefore shed labour on a very large scale, and this labour included the less efficient (typically the smaller-scale) farmers as well as agricultural labourers. The process worked through economies of scale: it made it possible for one man to manage a much larger area of farmland than had previously been the case. But in order to take advantage of these economies of scale, farmers needed not only the capital to invest in the expensive new labour-saving machinery, but also a large enough farm so that full advantage could be taken of the economies of scale offered by machinery. Those farmers whose farms were too small to do this were in effect undercut by larger farmers who were able to reap the full cost savings of mechanization. Thus many smaller farmers found their incomes progressively squeezed, and were inexorably forced off the land. This process was slowed and softened by the price support offered to agriculture by, first, the 1947 Agriculture Act, and after 1973 by the Common Agricultural Policy (CAP). Under both regimes real farm product prices still fell, even though more slowly than they would otherwise have done, and from the 1980s radical reform within the Common Agricultural Policy significantly intensified the pressure of the price squeeze, with the aim of eliminating the costly and embarrassing food surpluses which had built up under the CAP. Particularly significant were the MacSharry reforms of 1992, which cut price levels and emphasized set-aside of agricultural land regarded as surplus to production requirements. The effects of CAP reform unfortunately coincided with the BSE crisis. Farmers regarded both the difficulties stemming from CAP reform and those associated with the BSE crisis as directly the responsibility of government, at both European Union and national levels, since CAP reform was plainly a result of a top-down governmental process, while BSE, although not of course created by government, was seen as having been recognized and acted upon too late by government. The effects of BSE were more serious than most previous outbreaks of animal disease because of the link which was postulated between BSE in cattle and Creutzfeld-Jakob Disease (CJD), a rare but fatal and exceptionally unpleasant human disease. It was regarded as likely that the increase in CJD in Britain in the 1990s was a consequence of BSE-infected beef entering the food chain. In consequence, British beef was banned for export to other European countries. Beef prices collapsed and British beef and dairy farmers found their incomes sharply reduced.

If the fall in farm incomes was a real phenomenon, so too was in many respects the decline of rural services. As with the fall in farm incomes, the decline in rural services was a long-term phenomenon with deep roots in powerful economic processes characteristic of advanced industrial societies. Once again, economies of scale played a major role. It was more efficient to provide both public and private services through a pattern of a limited number of outlets able to offer high-quality, specialized services than through a large number of outlets offering a lower quality of more generalized services. Until the mid-twentieth century, both government and the private sector had been impeded in moving in this direction by limited consumer mobility. Before the era of mass car ownership, few people were willing or able to shop, or send their children to school, at any distance from the village in which they lived, but once the majority of the rural population gained access to car transport, they were able to travel to services. This process could be seen at work very clearly in the case of village shops, which closed in large numbers in the second half of the twentieth century as they were out-competed by supermarkets. With their economies of scale, efficient supply mechanisms and powerful purchasing strength, the supermarkets were able to offer a far wider range of products at lower cost than village shops. Furthermore, these products were typically of a higher, rather than a lower, quality. Villagers unsurprisingly chose to drive to the nearest supermarket rather than continue to use the village shop. But similar processes applied in the case of public services. A primary school in a small village might have only one teacher, who would perforce have to be a generalist; but it could scarcely be hoped that her expertise could match that of a specialist teacher in any given subject. Closing schools in small villages in favour of larger schools in the bigger villages was not only cost-effective but also allowed more children to be taught by specialist teachers. Similar arguments applied in the case of GP surgeries. The decline in rural services did not, however, accelerate as markedly in the late 1980s and 1990s as the fall in farm incomes.

Degradation of the rural environment was as we saw in Chapter 14 also a serious and real, if complex, problem of the countryside in the post-1945 era, with losses to habitats such as hedgerows, woods, ponds, moorland and their associated species a particular concern. Loss of rural land to non-agricultural and 'urban' developments similarly occurred after the Second World War, although in fact the planning controls introduced in 1947 proved effective enough to ensure that despite the rate of economic growth between the 1940s and the end of the twentieth century the rate of loss of rural land was lower than it had been in the depressed interwar years. The other complaints voiced by individuals and organizations associated with the Countryside Alliance also had a greater or lesser degree of basis in fact: there was indeed a mounting and increasingly effective attack by animal welfare organizations on rural sports (especially fox hunting and hare coursing), and on more mainstream aspects of the economic life of agriculture such as live animal exports.

So most of the concerns expressed by the Countryside Alliance were grounded in real processes of change. Yet it was also clear that many of the claims made by the alliance were of dubious validity. Most obviously, the insistence that the countryside had been politically disadvantaged was a re- markable one. Many of Britain's wealthiest and best-connected figures were landowners and supporters of the alliance; the Duke of Westminster, often rated as Britain's richest private individual, was a leading member of the organization. Any objective reading of nineteenth- and twentieth-century British history would accept that rural landowners had wielded influence quite out of proportion to their numbers, largely because of connections, knowledge and influence deriving from their former role as Britain's governing class, but perpetuated also by their wealth. There was a certain absurdity in members of the House of Lords complaining about their unfair exclusion from power, particularly when their access to political influence was compared with that of truly excluded social groups such as the homeless. The claim made by tenant and small farmers that they had been politically marginalized was not much more convincing. On the contrary, a notable feature of British politics in the second half of the twentieth century was the extraordinary relationship which farmers enjoyed with government policy-making. This operated primarily through the axis between the National Farmers Union (NFU) and the Ministry of Agriculture, Fisheries and Food (MAFF). Under the terms of the 1947 Agriculture Act, the ministry was obliged to consult with farmers' representatives (and this in practice meant the NFU) in con- ducting its annual price review to determine what the level of agricultural prices for the next year should be. A close relationship developed between civil servants within MAFF and the NFU, skilfully fostered by the leadership of the latter, which gave the NFU unparalleled influence in determining the level of prices of its own industry. No other industry has its own ministry with cabinet-level representation, and no other industry was able to obtain such enduringly favourable treatment from government. While entry into the European Economic Community reduced the efficacy of the NFU's close links with MAFF, these continued to be of value to farmers, and through collaboration with the farmers' unions of other European countries the NFU was also able to have an influence on European agricultural policy. As a result of the strong ties between the NFU and government policy-makers, British farmers were able to obtain huge subsidies on an ongoing basis, dwarfing the scale of subsidy to any other industry of comparable size. The suggestion that farmers had been discriminated against was therefore a somewhat astonishing one; far more plausible was that official policy had discriminated in favour of them.[3]

If landowners and farmers had few persuasive grounds for alleging that they had suffered from an urban bias in policy-making, rural residents with no such direct ties to agriculture were not in a very much better position to argue that they were disadvantaged. On the contrary, the average income per household in most rural counties was far above that in the inner cities, while unemployment rates were lower. Both population and employment grew much faster in the countryside than in the cities in the 1980s and 1990s, and Britain's wealthiest inhabitants were disproportionately rural in their habitation. The countryside taken as a whole was booming in comparison with the cities for most of the 1980s and 1990s; the transfer of resources was very much from the cities to the countryside. To claim that the countryside was at an economic disadvantage compared to the towns was therefore as implausible as to claim that landowners had suffered from political exclusion or that government had paid no heed to protecting farmers' incomes.

Furthermore, despite the real social basis of many of the complaints expressed by the Countryside Alliance, it was impossible not to be struck by the disparateness and even contradictoriness of many of the demands which the alliance and the broad coalition associated with it made. It was, for example, quite unclear what united the threat to hunting with the decline of rural service provision; these were two quite separate phenomena, the one rooted in changes in public attitudes towards nature and animals, and the other in market forces and economies of scale. The lengthy list of problems the Countryside Alliance pointed to seemed more like a melting pot into which any and every grievance with the slightest connection to the countryside had been tossed than it did like a coherent programme. Worse still, some of the demands being made by those associated with the countryside movement were in blatant contradiction of each other. On the countryside marches, both hunters and environmentalists marched together, but the latter were mostly sympathetic to animal welfare arguments, and opposed to hunting. Similarly, the environmentalist strand to the movement sat well with the demand for better public transport (especially bus services) for the countryside, but was difficult to reconcile with the vociferous complaint that high taxes on petrol were unfair to country people, since lower petrol taxes would have shifted the balance of advantage away from public transport back towards the private car. Again, was the countryside movement dedicated to the preservation and appreciation of England's rural landscapes, and thus to improving footpaths and facilitating access, or were ramblers symptomatic of the invading urban hordes who supposedly abused the countryside without understanding its rationale or values? Both positions were argued by supporters of the movement, yet the two were starkly contradictory.

Most of all, however, the claim which lay at the heart of the countryside movement – that 'town' and 'country' were separate and opposed entities – was deeply flawed. At the most basic level it was quite obvious that farmers depended on urban consumers to purchase the food they produced just as the inhabitants of cities depended on farmers to produce the food they ate. But the interdependence between town and country was of course far more extensive, subtle and ramified than this. Virtually everything consumed in the countryside had at some stage passed through urban factories or processing units in the course of production and distribution. Town and country were inextricably economically intertwined in the late twentieth century. They always had been so, of course, but in the sophisticated and diverse economy of late twentieth-century Britain the myriad threads which linked the two were more numerous and complex than they ever had been before.

More important, however, than the inseparable economic interconnectedness of town and country was the social and cultural convergence of the two in the course of the twentieth century. For, ironically, just at the time when the town versus country distinction was being voiced with most vehemence, the divide between the two was becoming less discernible than it had ever been before. In almost all respects other than land use, the countryside was becoming urbanized. This occurred perhaps most notably through the revolution in communications in the late nineteenth and twentieth centuries. The effects of the transport revolution, above all the advent of the car, have already been mentioned: this brought rural people within physical range of urban services, goods, leisure and cultural activities. Perhaps even more important was the development of electronic communications: initially the radio, which had a dramatic effect in breaking down the cultural isolation of the countryside, and later the telephone, television and computer. These brought urban voices, names, events, assumptions and attitudes into the farmhouse and the cottage, and did perhaps more than anything else to foster and establish a single overarching increasingly homogeneous national culture, which took no cognisance of the urban–rural divide.

These effects were accelerated, especially after the Second World War, by the decline of agricultural employment and by counterurbanization. As a result of these two linked processes, by the 1990s agriculture produced only a tiny fraction of the economic output, not only of Britain as a whole, but even of the countryside. The significance of agriculture in the rural employment structure had become similarly marginal: in 1999 under 4 per cent of the employed population in rural England worked in agriculture (compared to 1.7 per cent in England as a whole).[4] At the end of the twentieth century, therefore, the great majority of people in the countryside had no significant connection with agriculture. On the contrary, they worked in office or industrial jobs, often actually in towns and cities. In many cases they had been born and brought up in cities and could be considered as rural in virtue of one quality only: that they happened to live in the countryside rather than in a town. Rural Britain had become thoroughly urbanized in terms of the cultural values which held sway there, and in terms of its socio-economic structure.[5]

The political stance of the Countryside Alliance was therefore a deeply fractured and flawed one. An obvious interpretation of the movement, and one which was developed by several left-wing commentators, was that most of the positions advanced by the alliance were epiphenomenal, and should be seen as motivated purely or primarily by tactical considerations. On this interpretation, what was happening was that the new rural population was being manipulated by the wily political manoeuvring of the traditional elite, who were in fact just acting in defence of their economic interests as landowners and farmers and the maintenance of their amusements, principally hunting. The protests about declining rural services and the threat to the rural landscape were, according to this view, merely designed to recruit a broad coalition, behind which the old elite could shelter while directing the movement to their advantage.

There was clearly something in this position: the leadership of the Countryside Alliance was indeed disproportionately made up of members of the old elite, and its financial backing came very largely from the same sources and from advocates of blood sports. The argument gained in force if the interests which were being covertly defended were seen not just in terms of hunting, but with regard to farmer (and hence landowner) incomes more broadly. During the twentieth century an important convergence had taken place between farmers and landowners, with many landowners becoming farmers of their own land (largely for tax and other financial reasons), while most tenant farmers bought their land and so became landowners. The political and economic tensions between farmers and landowners evident in the nineteenth century were much less characteristic of the twentieth century, and it became correspondingly easier for landowners and farmers to act together as a single political interest group.

Nevertheless, the conspiracy-theory explanation of the countryside movement is too simplistic. It cannot explain how such remarkable numbers of people could be mobilized in defence of the narrow economic and sporting interests of farmers and landowners, who as we have seen constituted a very small proportion of the rural population by the late twentieth century. Nor can this explanation account for the success of the movement in intimidating government; had this really been no more than a front for elite interests, it seems improbable that a Labour government would have been swayed by the seemingly disparate and, as we have seen, often contradictory demands made by the Countryside Alliance. In fact, the movement not only succeeded in dominating media attention, but also very nearly in setting the political agenda for the late 1990s. The Labour government, elected with a record and seemingly impregnable majority in 1997, and enjoying unprecedented opinion poll leads for an in-office party, showed itself desperate to conciliate the Countryside Alliance. Michael Meacher, the Minister of the Environment, actually marched on one of the London demonstrations, and, even more strikingly, within a short time of the demonstrations the government had drawn back from its plans to legislate against hunting and in favour of a right to roam. This was all the more striking in view of the fact that both issues were dear to the heart of a significant section of the Labour electorate; the latter in particular was associated with the memory of John Smith, the labour leader who died prematurely in 1994.[6] Eventually the government did enact legislation which, subject to important restrictions, implemented the right to roam, but only after a two-year delay. The bill to ban hunting, despite manifesto commitments, was not given time by the government to pass through all its stages within the lifetime of the 1997 parliament, and as of October 2001, the future prospects of legislation to ban hunting remained uncertain.

Just how central ideas about the countryside had become to contemporary British politics was underlined by the outbreak of foot-and-mouth disease that affected large parts of England in 2001. While there is no questioning the severity of the outbreak, the scale of the government's response to what was ostensibly a crisis in a very minor sector of the economy was interesting. Within a few days the government had taken the unprecedented step of 'closing the countryside' to those without essential business there. The general election, which most commentators assumed the government had intended to hold on 3 May, was postponed until 7 June. Much of the countryside, including thousands of miles of footpaths and many tourist attractions, remained closed for several months, with devastating economic consequences for tourism. Foot-and-mouth disease dominated the media for several weeks, with coverage being overwhelmingly sympathetic to farmers. There was a strong public reaction and a range of benefit activities to help farmers was organized, including a royal gala concert in the Albert Hall. The government implemented a massive slaughter policy but offered sufficiently generous compensation to give credence to allegations that some farmers had purposely infected their animals to take advantage of this. The economic cost to the treasury was such as seriously to affect the government's projected spending plans. Nevertheless, many people in both rural and urban areas continued to see the government's handling of the epidemic as exemplifying the unfair treatment of 'the countryside' by an uncomprehending urban-dominated establishment. The response of both government and the public to the outbreak therefore demonstrated the pervasive influence of the range of attitudes associated with the country-side movement.

The popular and political impact of the countryside movement make it clear, then, that there was much more to it than the conspiracy theory would allow. Yet at the same time, the contradictory and incoherent demands made by the movement make it difficult to explain the massive support and effective political purchase the movement exhibited in terms of its ostensible pro-gramme. What underpinned the countryside movement and gave it such weight and influence was, it would seem, the powerful symbolism and meanings with which the term 'countryside' came to be invested in the late nineteenth and twentieth centuries, and which we have examined in the preceding chapters of this book. By the 1990s the countryside had come to stand for far more than the by then almost negligible socio-economic interests directly connected with agriculture. On the contrary, it had come to represent the dreams, aspirations, hopes and utopian yearnings of a large part of the population, including millions of people living in cities. The countryside had become a refuge in the mind from the disappointments, difficulties and emotional wounds inflicted by the fraught processes of urbanized and in-dustrialized modernity. In this way, the countryside had come to play a vital part in the psychic economy both of those who had not yet moved to the countryside, but wanted to, and of those who had. For the former, the country-side was a mental refuge which they might seek out in their leisure hours and days, and to which they might aspire to move should their economic circum-stances allow.[7] For the latter, the experience was more complex. In general, their inner lives had not changed in the way they had hoped when they had moved out from urban England into the countryside. But, as we saw in Chapters 14, 15 and 16, this disappointment was often projected into anger at what was allegedly being done to the countryside (whether by irresponsible farmers, as with rural environmentalism in the 1970s and 1980s, or by a neglectful government, as in the 1990s). For these reasons, a powerful commun-ity of imagined feeling was precipitated by the town versus country symbolism evoked by the organizers of the countryside movement, fundamentally false and misleading though this dichotomy was.

The contradictory political stance and programme of the countryside movement was in fact an indication that the real sources of the movement lay not in the medley of grievances it explicitly voiced, but in the symbolism, traditions and cultural meanings evoked in the expression of these grievances, and the hopes, fears and discontents these meanings embodied. This helps to explain how a politically incoherent movement, with no viable programme, was able to force changes in the policy of one of the most strongly established and popular government administrations of the twentieth century; such was the extraordinary ideological force with which notions of the countryside and of the rural had become endowed, that a campaign which successfully invoked them had a potency no government, however strong, could afford to ignore. Once again, therefore, we see the profound and dynamic interplay between social change on the one hand, and attitudes to the countryside on the other. At the very end of the period treated in this book, attitudes to the countryside were reshaping and constituting English society as powerfully as they ever had done.

Notes

Introduction

1. Howard Newby, *Green and Pleasant Land? Social Change in Rural England*, London, 1980.

2. B. A. Holderness, *British Agriculture Since 1945*, Manchester, 1985, pp. 103–5, 110.

3. Keith Thomas, *Man and the Natural World. Changing Attitudes in England 1500–1800*, London, 1983, pp. 17–50.

4. Marjorie Hope Nicholson, *Mountain Gloom and Mountain Glory*, London, 1959.

5. Thomas, *Man and the Natural World*, pp. 51–92.

6. The poetry of John Clare is a notable expression of the sense of loss and of nature banished in the interests of production occasioned by enclosure. See John Barrell, *The Idea of Landscape and the Sense of Place 1730–1840. An Approach to the Poetry of John Clare*, Cambridge, 1972.

7. D. Jacques, *Georgian Gardens: the Reign of Nature*, London, 1983.

8. Ann Bermingham, *Landscape and Ideology: the English Rustic Tradition, 1740–1860*, London, 1987.

1. Industrialization and Urbanization

1. [Arnold Toynbee], *Toynbee's Industrial Revolution: a Reprint of 'Lectures on the Industrial Revolution in England, Popular Addresses, Notes and other Fragments'. With a new introduction by the late T. S. Ashton*, Newton Abbot, 1969.

2. W. W. Rostow, *How It All Began: Origins of the Modern Economy*, London, 1975.

3. P. Deane and W. A. Cole, *British Economic Growth 1688–1959: Trends and Structure*, Cambridge, 1962.

4. N. F. R. Crafts, *British Economic Growth During the Industrial Revolution*, London, 1985.

5. J. C. D. Clark, *Revolution and Rebellion*, Cambridge, 1986, p. 66.

6. J. Mokyr, 'Editor's Introduction: the New Economic History and the Industrial Revolution', in J. Mokyr (ed.), *The British Industrial Revolution. An Economic Perspective*, 2nd edn, Boulder, Colorado, 1999, p. 3.

7. J. Winter, *Secure from Rash Assault. Sustaining the Victorian Environment*, Berkeley, California, 1999, pp. 161–3.

8. C. Hamlin, *Public Health and Social Justice in the Age of Chadwick. Britain, 1800–1854*, Cambridge, 1998, pp. 204–6.

9. R. M. Hartwell et al., *The Long Debate on Poverty. Eight Essays on Industrialization and 'the Condition of England'*, London, 1972.

10. P. H. Lindert and J. G. Williamson, 'English Workers' Living Standards During the Industrial Revolution: a New Look', *Economic History Review*, 36 (1), 1983, pp. 1–25.

11. R. Floud, K. Wachter and A. Gregory, *Height, Health and History*, Cambridge, 1990.

12. J. Komlos, 'The Secular Trend in the Biological Standard of Living in the United Kingdom, 1730–1860', *Economic History Review*, 2nd series, 46, 1993, pp. 115–44.

13. P. Huck, 'Infant Mortality and Living Standards of English Workers During the Industrial Revolution', *Journal of Economic History*, 55 (3), 1995, pp. 528–50; S. Sretzer and G. Mooney, 'Urbanization, Mortality and the Standard of Living Debate: New Estimates of the Expectation of Life at Birth in Nineteenth-century British Cities', *Economic History Review*, 2nd series, 51, 1998, pp. 84–112.

14. C. H. Feinstein, 'Pessimism Perpetuated: Real Wages and the Standard of Living in Britain During and After the Industrial Revolution', *Journal of Economic History*, 58 (3), 1998, pp. 625–58.

15. A recent summary of this debate can be found in S. Horrell and J. Humphries, 'The Origins and Expansion of the Male Breadwinner Family: the Case of Nineteenth-century Britain', *International Review of Social History*, 42, 1997, Supplement, pp. 25–64.

16. E. P. Thompson, 'Time, Work-discipline and Industrial Capitalism', *Past and Present*, 50, 1971.

17. E. Hopkins, 'Working Hours and Conditions During the Industrial Revolution: a Re-appraisal', *Economic History Review*, 2nd series, 35, 1982, pp. 52–66.

2. Literature and the Countryside

1. Raymond Williams, *The Country and the City*, London, 1973, pp. 14–19; Robert Graves, *The Common Asphodel: Collected Essays on Poetry, 1922–49*, London, 1949, pp. 252–3.

2. Williams, *The Country and the City*, pp. 22–6; Michael Bunce, *The Countryside Ideal. Anglo-American Images of Landscape*, London, 1994, p. 39.

3. Recent scholarship has, however, identified an interesting dissident tradition of proletarian anti-pastoral, in which the complacency and evasion of the mainstream pastoral tradition was unmasked. The best-known exponents of this were Stephen Duck and Mary Collier. See Donna Landry, *The Muses of Resistance*, Cambridge, 1990; and John Goodridge, *Rural Life in Eighteenth-century English Poetry*, Cambridge, 1995, pp. 11–90.

4. John Stuart Mill, *Autobiography*, London, 1886, pp. 146–9; Mark Rutherford, *Autobiography*, quoted in Basil Wiley, *The Eighteenth-century Background: Studies on the Idea of Nature in the Thought of the Period*, London, 1946, p. 291.

5. William Wordsworth, *Lines Written a Few Miles Above Tintern Abbey*, and *The Prelude* (1805), VII, 659–62, quoted in James A. W. Heffernan, 'Wordsworth's London: the Imperial Monster', *Studies in Romanticism*, 37, 1998, p. 421.

6. Williams, *The Country and the City*, pp. 149–52.

7. James Mulvihill, 'The Medium of Landscape in Cobbett's *Rural Rides*', *Studies in English Literature 1500–1800*, 33, 1993, pp. 825–6.

8. William Cobbett, *Rural Rides*, London, n.d. (*c.*1960), p. 42.

9. Thomas Carlyle, *Past and Present*, London, 1843.

10. Benjamin Disraeli, *Sybil* (1845), Harmondsworth, 1985, p. 226.

11. Charles Dickens, *Hard Times* (1854), Harmondsworth, 1985, p. 65.

12. Ibid., p. 146.

13. Elizabeth Gaskell, *North and South* (1855), Harmondsworth, 1986, p. 96.

3. Radicalism and the Land

1. The most distinguished exponent of the view that late eighteenth- and early nineteenth-century political radicalism built on the traditions of seventeenth-century dissent was E. P. Thompson. See E. P. Thompson, *Witness Against the Beast. William Blake and the Moral Law*, Cambridge, 1993, and *The Making of the English Working Class*, London, 1968, especially Part I.

2. For this and the following paragraphs on Spence, see M. Chase, *The People's Farm: English Radical Agrarianism 1775–1840*, Oxford, 1988, especially pp. 32–7, 45–63 and 68–145. Dr Chase's research has rehabilitated Spence as a serious political thinker and recovered the political tradition of English radical agrarianism, and this chapter is much indebted to his work.

3. Peter Linebaugh, 'Jubilating; or, How the Atlantic Working Class Used the Biblical Jubilee Against Capitalism, with Some Success', *Radical History Review*, 50, Spring 1991, p. 144.

4. *New Moral World*, 28 May 1842, quoted in J. F. C. Harrison, *Robert Owen and the Owenites in Britain and America. The Quest for a New Moral World*, London, 1969, pp. 56–7. See also ibid., pp. 24–5; and Edward Royle, *Robert Owen and the Commencement of the Millennium. A Study of the Harmony Community*, Manchester, 1998, p. 157.

5. Vincent Geoghegan, 'Ralahine: an Irish Owenite Community (1831–1833)', *International Review of Social History*, 36, 1991, pp. 377–411.

6. The literature on the Chartist Land Plan is extensive. See W. H. G. Armytage, 'The Chartist Land Colonies, 1846–48', *Agricultural History Review*, 32, 1958, pp. 87–96; J. MacAskill, 'The Chartist Land Plan', in A. Briggs (ed.), *Chartist Studies*, London, 1959, pp. 304–41; P. Searby, 'Great Dodford and the Later History of the Chartist Land Scheme', *Agricultural History Review*, 16, 1968, pp. 32–45; A. Hadfield, *The Chartist Land Company*, London, 1970; O. R. Ashton 'Chartism in Gloucestershire. The Contribution of the Chartist Land Plan, 1843–50', *Transactions of the Bristol and Gloucestershire Archaeological Society*, 104, 1986, pp. 201–8; M. Chase, 'The Chartist Land Plan and the Local Historian', *Local Historian*, 18, 1988, pp. 76–9; idem, '"We Wish Only to Work for Ourselves": the Chartist Land Plan', in M. Chase and I. Dyck (eds), *Living and Learning. Essays in Honour of J. F. C. Harrison*, Aldershot, 1996, pp. 133–48.

7. D. Eastwood, 'The Age of Uncertainty: Britain in the Early-nineteenth Century', *Transactions of the Royal Historical Society*, 6th series, 8, 1998, pp. 113–14.

8. Thompson, *The Making of the English Working Class*, pp. 581–604.

9. R. Wells, *Wretched Faces: Famine in Wartime England, 1793–1803*, Gloucester, 1988, pp. 55–70; Chase, *The People's Farm*, pp. 7–8.

10. Jamie L. Bronstein, *Land Reform and Working-class Experience in Britain and the United States 1800–1862*, Stanford, California, 1999, pp. 54–63, 84–5.

11. J. Burchardt, 'The Allotment Movement in England and Wales, 1793–1873', PhD thesis, University of Reading, pp. 409–14; C. S. Hallas, 'Yeomen and Peasants? Land-ownership Patterns in the North Yorkshire Pennines c.1770–1900', *Rural History*, 9 (2), 1998, pp. 157–77; Chase, *The People's Farm*, pp. 9–13.

12. Chase, *The People's Farm*, pp. 16–17.

13. Ibid., p. 188.

4. Gardens, Allotments and Parks

1. Henry W. Lawrence, 'The Greening of the Squares of London: Transformation of Urban Landscapes and Ideals', *Annals of the Association of American Geographers*, 83 (1), 1993, pp. 98–9.

2. H. L. Malchow, 'Public Gardens and Social Action in Late Victorian London', *Victorian Studies*, 29 (1), pp. 98–9.

3. Harriet Jordan, 'Public Parks, 1885–1914', *Garden History*, 22 (1), 1994, pp. 85–6.

4. Colin Young, 'The Acquisition of Weston-super-Mare's Victorian Parks', *Local Historian*, 20 (4), 1990, pp. 158–65.

5. Jeremy Burchardt, 'Land for the Labourer: Potato Grounds and Allotments in Nineteenth-century Southern England', *Agricultural History*, forthcoming.

6. David Crouch and Colin Ward, *The Allotment: Its Landscape and Culture*, London, 1988, pp. 66–7.

7. Jeremy Burchardt, 'The Allotment Movement in England and Wales, 1793–1873', PhD thesis, University of Reading, pp. 394–426.

8. Stephen Constantine, 'Amateur Gardening and Popular Recreation in the Nineteenth and Twentieth Centuries', *Journal of Social History*, 14 (3), 1981, pp. 387–406.

9. Martin Daunton, *House and Home in the Victorian City: Working-class Housing 1850–1914*, London, 1983.

10. Edward Thompson, *Customs in Common*, London, 1991, pp. 111–14.

11. Lawrence, 'The Greening of the Squares of London', pp. 92–109.

12. Anthea Taigel and Tom Williamson, *Parks and Gardens*, London, 1993, pp. 119–21.

13. Susan Lasdun, *The English Park. Royal, Private and Public*, London, 1991, pp. 129–31.

14. Moor Park, Preston, predates Birkenhead Park as a municipal project intended to improve social welfare but did not couple this so successfully with middle-class housing and was less influential than the latter as a model for subsequent municipal park development. Hazel Conway, *People's Parks. The Design and Development of Victorian Parks in Britain*, Cambridge, 1991.

15. Taigel and Williamson, *Parks and Gardens*, pp. 123–5.

16. Lasdun, *The English Park*, pp. 157–9; Phillada Ballard, *An Oasis of Delight: the History of the Birmingham Botanical Gardens*, London, 1983, pp. 35, 38; Richard Drayton, *Nature's Government. Kew Gardens, Science and Imperial Britain*, New Haven, Connecticut, 2000.

17. Malchow, 'Public Gardens and Social Action in Late Victorian London', p. 123.

18. Jordan, 'Public Parks, 1885–1914', pp. 90–91, 96–7.

5. Model Villages and Garden Cities

1. Gillian Darley, *Villages of Vision*, London, 1978, pp. 25–9, 35–7.

2. Tom Williamson, *Polite Landscapes. Gardens and Society in Eighteenth-century England*, Baltimore, 1995, pp. 148–50. David Jacques, *Georgian Gardens: the Reign of Nature*, London, 1983.

3. Darley, *Villages of Vision*, pp. 63–82.

4. David Roberts, *Paternalism in Early Victorian England*, London, 1979, pp. 129–48.

5. Patrick Joyce, *Work, Society and Politics. The Culture of the Factory in Later Victorian England*, Hassocks, 1980, esp. pp. 90–200.

6. James Hole, *The Homes of the Working Classes, with Suggestions for Their Improvement*, London, 1866, frontispiece.

7. Darley, *Villages of Vision*, pp. 130–32, 137–47.

8. Ebenezer Howard, *Tomorrow: A Peaceful Path to Real Reform*, London, 1898; Peter Hall and Colin Ward, *Sociable Cities: the Legacy of Ebenezer Howard*, Chichester, 1998, pp. 9–13.

9. Stanley Buder, *Visionaries and Planners. The Garden City Movement and the Modern Community*, Oxford, 1990, pp. 87–9; Hall and Ward, *Sociable Cities*, pp. 34–6.

10. Hall and Ward, *Sociable Cities*, pp. 42, 46; Robert Beevers, *The Garden Cites Utopia. A Critical Biography of Ebenezer Howard*, London, 1988, pp. 163–76.

6. Literary Attitudes to the Countryside

1. The best discussion of regionalism in the English novel is W. J. Keith, *Regions of the Imagination. The Development of British Rural Fiction*, Toronto, 1988.

2. M. J. Wiener, *English Culture and the Decline of the Industrial Spirit*, Cambridge, 1981, p. 53.

3. E. M. Forster, *Howards End* (1910), Harmondsworth, 1983, pp. 29–30, 329.

4. Thomas Hardy, *Tess of the d'Urbervilles* (1891), London, 1984, p. 309.

5. G. Sturt, *Change in the Village* (1912), London, 1984.

6. Raymond Williams, *The Country and the City*, London, 1973, especially Chs 15, 19 and 20.

7. G. Sturt, *The Wheelwright's Shop* (1923), Cambridge, 1993.

8. F. R. Leavis and D. Thompson, *Culture and Environment. The Training of Critical Awareness*, London, 1933.

9. L. James, 'Landscape in Nineteenth-century Literature', in G. E. Mingay (ed.), *The Rural Idyll*, London, 1989, p. 72.

10. G. Cavaliero, *The Rural Tradition in the English Novel 1900–1939*, London, 1977, Chs 4 and 9; W. J. Keith, *The Poetry of Nature. Rural Perspectives in Poetry from Wordsworth to the Present*, Toronto, 1980, Ch. 7; D. Gervais, *Literary England: Versions of 'Englishness' in Modern Writing*, p. 8.

11. P. Brooker and P. Widdowson, 'A Literature for England', in R. Colls and P. Dodd (eds), *Englishness: Politics and Culture 1880–1920*, London, 1986, pp. 122, 126–33.

12. Keith, *The Poetry of Nature*, pp. 151–6.

7. Land Reform After 1850

1. Malcolm Chase, 'Out of Radicalism: the Mid-Victorian Freehold Land Movement', *English Historical Review*, 106, 1991, pp. 319–45.

2. Sadie B. Ward, 'Land Reform in England 1880–1914', PhD Thesis, University of Reading, 1976, pp. 52–6.

3. John Prest, *Politics in the Age of Cobden*, London, 1977, Ch. 6; Avner Offer, *Property and Politics 1870–1914. Landownership, Law, Ideology and Urban Development in England*, Cambridge, 1981, pp. 182–3.

4. Offer, *Property and Politics*, pp. 40–41; Roy Douglas, *Land, People and Politics. A History of the Land Question in the United Kingdom, 1878–1952*, London, 1976, pp. 40–42, 48–58; Ward, 'Land Reform in England', pp. 58–69; Andrew Adonis, 'Aristocracy, Agriculture and Liberalism: the Politics, Finances and Estates of the Third Lord Carrington', *Historical Journal*, 31 (4), 1988, pp. 888–97.

5. Ward, 'Land Reform in England', pp. 65–6, 81–102.

6. Henry George, *Progress and Poverty*, New York, 1880; Offer, *Property and Politics*, pp. 184–5.

7. Ward, 'Land Reform in England', pp. 139–86.

8. Ibid., pp. 125–38, 366–461; Douglas, *Land, People and Politics*, pp. 48–9.

9. Douglas, *Land, People and Politics*, pp. 114–15.

10. E. H. H. Green, *The Crisis of Conservatism: the Politics, Economics, and Ideology of the Conservative Party, 1880–1914*, London, 1995, pp. 128, 192.

11. Ward, 'Land Reform in England', pp. 292–337.

12. Douglas, *Land, People and Politics*, pp. 134–45.

13. Green, *The Crisis of Conservatism*, pp. 209–10, 218–19.

14. Michael Tichelar, 'Socialists, Labour and the Land: the Response of the Labour Party to the Land Campaign of Lloyd George Before the First World War', *Twentieth Century British History*, 8 (2), 1997, pp. 127–30, 142–4.

15. David Spring, 'Land and Politics in Edwardian England', *Agricultural History*, 58 (1), 1984, pp. 30–42.

16. Bentley B. Gilbert, 'David Lloyd George: the Reform of British Landholding and the Budget of 1914', *Historical Journal*, 21 (1), 1978, pp. 117–41.

17. Carol Lockwood, 'From Soldier to Peasant? The Land Settlement Scheme in East Sussex, 1919–1939', *Albion*, 30, 1998, pp. 439, 443–4.

18. Douglas, *Land, People and Politics*, pp. 169–214.

19. Brian Short, *Land and Society in Edwardian Britain*, Cambridge, 1997, pp. 27–37.

20. Offer, *Property and Politics*, p. 406.

8. Preservationism, Englishness and the Rise of Planning

1. Mark Clapson, *Invincible Green Suburbs, Brave New Towns: Social Change and Urban Dispersal in Postwar England*, Manchester, 1998, p. 33.

2. John Sheail, *Rural Conservation in Interwar Britain*, Oxford, 1981, pp. 14–15; David Matless, *Landscape and Englishness*, London, 1998, pp. 37–8.

3. David Prynn, 'The Clarion Clubs, Rambling and the Holiday Associations in Britain Since the 1890s', *Journal of Contemporary History*, 11, 1976, pp. 66–9.

4. D. N. Jeans, 'Planning and the Myth of the English Countryside in the Interwar Period', *Rural History*, 1 (2), 1990, pp. 251–8; Dennis Hardy and Colin Ward, *Arcadia for All: the Legacy of a Makeshift Landscape*, London, 1984.

5. Philip Lowe, 'The Rural Idyll Defended: from Preservation to Conservation', in G. E. Mingay (ed.), *The Rural Idyll*, London, 1989, p. 114; John Ranlett, '"Checking Nature's Desecration": Late-Victorian Environmental Organisations', *Victorian Studies*, 26 (2), 1983, pp. 197–222.

6. M. J. Wiener, *English Culture and the Decline of the Industrial Spirit*, Cambridge, 1981.

7. For a recent critique of Wiener's views on the effects of public school education, see Hartmut Berghoff, 'Public Schools and the Decline of the British Economy 1870–1914', *Past and Present*, 129, 1990, pp. 148–67.

8. Alun Howkins, 'The Discovery of Rural England', in Robert Colls and Philip Dodd (eds), *Englishness: Politics and Culture 1880–1920*, London, 1986, pp. 62–88.

9. Georgina Boyes, *The Imagined Village: Culture, Ideology and the English Folk Revival*, Manchester, 1993, pp. 95, 103, 108, 112–13.

10. Patrick Wright, *On Living in an Old Country. The National Past in Contemporary Britain*, London, 1985. See also Frank Trentmann, 'Civilization and Its Discontents: English Neo-Romanticism and the Transformation of Anti-modernism in Twentieth-century Western Culture', *Journal of Contemporary History*, 29, 1994, pp. 583–625. Like Wright, Trentmann locates pro-rural sentiment in a general Western (rather than specifically English) reaction against modernity, but he denies its conservative character.

11. Peter Mandler, '"Against Englishness": English Culture and the Limits to Rural Nostalgia, 1850–1940', *Transactions of the Royal Historical Society*, 6th series, 7, 1997, pp. 155–77.

12. Paul Readman, 'Landscape Preservation, "Advertising Disfigurement", and English National Identity c. 1890–1914', *Rural History*, 12, 2001, p. 63.

13. Boyes, *The Imagined Village*.

14. Anthony Taylor, '"Commons-stealers", "Land-grabbers" and "Jerry-builders": Space, Popular Radicalism and the Politics of Public Access in London, 1848–1880', *International Review of Social History*, 40, 1995, pp 383–407; Peter Mandler, *The Fall and Rise of the Stately Home*, New Haven, Connecticut, 1997, pp. 109–263.

15. Matless, *Landscape and Englishness*, pp. 50–54.

16. Ibid.; H. Peach and N. Carrington, *The Face of the Land*, London, 1930.

17. The relationship between rambling and preservationism is considered at more length in the next chapter. See also Tom Stephenson, *Forbidden Land: the Struggle for Access to Moorland and Mountain*, Manchester, 1989, pp. 168–75.

18. John K. Walton, 'The National Trust Centenary: Official and Unofficial Histories', *Local Historian* 26 (2) 1996, pp. 83–4.

19. Howard Hill, *Freedom to Roam: the Struggle for Access to Britain's Moors and Mountains*, Ashbourne, 1980, p. 77.

20. M. Pugh, *The Tories and the People 1880–1935*, Oxford, 1985; R. McKibbin, *The Ideologies of Class. Social Relations in Britain, 1880–1950*, Oxford, 1990, Ch. 9.

21. Simon Miller, 'Urban Dreams and Rural Reality: Land and Landscape in English Culture, 1920–45', *Rural History*, 6 (1), 1995, pp. 89–102. See also Philip Williamson, *Stanley Baldwin. Conservative Leadership and National Values*, Cambridge, 1999, pp. 244–50.

22. Williamson, *Stanley Baldwin*, p. 247.

23. Miller, 'Urban Dreams and Rural Reality', pp. 89–102. Miller's claim that Baldwin was inattentive to the socio-economic problems of the interwar countryside is echoed by Williamson, *Stanley Baldwin*, p. 245.

24. Edmund C. Penning-Rowsell, 'Who "Betrayed" Whom? Power and Politics in the 1920/21 Agricultural Crisis', *Agricultural History Review*, 45 (2), 1997, pp. 176–94.

25. Alan Armstrong, *Farmworkers. A Social and Economic History 1770–1980*, London, 1988, Ch. 8.

26. Raymond Williams, *The Country and the City*, London, 1973; Howard Newby,

Green and Pleasant Land? Social Change in Rural England, London, 1980; John Barrell, *The Dark Side of the Landscape. The Rural Poor in English Painting 1730–1840*, Cambridge, 1983.

27. C. Griffiths, '"Red Tape Farm"? The Labour Party and the Farmers, 1918–1939', in J. R. Wordie (ed.), *Agriculture and Politics in England 1815–1939*, London, 2000, pp. 199–241.

28. Sheail, *Rural Conservation*, pp. 66–70.

29. Ibid., pp. 85–6.

30. John Lowerson, 'Battles for the Countryside', in Frank Gloversmith (ed.), *Class, Culture and Social Change: a New View of the 1930s*, Brighton, 1980, p. 258.

9. The Economic Consequences of Rural Nostalgia

1. A. Sampson, *The Essential Anatomy of Britain: Democracy in Crisis*, London, 1992; W. Hutton, *The State We're In*, London, 1995; C. Barnett, *The Lost Victory: British Dreams, British Realities, 1945–1950*, London, 1995; M. J. Wiener, *English Culture and the Decline of the Industrial Spirit*, Cambridge, 1981.

2. For a good recent summary of the arguments on British economic decline, see M. Dintenfass, *The Decline of Industrial Britain, 1870–1980*, London, 1992.

3. Hutton, *The State We're In*, pp. 114–131; Barnett, *The Lost Victory*, pp. 123–64.

4. L. G. Sandberg, *Lancashire in Decline. A Study in Entrepreneurship, Technology, and International Trade*, Colombus, Ohio, 1974.

5. M. Sanderson, *Education and Economic Decline in Britain, 1870 to the 1990s*, Cambridge, 1999; Hartmut Berghoff, 'Public Schools and the Decline of the British Economy 1870–1914', *Past and Present*, 129, 1990, pp. 148–67.

6. W. D. Rubinstein, *Capitalism, Culture and Decline in Britain 1750–1990*, London, 1993.

7. C. H. Feinstein, 'Success and Failure: British Economic Growth Since 1948', in Roderick Floud and Donald McCloskey (eds), *The Economic History of Britain Since 1700*, 2nd edn, Cambridge, 1994, pp. 95–122.

10. Rambling

1. Marion Shoard, *A Right to Roam?*, Oxford, 1999, pp. 149–50.

2. In an important new study which appeared after this book had gone to press, Donna Landry argues that field sports, especially hunting, were among the primary constitutive influences on late eighteenth- and early nineteenth-century rural walking. Donna Landry, *The Invention of the Countryside*, Basingstoke, 2001.

3. W. J. Keith, *The Poetry of Nature. Rural Perspectives in Poetry from Wordsworth to the Present*, Toronto, 1980, pp. 11–37.

4. Marion Shoard, *This Land is Our Land. The Struggle for Britain's Countryside*, London, 1987, p. 113.

5. Tom Stephenson, *Forbidden Land: the Struggle for Access to Mountain and Moorland*, Manchester, 1989, pp. 60–69.

6. Elizabeth Gaskell, *Mary Barton. A Tale of Manchester Life*, London, 1848.

7. Louis James, 'Landscape in Nineteenth-century Literature', in G. E. Mingay (ed.), *The Rural Idyll*, London, 1989, pp. 70–71.

8. Gordon Cherry and John Sheail, 'The Urban Impact on the Countryside', in E. J. T. Collins (ed.), *The Agrarian History of England and Wales VII (part II), 1850–1914*, Cambridge, 2000, pp. 1655–7.

9. Shoard, *A Right to Roam?*, pp. 169–74.

10. David Matless, *Landscape and Englishness*, London, 1998, pp. 70–73.

11. Trentmann, 'Civilization and Its Discontents: English Neo-Romanticism and the Transformation of Anti-modernism in Twentieth-century Western Culture', *Journal of Contemporary History*, 29, 1994, pp. 589–91.

12. David Prynn, 'The Clarion Clubs, Rambling and the Holiday Associations in Britain Since the 1890s', *Journal of Contemporary History*, 11, 1976, pp. 71–5.

13. Catherine Brace, 'A Pleasure Ground for the Noisy Herds? Incompatible Encounters with the Cotswolds and England, 1900–1950', *Rural History*, 11, 2000, pp. 75–94.

14. Stephenson, *Forbidden Land*, pp. 153–64.

15. Ibid., pp. 153–64; Benny Rothman, *The 1932 Kinder Trespass: a Personal View of the Kinder Scout Mass Trespass*, Altrincham, 1982, pp. 23–36.

16. Rothman, *The 1932 Kinder Trespass*, p. 20.

17. Matless, *Landscape and Englishness*, p. 71; Stephenson, *Forbidden Land*, pp. 88–100.

18. Stephenson, *Forbidden Land*, p. 163; Howard Hill, *Freedom to Roam: the Struggle for Access to Britain's Moors and Mountains*, Ashbourne, 1980, pp. 74–5, 81–2.

11. The Organic Movement Before and During the Second World War

1. Philip Conford, 'A Forum for Organic Husbandry: the *New English Weekly* and Agricultural Policy, 1939–49', *Agricultural History Review*, 46 (2), 1998, p. 198.

2. Philip Conford, 'The Alchemy of Waste: the Impact of Asian Farming on the British Organic Movement', *Rural History*, 6 (1), 1995, pp. 107–10.

3. David Matless, *Landscape and Englishness*, London, 1998, pp. 155–60.

4. Ibid., p. 109; Philip Conford, 'Good Husbandry', *Henry Williamson Society Journal*, 35, September 1999, p. 31.

5. Ibid., p. 29.

6. Matless, *Landscape and Englishness*, pp. 103–4, 136.

7. King's book was not published in Britain until after the First World War. F. H. King, *Farmers of Forty Centuries, or Permanent Agriculture in China, Korea and Japan*, London, 1927; Conford, 'The Alchemy of Waste', pp. 103–4, 106–7.

8. R. D. Brigden, 'Farming in Partnership. The Leckford Estate and the Pursuit of Profit in Inter-war Agriculture', PhD thesis, University of Reading, 2000, p. 330. The method used by the Wilson brothers was described as 'evil' in one of the most widely read organicist works of the interwar years, W. Beach Thomas's *How England Becomes Prairie* (London, 1927), pp. 32, 38, 56.

9. As was brought graphically to the attention of the interwar generation by G. V. Jacks and R. O. Whyte, *The Rape of the Earth*, London, 1939, a worldwide survey of soil erosion.

10. Matless, *Landscape and Englishness*, pp. 162–6; Conford, 'The Alchemy of Waste', p. 111.

11. Conford, 'Good Husbandry', p. 30.

12. Ibid., p. 28.

12. Rural Reconstruction Between the Wars

1. P. A. Graham, *The Rural Exodus: the Problem of the Village and the Town*, London, 1892; S. R. Haresign, 'Small Farms and Allotments as a Cure for Rural Depopulation on the Lincolnshire Fenland 1870–1914', *Lincolnshire History and Archaeology*, 18, 1983, pp. 27–36.

2. H. Rider Haggard, *Rural England*, London, 1902; Edmund C. Penning-Rowsell, 'Who "Betrayed" Whom? Power and Politics in the 1920/21 Agricultural Crisis', *Agricultural History Review*, 45 (2), 1997, pp. 176–94.

3. Carol A. Lockwood, 'From Soldier to Peasant? The Land Settlement Scheme in East Sussex, 1919–1939', *Albion*, 30, 1998, pp. 448–62.

4. R. D. Brigden, 'Farming in Partnership. The Leckford Estate and the Pursuit of Profit in Inter-war Agriculture', PhD Thesis, University of Reading, 2000, pp. 65–88.

5. On the Women's Institutes, see M. Morgan, *The Acceptable Face of Feminism*, London, 1996. Valuable data relating to rural leisure organizations between the wars is in H. E. Bracey, *Social Provision in Rural Wiltshire*, London, 1952.

6. J. Burchardt, 'Deference and Democracy: Village Social Organizations in England 1870–1940', in J. Bielemann (ed.), *Rural Institutions: Proceedings of the CORN-Wageningen Conference, 1999*, Wageningen, forthcoming.

7. Margaret Brasnett, *Voluntary Social Action. A History of the National Council of Social Service 1919–1969*, London, 1969, pp. 32–3; J. Burchardt, 'Reconstructing the Rural Community: Village Halls and the National Council of Social Service, 1919 to 1939', *Rural History*, 10 (2), 1999, pp. 195–6.

8. Inez Jenkins, *The History of the Women's Institute Movement of England and Wales*, Oxford, 1953, pp. 55–6.

9. Nick Mansfield, 'Class Conflict and Village War Memorials, 1914–24', *Rural History*, 6 (2), 1995, pp. 67–87.

10. An interesting example of an organicist approach to rural reconstruction, placing the emphasis firmly on agriculture rather than social life, is R. G. Stapledon, *The Land. Now and Tomorrow*, London, 1935. See also Philip Conford, *The Origins of the Organic Movement*, Edinburgh, 2001.

11. Burchardt, 'Deference and Democracy'.

12. Burchardt, 'Reconstructing the Rural Community', pp. 205, 211–12.

13. Rural Change and the Legislative Framework, 1939 to 2000

1. R. D. Brigden, 'Farming in Partnership. The Leckford Estate and the Pursuit of Profit in Inter-war Agriculture', PhD Thesis, University of Reading, 2000, p. 191; E. J. T. Collins, 'The Uptake of the Milking Machine in England and Wales', in Klaus Herrmann and Harald Winkel (eds), *Vom 'Fleissigen' zum 'Produktiven' Bauern. Aspekte zum Wandel der europäischen Landwirtschaft des 19./20. Jahrhunderts*, n.d., p. 3.

2. Unpublished research by the author based on Hampshire trade directories.

3. A. Burrell, B. Hill and J. Medland, *Statistical Handbook of UK Agriculture*, Wye College, 1987, p. 43.

4. Howard Newby, *The Deferential Worker. A Study of Farm Workers in East Anglia*, London, 1977, pp. 309–16.

5. Alan Armstrong, *Farmworkers. A Social and Economic History 1770–1980*, London, 1988, pp. 238–43.

6. Thomas Hardy, *Far from the Madding Crowd*, London, 1874; W. H. Hudson, *A Shepherd's Life. Impressions of the South Wiltshire Downs*, London, 1910.

7. Many farms, especially in eastern England, no longer even have livestock.

8. William Wordsworth, letters to the *Morning Post*, quoted in James Winter, *Secure from Rash Assault: Sustaining the Victorian Environment*, Berkeley, California, 1999, p 107; Dickens, *Hard Times*; John Ruskin, *The Crown of Wild Olive. Four Lectures on Industry and War*, London, 1898; E. M. Forster, *Howards End*, 1910, D. H. Lawrence, *The Rainbow*, 1915.

9. Brian Short (ed.), *The English Rural Community: Image and Analysis*, Cambridge, 1992, p. 2.

10. A good discussion of the effects of the price regime established under the 1947 Agriculture Act can be found in P. Self and H. J. Storing, *The State and the Farmer*, London, 1962. See also Michael Winter, *Rural Politics. Policies for Agriculture, Forestry and the Environment*, London, 1996.

11. Gordon E. Cherry and Alan Rogers, *Rural Change and Planning. England and Wales in the Twentieth Century*, London, 1996, pp. 83–7.

12. *Report of the Committee on Land Utilisation in Rural Areas*, cmd 6378, London, 1942.

13. Andrew Flynn, Philip Lowe and Michael Winter, 'The Political Power of Farmers: an English Perspective', *Rural History*, 7, 1996, pp. 15–32, esp. p. 24.

14. Paul A. Crompton, 'The Changing Population', in R. J. Johnston and Vince Gardiner (eds), *The Changing Geography of the United Kingdom*, London, 1991, pp. 35–82; Malcolm J. Moseley, 'The Rural Areas', in ibid., pp. 294–315.

15. Ruth Gasson, *Mobility of Farm Workers. A Study of the Effects of Towns and Industrial Employment on the Supply of Farm Labour*, Cambridge, 1974, pp. 16–18.

16. Ray Pahl, *Urbs in Rure. The Metropolitan Fringe in Hertfordshire*, London, 1965.

14. Agriculture and the Environment

1. Rachel Carson, *Silent Spring*, London, 1963.

2. Ian Hodge, 'The Changing Place of Farming', in Denis Britton (ed.), *Agriculture in Britain: Changing Pressures and Policies*, Wallingford, 1990, pp. 34–44.

3. Philip Lowe, Graham Cox, Malcolm MacEwen, Tim O'Riordan and Michael Winter, *Countryside Conflicts. The Politics of Farming, Forestry and Conservation*, Aldershot, 1986, pp. 265–300.

4. B. A. Holderness, *British Agriculture Since 1945*, Manchester, 1985, pp. 110–20.

5. Between 1984 and 1993 there was a net loss of 158,000 km of hedgerows in England. Countryside Agency, *The State of the Countryside 1999*, London, 1999, p. 11.

6. Quentin Seddon, *The Silent Revolution*, London, 1989, pp. 35–40, 97–114.

7. Lowe et al., *Countryside Conflicts*, pp. 191–208.

8. J. K. Bowers and Paul Cheshire, *Agriculture, the Countryside and Land Use: an Economic Critique*, London, 1983, pp. 29–51. However, it should be pointed out that the original purpose of the AONBs was to preserve landscape characteristics, particularly by keeping industrial and residential development out of the villages, and in this respect they have been more successful than environmentalist critics usually allow.

9. E. J. T. Collins, 'Agriculture and Conservation in England: an Historical Overview, 1880–1939', *Journal of the Royal Agricultural Society of England*, 146, 1985, pp. 38–46.

10. Howard Newby, *Green and Pleasant Land? Social Change in Rural England*, London, 1980, pp. 20–23, 167–8.

15. Recreation in the Countryside since the Second World War

1. J. Davidson and G. Wibberley, *Planning and the Rural Environment*, Oxford, 1977, p. 6.

2. John Blunden and Nigel Curry, *A People's Charter? Forty Years of the National Parks and Access to the Countryside Act, 1949*, London, 1990, p. 53.

3. Sue Glyptis, *Countryside Recreation*, Harlow, 1991, p. 23.

4. Davidson and Wibberley, *Planning and the Rural Environment*, pp. 52–5.

5. Countryside Agency, *The State of the Countryside 1999*, London, 1999, p. 32.

6. Glyptis, *Countryside Recreation*, p. ix.

7. Nigel Curry, *Countryside Recreation, Access and Land Use Planning*, London, 1994, p. 209.

8. Gordon E. Cherry, *Environmental Planning 1939–69. Volume II: National Parks and Recreation in the Countryside*, London, 1975, pp. 154–5.

9. John Sheail, 'The Concept of National Parks in Great Britain 1900–1950', *Transactions of the Institute of British Geographers*, 66, 1975, pp. 41–56.

10. Blunden and Curry, *A People's Charter?*, p. 103.

11. Paul Cloke, 'The Countryside as Commodity: New Spaces for Rural Leisure', in Sue Glyptis (ed.), *Leisure and the Envoironment, Essays in Honour of Professor J. A. Patmore*, London, 1993, pp. 53–67.

16. Intra-village Social Change and Attitudinal Conflict in the Twentieth Century

1. Countryside Agency, *The State of the Countryside 1999*, London, 1999, p. 27.

2. Philip Rieden, 'The End of a Great Estate: the Honour of Grafton in the Twentieth Century', unpublished conference paper delivered 9 October 1999 at 'The VCH and the Study of Rural Change', Cheltenham and Gloucester College of Higher Education.

3. In 1997, 42 per cent of rural parishes had no shop, 43 per cent no post office, 29 per cent no pub, 83 per cent no GP based in the parish and 49 per cent no school (for any age). Countryside Agency, *The State of the Countryside 1999*, p. 26.

4. Guy Robinson, *Conflict and Change in the Countryside. Rural society, Economy and Planning in the Developed World*, London, 1990, pp. 376–81.

5. James Littlejohn, *Westrigg. The Sociology of a Cheviot Parish*, London, 1963, pp. 152–3; R. M. Crichton, *Commuters' Village. A Study of Community and Commuters in the Berkshire Village of Stratfield Mortimer*, Dawlish, 1964, p. 86.

6. Howard Newby, *The Countryside in Question*, London, 1988, p. 39.

7. Jonathan Murdoch and Terry Marsden, *Reconstituting Rurality. Class, Community and Power in the Development Process*, London, 1994.

8. Howard Newby, *Country Life: a Social History of Rural England*, London, 1987,

pp. 220–33; *Green and Pleasant Land? Social Change in Rural England*, London, 1980, pp. 164–90.

9. P. Ambrose, *The Quiet Revolution*, London, 1974, pp. 81–2.

10. Ibid., pp. 80–81, 86–7.

11. Ibid., pp. 83–5.

12. Ibid., p. 87.

13. Ibid., p. 88.

14. Ibid., pp. 91–3.

15. Jean Robin, *Elmdon. Continuity and Change in a North-west Essex Village 1861–1964*, Cambridge, 1980, pp. 228–33.

16. Ibid., pp. 219–21.

17. Ibid., pp. 224–6.

18. Ibid., pp. 233–4.

19. Ibid., pp. 237–8.

17. Town, Country and Politics at the End of the Twentieth Century

1. *Observer*, 1 March 1998, p. 8, col. 8.

2. Ibid., col. 5–6; *Financial Times*, 28 February 1998, p. 8, col. 3; *The Times*, 2 March 1998, p. 3.

3. P. Self and H. J. Storing, *The State and the Farmer*, London, 1962; W. Grant, 'The National Farmers Union: the Classic Case of Incorporation?', in D. Marsh (ed.), *Pressure Politics*, London, 1983, pp. 129–43; Graham Cox, 'Agriculture and Conservation in Britain: a Policy Community Under Siege', in Graham Cox, Philip Lowe and Michael Winter (eds), *Agriculture: People and Politics*, London, 1986, pp. 184–99; Philip Lowe, Graham Cox, Malcolm MacEwen, Tim O'Riordan and Michael Winter, *Countryside Conflicts. The Politics of Farming, Forestry and Conservation*, Aldershot, 1986, pp. 85–111; Martin J. Smith, *The Politics of Agricultural Support: Britain. The Development of the Agricultural Policy Community*, Brookfield, Vermont, 1990.

4. Countryside Agency, *The State of the Countryside 1999*, London, 1999, pp. 13, 20.

5. Howard Newby, *Country Life: a Social History of Rural England*, London, 1987, p. 236.

6. *Observer*, 7 March 1999, p. 8.

7. Research carried out by the Countryside Commission in 1997 suggested that over half the population wanted to live in the countryside. The Countryside Agency, *The State of the Countryside 1999*, p. 8.

Select Bibliography

Ambrose, P., *The Quiet Revolution*, London, 1974.

Armstrong, A., *Farmworkers. A Social and Economic History 1770–1980*, London, 1988.

— 'The Countryside', in F. M. L. Thompson (ed.), *The Cambridge Social History of Britain, 1750–1950. Volume 1: Regions and Communities*, Cambridge, 1990.

Barnett, A. and R. Scruton, *Town and Country*, London, 1998.

Barrell, J., *The Idea of Landscape and the Sense of Place 1730–1840. An Approach to the Poetry of John Clare*, Cambridge, 1972.

Beevers, R. *The Garden City Utopia. A Critical Biography of Ebenezer Howard*, London, 1988.

Bensusan, S. L., *Latter-day Rural England*, London, 1927.

Bermingham, A., *Landscape and Ideology: the English Rustic Tradition, 1740–1860*, London, 1987.

Blunden, J. and N. Curry, *A People's Charter? Forty Years of the Parks and Access to the Countryside Act, 1949*, London, 1990.

Blythe, R., *Akenfield*, London, 1969.

Bonham-Carter, V., *The Survival of the English Countryside*, London, 1971.

Bowers, J. K. and P. Cheshire, *Agriculture, the Countryside and Land Use: an Economic Critique*, London, 1983.

Boyes, G., *The Imagined Village: Culture, Ideology, and the English Folk Revival*, Manchester, 1993.

Brace, C., 'A Pleasure Ground for the Noisy Herds? Incompatible Encounters with the Cotswolds and England, 1900–1950', *Rural History*, 11, 2000, pp. 75–94.

Bracey, H. E., *English Rural Life: Village Activities, Organizations and Institutions*, London, 1959.

— *People and the Countryside*, London, 1972.

Britton, D. (ed.), *Agriculture in Britain: Changing Pressures and Policies*, Wallingford, 1990.

Bronstein, J. L., *Land Reform and Working-class Experience in Britain and the United States 1800–1862*, Stanford, California, 1999.

Brooker, P., 'A Literature for England', in R. Colls and P. Dodd (eds), *Englishness: Culture and Politics 1880–1920*, London, 1986.

Buder, S., *Visionaries and Planners. The Garden City Movement and the Modern Community*, Oxford, 1990.

Bunce, M., *The Countryside Ideal: Anglo-American Images of Landscape*, London, 1994.

Burchardt, J., 'The Allotment Movement in England and Wales, 1793–1873', University of Reading, PhD Thesis, 1997.

Chadwick, G. F., *The Park and the Town: Public Landscape in the Nineteenth and Twentieth Centuries*, London, 1966.

Chase, M., *The People's Farm: English Radical Agrarianism 1775–1840*, Oxford, 1988.

— 'Out of Radicalism: The Mid-Victorian Freehold Land Movement', *English Historical Review*, 106, 1991, pp. 319–45.

— 'The Chartist Land Plan and the Local Historian', *Local Historian*, 18, 1988, pp. 76–9.

Cherry, G. E., *Environmental Planning 1939–69: Volume II. National Parks and Recreation in the Countryside*, London, 1975.

Cherry, G. E. and A. Rogers, *Rural Change and Planning. England and Wales in the Twentieth Century*, London, 1996.

Cherry G. E. and J. Sheail, 'The Urban Impact on the Countryside', in E. J. T. Collins (ed.), *The Agrarian History of England and Wales VII (Part II), 1850–1914*, Cambridge, 2000, pp. 1515–756.

Church, R. A., 'James Orange and the Allotment System in Nottingham', *Transactions of the Thoroton Society*, LXIV, 1960.

Clapson, M., *Invincible Green Suburbs, Brave New Towns: Social Change and Urban Dispersal in Post-war England*, Manchester, 1998.

Cloke, P. and J. Little (eds), *Contested Countryside Cultures. Otherness, Marginalisation and Rurality*, London, 1997.

Collins, E. J. T., 'The Uptake of the Milking Machine in England and Wales', in Klaus Herrmann and Harald Winkel (eds), *Vom 'fleissigen' zum 'produktiven' Bauern. Aspekte zum Wandel der europäischen Landwirtschaft des 19./20. Jahrhunderts*, no place of publication or date.

— (ed.), *The Agrarian History of England and Wales VII (Part II), 1850–1914*, Cambridge, 2000.

Colls, R. and P. Dodd (eds), *Englishness: Politics and Culture 1880–1920*, London, 1986.

Conford, P., 'The Alchemy of Waste: the Impact of Asian Farming on the British Organic Movement', *Rural History*, 6 (1), 1995, pp. 103–14.

— 'A Forum for Organic Husbandry: the *New English Weekly* and Agricultural Policy, 1939–49', *Agricultural History Review*, 46 (2), 1998, pp. 197–210.

— 'Good Husbandry', *Henry Williamson Society Journal*, 35, September 1999, pp. 27–34.

— *The Origins of the Organic Movement*, Edinburgh, 2001.

Constantine, S., 'Amateur Gardening and Popular Recreation in the Nineteenth and Twentieth Centuries', *Journal of Social History*, 14 (3), 1981, pp. 387–406.

Conway, H., *People's Parks. The Design and Development of Victorian Parks in Britain*, Cambridge, 1991.

— 'Everyday Landscapes: Public Parks from 1930 to 2000', *Garden History*, 28, 2000, pp. 117–34.

Cosgrove, D. and S. Daniels (eds), *The Iconography of Landscape. Essays on the Symbolic Representation, Design and Use of Past Environments*, Cambridge, 1988.

Countryside Agency, *The State of the Countryside 1999*, London, 1999.

Cox, G., 'Agriculture and Conservation in Britain: a Policy Community Under Siege', in G. Cox, P. Lowe and M. Winter (eds), *Agriculture: People and Policies*, London, 1986.

Crichton, R., *Commuter Village*, Newton Abbot, 1964.

Crouch, D. and Colin Ward, *The Allotment: Its Landscape and Culture*, London, 1988.

Curry, N., *Countryside Recreation, Access and Land Use Planning*, London, 1994.

Daniels, S., *Fields of Vision: Landscape Imagery and National Identity in England and the U.S.*, London, 1993.

Darley, G., *Villages of Vision*, London, 1978.

Davidson, J. and G. Wibberley, *Planning and the Rural Environment*, Oxford, 1977.

Eastwood, D., 'The Age of Uncertainty: Britain in the Early-nineteenth Century', *Transactions of the Royal Historical Society*, 6th series, 8, 1998, pp. 91–116.

Geoghegan, V., 'Ralahine: an Irish Owenite Community (1831–1833)', *International Review of Social History*, 36, pp. 377–411.

Gervais, D., *Literary England: Versions of 'Englishness' in Modern Writing*, Cambridge, 1993.

Gilg, A. W., *Countryside Planning. The First Three Decades 1945–76*, London, 1978.

Gloversmith, F. (ed.), *Class, Culture and Social Change: a New View of the 1930s*, Brighton, 1980.

Glyptis, S., *Leisure and the Environment: Essays in Honour of Professor J. A. Patmore*, London, 1993.

— *Planning and Rural Recreation in Britain*, Aldershot, 1993.

Goodridge, J., *Rural Life in Eighteenth-century English Poetry*, Cambridge, 1995.

Gould, P. C., *Early Green Politics: Back to Nature, Back to the Land, and Socialism in Britain, 1880–1900*, Brighton, 1988.

Hadfield, A., *The Chartist Land Company*, London, 1970.

Hall, P., *Sociable Cities: the Legacy of Ebenezer Howard*, Chichester, 1998.

Hallas, C. S., 'Yeomen and Peasants? Landownership Patterns in the North Yorkshire Pennines c.1770–1900', *Rural History*, 9 (2), 1998, pp. 157–77.

Hardy, D., *From Garden Cities to New Towns. Campaigning for Town and Country Planning, 1899–1946*, London, 1991.

Hardy, D. and Colin Ward, *Arcadia for All: the Legacy of a Makeshift Landscape*, London, 1984.

Harrison, J. F. C., *Robert Owen and the Owenites in Britain and America. The Quest for a New Moral World*, London, 1969.

Heathorn, S., 'An English Paradise to Regain? Ebenezer Howard, the Town and Country Planning Association and English Ruralism', *Rural History*, 11, 2000, pp. 113–28.

Hill, H., *Freedom to Roam: the Struggle for Access to Britain's Moors and Mountains*, Ashbourne, 1980.

Holderness, B. A., *British Agriculture Since 1945*, Manchester, 1985.

Howard, E., *Tomorrow: a Peaceful Path to Real Reform*, London, 1898.

Howkins, A., 'The Discovery of Rural England', in R. Colls and P. Dodd (eds), *Englishness: Culture and Politics 1880–1920*, London, 1986.

— *Reshaping Rural England. A Social History 1850–1925*, London, 1991.

Hunter, M., *Preserving the Past. The Rise of Heritage in Modern Britain*, Gloucester, 1996.

Jacks, G. V., and R. O. Whyte, *The Rape of the Earth. A World Survey of Soil Erosion*, London, 1939.

Jacques, D., *Georgian Gardens: the Reign of Nature*, London, 1983.

Jeans, D. N., 'Planning and the Myth of the English Countryside in the Interwar Period', *Rural History*, 1 (2), 1990, pp. 249–64.

Jordan, H., 'Public Parks, 1885–1914', *Garden History*, 22 (1), 1994, pp. 85–113.

Landry, D., *The Muses of Resistance*, Cambridge, 1990.

— *The Invention of the Countryside*, Basingstoke, 2001.

Lasdun, S., *The English Park, Royal, Private and Public*, London, 1992.

Lawrence, H. W., 'The Greening of the Squares of London: Transformation of Urban Landscapes and Ideals', *Annals of the Association of American Geographers*, 83 (1), 1993, pp. 90–118.

Lebas, E., 'The Making of a Socialist Arcadia: Arboriculture and Horticulture in the London Borough of Bermondsey After the Great War', *Garden History*, 27 (1), summer 1999, pp. 219–37.

Light, A., *Forever England: Femininity, Literature and Conservatism Between the Wars*, Cambridge, 1991.

Linebaugh, P., 'Jubilating; or, how the Atlantic Working Class Used the Biblical Jubilee Against Capitalism, with Some Success', *Radical History Review*, 50, spring 1991, pp. 143–80.

Littlejohn, J., *Westrigg. The Sociology of a Cheviot Parish*, London, 1963.

Lockwood, C. A., 'From Soldier to Peasant? The Land Settlement Scheme in East Sussex, 1919–1939', *Albion*, 30, 1998, pp. 439–62.

Lowe, P., 'The Rural Idyll Defended: from Preservation to Conservation', in G. E. Mingay (ed.), *The Rural Idyll*, London, 1989.

Lowenthal, D., 'British National Identity and the English Landscape', *Rural History*, 2, 1991, pp. 205–30.

Lowerson, J., 'Battles for the Countryside', in Frank Gloversmith (ed.), *Class, Culture and Social Change: a New View of the 1930s*, Brighton, 1980.

Lucas, J., 'Places and Dwellings: Wordsworth, Clare and the Anti-picturesque', in D. Cosgrove and S. Daniels (eds), *The Iconography of Landscape. Essays on the Symbolic Representation, Design and Use of Past Environments*, Cambridge, 1988.

Lutz, A., 'The Deserted Village and the Politics of Genre', *Modern Language Quarterly*, 55 (2), 1994, pp. 149–68.

Maclean, G., D. Landry and J. P Ward, *The Country and the City Revisited. England and the Politics of Culture, 1550–1850*, Cambridge, 1999.

Macnaghten, P. and J. Urry, *Contested Natures*, London, 1998.

Malchow, H. L., 'Public Gardens and Social Action in Late Victorian London', *Victorian Studies*, 29 (1), 1985, pp. 97–124.

Mandler, P., 'Against Englishness: English Culture and the Limits to Rural Nostalgia, 1850–1940', *Transactions of the Royal Historical Society*, 6th series, 7, 1997, pp. 155–75.

Marsh, J., *Back to the Land: the Pastoral Impulse in Britain from 1880 to 1914*, London, 1982.

Martin, E. W., *The Shearers and the Shorn: Life in a Devon Community*, London, 1965.

Masser, F. I., *The Metropolitan Village*, London, 1973.

Matless, D. *Landscape and Englishness*, London, 1998.

Meacham, S., *Regaining Paradise: Englishness and the Early Garden City Movement*, New Haven, Connecticut, 1999.

Metcalf, S., 'The Idea of a Park: the Select Committee and the First Public Parks', *Journal of Regional and Local Studies*, 4, 1984, pp. 18–30.

Michie, R. C., 'Insiders, Outsiders and the Dynamics of Change in the City of London Since 1900', *Journal of Contemporary History*, 33 (4), 1998, pp. 547–71.

Miller, S., 'Urban Dreams and Rural Reality: Land and Landscape in English Culture, 1920–45', *Rural History*, 6 (1), 1995, pp. 89–102.

Mingay, G. E (ed.), *The Rural Idyll*, London, 1989.

Mokyr, J. (ed.), *The British Industrial Revolution. An Economic Perspective*, 2nd edn, Boulder, Colorado, 1999.

Moore-Colyer, R. J., 'Feathered Women and Persecuted Birds: the Struggle Against the Plumage Trade, c.1860–1922', *Rural History*, 11, 2000, pp. 57–74.

Mumford, L., *The City in History*, London, 1966.

Murdoch J. and T. Marsden, *Reconstituting Rurality. Class, Community and Power in the Development Process*, London, 1994.

Newby, H., *Green and Pleasant Land? Social Change in Rural England*, London, 1980.

— *Country Life: a Social History of Rural England*, London, 1987.

Nicholson, M. H., *Mountain Gloom and Mountain Glory. The Development of the Aesthetics of the Infinite*, London, 1959.

Offer, A., *Property and Politics, 1870–1914. Landownership, Law, Ideology and Urban Development in England*, Cambridge, 1981.

Orwin, C. S., *Problems of the Countryside*, Cambridge, 1945.

Pahl, R. E., 'The Rural–Urban Continuum', *Sociologia Ruralis*, 6 (3–4), 1966.

— 'The Rural–Urban Continuum: a Reply to Eugen Lupin', *Sociologia Ruralis*, 7 (1), 1967.

Parry, M. L., *The Changing Use of Land*, London, 1991.

Patmore, J. A., *Land and Leisure in England and Wales*, Newton Abbot, 1970.

— *Recreation and Resources: Leisure Patterns and Leisure Places*, Oxford, 1983.

Pedley, W. H., *Labour on the Land. A Study on the Developments Between the Two Great Wars*, Oxford, 1942.

Penning-Rowsell, E. C., 'Who "Betrayed" Whom? Power and Politics in the 1920/21 Agricultural Crisis', *Agricultural History Review*, 45 (2), 1997.

Peters, G., 'British Agriculture Under Attack', in G. Cox, P. Lowe and M. Winter (eds), *Agriculture: People and Policies*, London, 1986.

Potts, A., '"Constable Country" Between the Wars', in R. Samuel (ed.), *Patriotism: the Making and Unmaking of British National Identity, III: National Fictions*, London, 1989.

Prince, H., 'Art and Agrarian Change, 1710–1815', in D. Cosgrove and S. Daniels (eds), *The Iconography of Landscape. Essays on the Symbolic Representation, Design and Use of Past Environments*, Cambridge, 1988.

Prynn, D., 'The Clarion Clubs, Rambling and the Holiday Associations in Britain Since the 1890s', *Journal of Contemporary History*, 11, 1976, pp. 65–77.

Ranlett, J. '"Checking Nature's Desecration": Late Victorian Environmental Organisations', *Victorian Studies*, 26 (2), 1983, pp. 197–222.

Readman, P., 'Landscape Preservation, "Advertising Disfigurement" and English National Identity, c.1880–1914', *Rural History*, 12, 2001, pp. 61–84.

Robbins, K., *Great Britain: Identities, Institutions and the Idea of Britishness*, London, 1998.

Robin, J., *Elmdon. Continuity and Change in a North-west Essex Village 1861–1964*, Cambridge, 1980.

Robinson, G. M., *Conflict and Change in the Countryside. Rural Society, Economy and Planning in the Developed World*, London, 1990.

Rothmann, B., *The 1932 Kinder Trespass: a Personal View of the Kinder Scout Mass Trespass*, Altrincham, 1982.

Royle, E., *Robert Owen and the Commencement of the Millennium. A Study of the Harmony Community*, Manchester, 1998.

Rubinstein, W. D., *Capitalism, Culture and Decline in Britain, 1750–1990*, London, 1993.

Serpell, M. F., *A History of the Lophams*, London, 1980.

Sheail, J., 'The Concept of National Parks in Great Britain 1900–1950', *Transactions of the Institute of British Geographers*, 66, 1975, pp. 41–56.

— *Rural Conservation in Interwar Britain*, London, 1981.

Shoard, M., *This Land is Our Land. The Struggle for Britain's Countryside*, Oxford, 1987.

— *A Right to Roam*, Oxford, 1999.

Short, B., *Land and Society in Edwardian Britain*, Cambridge, 1997.

— (ed.), *The English Rural Community: Image and Analysis*, Cambridge, 1992.

Short, J. R., *Imagined Country: Society, Culture and Environment*, London, 1991.

Stapledon, R. G., *The Land Now and Tomorrow*, London, 1935.

Stephenson, T., *Forbidden Land: the Struggle for Access to Mountain and Moorland*, Manchester, 1989.

Taigel, A. and T. Williamson, *Parks and Gardens*, London, 1993.

Thomas, K., *Man and the Natural World. Changing Attitudes in England 1500–1800*, London, 1984.

Thomas, W. Beach, *How England Becomes Prairie*, London, 1927.

Thompson, E. P., *The Making of the English Working Class*, London, 1968.

— *Customs in Common*, London, 1991.

Tichelar, M., 'Socialists, Labour and the Land: the Response of the Labour Party to the Land Campaign of Lloyd George Before the First World War', *Twentieth Century British History*, 8 (2), 1997, pp. 127–44.

Tinker, C., *Nature's Simple Plan. A Phase of Radical Thought in the Mid-eighteenth Century*, Princeton, New Jersey, 1922.

Trentmann, F., 'Civilization and Its Discontents: English Neo-romanticism and the Transformation of Anti-modernism in Twentieth-century Western Culture', *Journal of Contemporary History*, 29, 1994, pp. 583–625.

Turner, T., *English Garden Design: Landscape and Styles Since 1660*, Woodbridge, 1986.

Walton, J. K., 'The National Trust Centenary: Official and Unofficial Histories', *Local Historian*, 26 (2), 1996, pp. 80–88.

Ward, C., *Goodnight Campers! The History of the British Holiday Camp*, London, 1986.

Wells, R., *Wretched Faces: Famine in Wartime England, 1793–1803*, Gloucester, 1988.

Wiener, M., *English Culture and the Decline of the Industrial Spirit*, Cambridge, 1981.

Williams, R., *The Country and the City*, London, 1973.

Williams, W. M., *The Sociology of an English Village*, London, 1956.

— *A West Country Village: Ashworthy*, London, 1964.

Williamson, P., *Stanley Baldwin. Conservative Leadership and National Values*, Cambridge, 1999.

Winter, J., *Secure from Rash Assault: Sustaining the Victorian Environment*, Berkeley, California, 1999.

Winter, M., *Rural Politics. Policies for Agriculture, Forestry and the Environment*, London, 1996.

Wright, P., *On Living in an Old Country. The National Past in Contemporary Britain*, London, 1985.

— *The Village That Died for England. The Strange Story of Tyneham*, London, 1995.

Young, C., 'The Acquisition of Weston-Super-Mare's Victorian Parks', *Local Historian*, 20, 1990, pp. 158–65.

Index